MW00443125

Pooled Ink

Pooled Ink

Celebrating the 2013 NCW Contest Winners

Edited by Jennifer Top

Northern Colorado Writers, LLC

© 2013 Northern Colorado Writers, LLC
Fort Collins, Colorado
www.NorthernColoradoWriters.com

Cover photo by Robert J. Blinderman
Cover design by Jennifer Top

ISBN-13: 978-1493662852
ISBN-10: 1493662856

CONTENTS

PREFACE &
ACKNOWLEDGMENTS

As these writing contests continue to grow I am continually humbled by all the beautiful creative work that writers from all over the country have shared with us. Because of that I approach this work of organizing the contests and putting together this anthology with reverence and great responsibility. It is important work, and the more I do it the more I feel that if my purpose in life is to help share these creative expressions with the world, that is a good life, and I'm honored to be able to do it.

I couldn't do it without help, of course, and I would like to extend my thanks to our esteemed judges for this year's series: Ms. Alyson Hagy for short fiction, Mr. David Shields for personal essay/creative nonfiction, and Mr. David Mason for poetry.

Also, I can't say enough about the founder and director of NCW, Ms. Kerrie Flanagan, for her constant support of fellow writers in and outside of NCW as well as her contributions to creative pursuits in the greater community. She's not only an accomplished writer, remarkably kind, and intelligent, she's a savvy and innovative business woman and I'm grateful for all that I've learned from her.

The pieces that follow include a wide range of styles and attitudes, a collection of unique voices that to me not only tell stories but paint pictures, evoke emotions without sentimentality, and leave us changed for knowing them. I hope you enjoy them.

—*Jennifer Top*

Man Camp

by Claire Boyles

short fiction 1st place

JUDD AWOKE, AGAIN, TO THE SOUND OF DUSTIN'S SMOKER'S HACK, exacerbated by a nasty bronchitis that Dustin had picked up on the bus ride from Montana. Through the thin plastic wall that separated their rooms, the kid sounded like a 60-year-old man. Judd had been in the North Dakota man camp for about two years, and he had to admit it lived up to the promises of the recruiter he had spoken to back in Colorado. The guy had promised a comfortable life (Amenities like you wouldn't believe! Better than home! Hassle-free!) and the chance to make his fortune driving water trucks for the rigs. It was Judd's nature to doubt these men, all salesmen, really, so he had kept his expectations about this part of his compensation package low. And he had to hand it to the guy, hassle free it had been for the past two years. Working 80–90 hour weeks, he had, in fact, made the small fortune he needed to pay for Annie's care. It was better than the situation he'd had in his first gig back in Colorado, living in a giant double wide with 11 other guys, the bunk beds lined up like army barracks, the shared kitchen covered in slopped Stagg chili and Dorito powder, the smell of burnt coffee and the never-ending overflow of the trash can. That had been free, too, provided by the company, but still there was so much time spent on shopping for and preparing food, the

1

cleanup duty that everyone shirked, the complete lack of privacy.

Judd got up, dressed, and used the bathroom he and Dustin shared, a Jack-and-Jill between their rooms. Judd wondered how many of the other guys knew that term, a Jack-and-Jill bathroom, from their lives at home with their wives or girlfriends. He wondered if knowing it made them as lonely as it made him. The gravel path to the cafeteria crunched under his boots, the overhead lights above the path glowing down like spotlights. The man camp was active at all hours. The men seemed quieter at night, presumably due to the human habit of their lives before the camp. But there were always men coming in and men heading out, a 24-hour stream of going to work and getting off work, sleeping and waking, being indoors and being outdoors. Even now there were guys watching *The Godfather* in the rec room, guys lifting weights in the fitness area, guys walking to the bunks, pulling their hoods over their heads to shield them from the relentless prairie wind. It was five a.m.

He'd broken a lace that morning and was hoping the camp store was open early enough for him to get a new set. The store didn't carry much save for things the men would need in a pinch—boot laces, work gloves, tobacco products, snack foods. He carried the boot laces into the cafeteria, which was near deserted. The place was designed to feed a couple hundred, but due to the irregular shifts, it was rare to see more than 20 or 30 guys eating there at once. Sitting on the bench of an empty table to lace his boot, he noticed one of the fluorescent lights flickering. Looking around, he didn't see Dustin anywhere, and hoped the kid was moving. They were going to ride together today, but Judd wasn't going to wait around if the moron couldn't get himself out of bed in time.

North Dakota was even more open than the eastern plains of Colorado; his rigs were nowhere near the small towns that were scattered across the prairie. Judd felt the expanse of empty land inside his ribs, a deep breath. He could feel himself spreading, opening into the territory. The work kept his mind and hands occupied, and between work and sleep, there wasn't time to think, or analyze, or, best of all, regret. He asked for extra shifts instead of his weeks off, and while the company insisted on a few days for every man, his supervisor was more than happy to shave a day or two off his breaks. Judd killed the empty days in the game room of the man camp, playing an old version of *Gran Turismo* on an ancient Playstation 2 and taking breaks on the smoker's plaza. The gas rigs were a new world . . . unceasing, unstoppable, around the clock. Just the way Judd had hoped it would be.

Dustin was new, barely 21 and fresh out of his parents' house, the biggest disappointment of his life so far having been an apparently unsuccessful search for a steady girlfriend. Every break he got, Dustin went home to his mother's chili and cinnamon rolls and to beers with his high school buddies. Judd hadn't been back to Greeley since he'd left. For Judd, Annie and DJ were still everywhere in Greeley, and Judd knew he'd see JB's Drive-In and picture his lovely wife, pregnant, laughing as a thick marshmallow flavored milkshake mustache dripped on her face. "Say it five times fast!" Annie had insisted, and they'd both tried it, giggling like fools, over and over. Marshmallow milkshake mustache marshmallow milkshake mustache marshmallow milkshake mustache. Judd could not imagine, now, having to drive past the junkyard off Highway 34, the one with the observation tower he had paid a buck to climb with DJ so the boy could marvel at the view of the Rockies on the western horizon. The one where the old Grand Caravan, Annie's car, the car he had spent nearly every day off working on, now sat rusting in the cruel sun. These early, happy memories were somehow less painful than the more recent ones from the year before the accident. Annie's maddening, dark, brooding silences. The TV, always on, blaring in the background. His anger and frustration as he grabbed her shoulders and yelled, "Pull it together, Annie. Jesus. Just do something. Do anything. If you can't be happy with this, make a fucking change."

Judd loaded a plate with bacon and eggs, a bagel with cream cheese, juice and coffee, and on a whim, a Danish. He saw the to-go food cart stocked and ready, but while the sack lunches were better than nothing, they didn't always hold him. Better to stuff himself full now and not have to worry about it for a few hours. He didn't know any of the other men, so he sat down at the end of a table, alone, and pulled out his phone to check the news. Smart phones were amazing to him. He was old enough to have helped his mother, a legal secretary, lug a typewriter home so she could work after he went to bed. He had used clunky DOS desktops in high school, had bought a laptop for the business that had failed, and now, as a water hauler, all he needed was a tiny, pocket-sized phone.

He pulled up CNN to check the headlines but got distracted by sponsored links and ended up on YouTube, watching something called a Whizbang chicken plucker that a farmer had built out of an old washing machine. It was random but compelling. The farmer fired up the motor, shot a garden hose into the basket, and dropped in the bird he had beheaded and bled out just before. Feathers splashed into the air and the bird emerged after only about a minute totally bare, like a rubber chicken from an old slapstick gag. The farmer, delighted, raved about the speed and quality of the pluck. Judd looked around for someone to show it to, but saw only one grizzled old codger, mid-60s maybe, reading a paper copy of the *Tribune* a few tables away. Judd watched him rub his hands on his thighs and pull a pencil, an actual lead pencil, the kind that needed to be sharpened in one of those rotary sharpeners from grade school, out of his shirt pocket. The man folded the paper into a small rectangle and started the crossword puzzle. Judd smiled to himself. He didn't know the man, had heard he was a retired history teacher from some high school in Bismarck. A little old for the rigs themselves, the man, a procurement officer or something, had arrived a week ago for a site visit. Judd figured he'd have to meet with him sooner or later, to talk about the service records it was Judd's job to file each week. At 38, Judd often felt like an old man, in camp and on site, surrounded by green, disillusioned millennial boys who thought they'd make their fortune as pro football stars or rappers, who had paid just enough attention in high school to graduate, and who had managed to leverage their diplomas into jobs on the rigs with training and good pay . . . pay that for the most part, the young guys seemed to take for granted, to feel they deserved somehow.

Judd and others his age, far enough along in life to know that you don't, especially post-2008, thumb your nose at any comfortable paycheck, often thought of themselves as father figures to these kids. Judd had entertained this illusion for a few days until Dustin had set him straight. "Dude," he'd said, "we don't want to be like you guys when we're your age. That would be, like, nothing. We're already like you guys. When I'm your age, I'm gonna have, like, a family, and my own business, and a fucking BMW. I'm going to work clean, dude. No more of this dirty shit all over my clothes." Dustin's plan, Judd knew, was to make enough money to pay for an education in alternative energy at the community college and then start his own business installing windmills or solar panels or "something like, we don't even imagine now, you know? Like, totally out of a space movie. Like in that old movie, *Back to the Future*, when Doc stuffs garbage into his DeLorean to make gas. That's what I'm doing in my thirties, man. Stacks of bills. No more of this raping the earth and shit."

This was a sentiment echoed by pretty much every twenty-something in the camp, an entire army of future entrepreneurs masquerading as water haulers and roustabouts. The oilfields were just a stepping stone for these young guys, who, honestly, had no idea how good they had it. Judd wondered if it was true, if one day he'd be calling a millionaire Dustin to see about a job when the drilling was done and this whole thing busted, as everyone knew it was bound to. Even the man camp, an entire prairie town, really, designed to be torn down and hauled away like fucking LEGOs.

Judd felt, rather than saw, a man sit down next to him. It was the codger, with his paper. Judd looked up, surprised.

"Happen to have any guesses about a product suffix suggesting noodles?" The man smiled an answer to Judd's astonished silence, held out his hand. "Ben Stone. Company recruiter. You're Judd Davis?"

Judd took the man's hand. "Good to meet you," he croaked, then cleared his throat to clear the sleep from his voice. "You out from Bismarck?"

"Yep. Turned me loose for a few days for field research. I have to say, I was expecting worse. The food is really quite good, though I would never tell my wife that. And it's quieter than I thought it would be. For whatever reason, I had a picture in my head of the man camp as something from a Steinbeck novel. Not quite *Grapes of Wrath* because, no family, you know? But maybe *Cannery Row.*"

Judd laughed. Steinbeck was the only author he remembered authentically liking in high school English. "Not near enough alcohol for that. Too many rules."

Stone laughed too. "That and you all have actual work to do. Less time and energy for frog hunting. Listen. You have any time for a meeting today?"

Judd considered. Stone was a recruiter, not procurement, which made his motives for the meeting less clear. "I've got a shift. Leave in about ten minutes. Could meet around lunch tomorrow, though, if that works for you."

Stone rose from the table. "I'm holding court in the conference room up by the front office. One or so? Tomorrow afternoon?"

Judd nodded. "Sure. Can I ask why?"

"I've got an offer I think you'll like. And since I can tell I'll still be working on this," he waved the folded crossword, "think on that noodle thing, will you?" Stone refilled his coffee mug, ceramic, with the faded gild of a logo on it, nodded to Doris, the giantess who served as the camp's head breakfast cook, and left the dining hall just as Dustin exploded into it, boots unlaced, shrugging into an insulated work jacket, waving an acknowledgment to Judd.

Dustin stuffed his pockets with sausage biscuits and filled his thermos with coffee while Judd grabbed sack lunches for them both. "You look like shit," Judd said to Dustin. "Sure you don't need a day?"

Dustin shrugged. "Nah. I'm alright. The cough is a real bitch at night, but it's better in the daytime."

The shift went by. The drilling rig had left the site the week before, and the injector, after a minor repair, was put back to work. There was a bit of tension and uncertainty about the flare until it was clear that all was working the way it should. All of the site activity was hidden from view by giant water tanks. In this case, Judd wondered whose view they were worrying about, as this particular site was so remote they hadn't seen any sign of humanity since they turned off the state highway 25 miles back. The truck convoys hauling water were one of the most visible things for local people to object to . . . so much traffic on once sleepy, rural roads. But it would be worse, Judd knew, if the entire drilling process was so tangible. It was an unspoken rule that the rigs should be hidden as much as possible, not, of course, that the company had anything to hide about their safe, environmentally sound businesses. What the public could see, the flare burning off the emissions, the giant drill rig, the 24-hour spotlights, was upsetting enough. The turmoil underneath it all, the underground explosives and the chemical soup and the invisible gasses, was far more frightening.

Still, this job was the only luck he'd had in the past few years. He knew the company had saved his ass and the asses of any number of other men who had been laid off from jobs in construction, in landscaping, in mortgage lending, for God's sake, during the recession. Judd had become, over the years, a master of control of his own thoughts. He refused to engage with complex moral conflict. He would not dwell on difficult things, not environmental issues, not politics, not his mother, not Annie, not DJ.

He thought of his mother, her face a perfect mask of serenity and contentment throughout his father's alcoholic rages. Realized too late, after he himself had run off and left home, how heartbreakingly lonely the eerie calm of the house must have been for her. He remembered himself, a frightened 10-year-old, approaching his mother as she scrubbed pans at the sink after dinner and asking her about the erections he had started getting on a regular basis. During math class. On the school bus. Riding his bike. "What's happening?" he asked her. "Am I okay?" His mother's hand in its yellow rubber glove had slowed only for a moment, her grip almost imperceptibly tightening on the sponge.

"Of course you're okay," she had said, refusing eye contact. "Just don't think about it and it will go away."

It was advice Judd returned to over and over again, the simple truth around which he organized his life. It was what had drawn him to trade the plains of Colorado for the North Dakota prairie, to ignore completely the earnest urgings of his therapist to "re-engage with society." At first, the man camp had been just the exact blissful escape he had searched for. Recently, though, there were the dreams. Dreams in which the real and the imaginary intertwined like fingers. Dreams in which his rig was leaking into a burning river, and it was his limp, lifeless body, not DJ's, being recovered from the roiling foam. Dreams of a withered, ghost-like Annie who pointed and scowled at him, so accusatory, so suddenly lucid, and it was Judd, not Annie, who had driven the Caravan off the bridge, and then he suddenly stood again on the bridge above the wreck, engulfed in guilt but frozen, unable to flee. Dreams in which DJ, his curly mop bouncing around his four-year-old innocence, scrambled around the bank rocks, asking, incessantly, if Judd wanted to try a different fly. In this dream, he could feel both the annoyance he had felt toward the boy in the real-life moment, the emotions of his past self, and also the agony and regret of his current being. He wanted to shake his past self into the moment, or scare him into it, like Marley to Scrooge. Judd as the ghost of his own empty future. Judd lost. And another, himself at DJ's age, hiking in the foothills, climbing to the top of a rock and spreading his arms as far as they would go. Spinning, like he'd seen people do on TV, the joy and pride of his own accomplishment streaming from his core, from somewhere near his boy heart, through the big sky, combining, in the end, with the giant, mysterious clouds.

Dreams were just dreams, but Judd found it harder and harder, in the morning, to shake off the emotion left in their wake. Even when the images receded, he was left with the pride, the desperation, the regret, and these emotions did not reconcile easily with life in the man camp. He thought about Dustin and the other young guys, and about himself at their age, so full of cocky confidence. Sure with absolute know-it-all certainty that the way they lived or ate or thought was the one right way to do any of those things. Dustin, to Judd, was nearly as innocent as the DJ of his dreams. Neither of them had lived enough time to fuck it all up, to fail at important things. Neither of them realized how much of life was the luck, good or bad, that flowed out of the crap choices you made before you understood what it all meant, before the stakes were clear, before you knew how to properly care for the things you held dear. Neither would have ever wondered, the way Judd did when his dreams woke him, breathless and sweaty, whether Annie had a real accident or whether she meant to drive into that river.

Dustin had picked up Judd's habit of ladling soup into a mug so that he could drink meals down on the walk from the cafeteria to the bunk before collapsing into sleep. They would head out again after Judd's meeting, back to switching tanks in the relentless howling wind that scoured the prairie. Today, Judd sat for a few minutes to eat mac and cheese before stumbling back to catch a nap. He wondered if Stone had eaten lunch yet, if he had found his suffix suggesting noodles. He wondered if Stone had known the solution all along but had needed a conversation starter.

When he awoke later, there was a film of dust and tears crusting his eyes nearly shut, and when he cleaned his ears after his shower, the swab came out blackened and greasy.

The lens coating on his sunglasses was scraped and scratched nearly off from the grit that pelted the men as they worked. It was one reason Judd had come to prefer the night shift; often, the winds were calmer at night than they were during the day. Dustin's alarm was still beeping, and Judd banged a few times on Dustin's locked door to get the kid moving before heading into his own bunk.

The bunks were small, a single bed, a closet with drawers inside, a small counter/desk with a mirror above it, something Annie would have called a vanity. In the middle, there was just enough space for one man to stand up. Visitors were naturally discouraged by the tightness of the space; men tended to socialize, if at all, in the dining and rec halls rather than in the bunks. Women, drugs, and alcohol, according to the rules, weren't allowed in the rooms at all. Judd had returned from shifts a few times to see subtle evidence that one of the company's promised spot inspections had taken place. Judd was grateful to have his own room, but he understood that he had traded real privacy for convenience here in the camp. He accepted it as a condition of employment, and didn't rail against the injustice of the inspections the way Dustin and the other young guys sometimes did. Judd had argued with Dustin, just once, that living at home with his parents had likely been even less private, that they had probably searched Dustin's room when he wasn't home, lurked on his Facebook account, eavesdropped on phone conversations . . . all without the courtesy of announcing that this was a possibility. Dustin had looked so crestfallen at this, so betrayed. "That's fucked up, man. I wonder if they're in my room, like, right now. I mean, I thought I lost a dime bag once, but maybe like my dad just took it and didn't have the balls to say anything, you know?" Judd had felt like such an ass, sowing the seeds of discontent between this kid and what was probably his perfectly well-meaning, loving father. It was exactly this contrariness, this need to point out flaws to others, that had driven Annie crazy. "Like your mother," she had said. "Just like her. Knock it off, will you?" And he had tried, he had, was still trying, really, but he never saw it until after the fact, when the razor-sharp effect of his bullshit had hit the people around him. When the wound was already inflicted and he had no idea how to stop the bleeding.

Stone was in the conference room looking every bit the retired history professor when Judd arrived. His ancient blazer had leather patches on the elbows, pencils stuck out of the breast pocket of his shirt. Judd wondered why Stone, who seemed to have been cultivating this look for years, neglected to use a pocket protector. The bottom seam of his pocket was marked and stained with ink and lead. Stone's eyebrows, his most prominent feature, like gray, bushy caterpillars, were furrowed over the crossword, while the conference room table was disheveled, so covered in stacks of manila folders and newspaper and reports that sitting across from Stone felt almost like having a conversation from opposite ends of a canyon.

They shook hands. "-aroni," Judd said as they both sat.

For a split second, Stone looked confused, then laughed heartily, studying his crossword. "Of course!" he exclaimed. "But that does mean that these two down answers can't be right." He attacked the page with a gum eraser, and Judd noticed that the metal eraser casing of every one of Stone's pencils was empty and bent.

Stone rubbed his hands together and opened the manila file nearest to him. "Now, from your file it appears you had quite the successful land appraisal business down Greeley way a few years back. How'd you end up hauling water up here?"

Judd didn't answer right away. What sort of answer did Stone want? Surely not the sordid personal details. "Turns out the water pays better than appraisals. I needed the money."

"Aims Community College. Associate degree?"

"Yes. Took a few business courses, gen ed stuff."

"But you didn't go on for a Bachelor's?"

"Nope. Thought I'd be a land surveyor, but didn't make it through."

"You still have family back in Colorado?"

Judd saw Annie, the specter Annie of his dreams. He pictured her speechless glare, so full of the depths of her hate, drilling straight into him. He never knew how much information to give, how much of his life people were prepared to take in response to such pleasantries. "In Greeley. My wife. In assisted living. She doesn't really . . . she has a brain injury."

"I'm sorry to hear that," Stone sighed. Judd was surprised by the older man's sincerity, and then was surprised by his surprise, by how long it had been since he had believed in anyone else's honesty. Stone continued, "Here's the thing, Judd. We need an advance land guy back there in Weld. Someone to secure easements from property owners, convince them to allow us to get the seismic testing done, reassure them that they won't start being able to light their water faucets on fire. Company policy says promote from within, we need someone who knows the area, and you seem to stand right out. You interested?"

Judd felt his hands start to shake, but managed to keep them hidden. "What's the offer?"

"Significant salary increase, with bonuses, you're looking at well above six figures. Stock options. Nice private office in our Greeley headquarters. I hear it's got a mountain view and everything. Company truck. Relocation paid, though looking at the, well, simplicity of your situation here, we may be able to swap out the moving expenses for a down payment credit toward a house. You keep your benefits. Get yourself back near your wife."

"When would I start?"

"End of the week. Two weeks off to get yourself settled down there, and then you're on the job."

Judd let out a low whistle. "When do you need to know?"

"First thing in the morning. I'll see you at breakfast, you let me know." Stone smiled. "You could do a lot worse than this, you know."

Judd smiled weakly and excused himself. He knew.

Dustin was in the dining hall, an empty tray in front of him save for half a bottle of chocolate milk, texting. Judd sat down. "You ready?"

Dustin didn't look up, his fingers nearly blurring across the touch screen of his phone. Judd hated the kid's distractibility, the assumption that the human in front of you, face to face, should wait in favor of the human on the other end of the digital world. Finally, Dustin put his phone in his pocket and looked up. "Dude. You would not believe this girl. Like she thinks we're going to get married, wants me to quit and come home and play house. And I was getting into that, you know, thinking about putting in my notice. And then my buddy tells me she's running around on me at home, out at the bars every night, sitting on guys' laps, and shit. I mean, what does she want from me?"

Judd briefly considered telling Dustin about Stone's offer, but rejected the idea. It would be a little like explaining algebra to a preschooler. Judd needed wisdom, and Dustin didn't have any to offer. Guys he knew his own age in the camp were mostly working for the money, living away from their presumably loving wives and living, healthy children, wanting desperately all the time to leave the camp and go back home. He'd be an asshole to ask any of those guys for advice.

He thought of Annie as he'd last seen her, over two years ago, in a wheelchair in the nursing home recreation room, a blanket on her lap, her hair greasy and stringy. Her eyes vacant, his once beautiful young wife just staring at him, silent. Judd believed that he was as unrecognizable to her as she was to him.

"Dude. Time to go, right?" Dustin said. "What's up?"

Judd got out his phone and handed it to Dustin. "You ever heard of a Whizbang chicken plucker? Maybe that's how you can make your millions and impress this girl."

"You're real funny, jackass."

The next morning, over Doris's famous biscuits and gravy and strong coffee, Judd told Stone he'd go home.

Claire Boyles is a writer, mom, teacher, and former farmer. She is a regular contributor to the Greeley Moms site at the Greeley Tribune *and blogs about life after farming on her personal blog, Barnyard to Backyard.*

DEEPS

by Annie Dawid

personal essay/creative nonfiction 1st place

"Thou hast laid me in the lowest pit, in darkness, in the deeps."

—from Psalm 88

DURING MY LAST SOJOURN IN THAT PLACE, I COULD LISTEN ONLY TO Marian Anderson and Paul Robeson singing mournful, soothing gospel. I could read only literature from the nineteenth century and earlier. In the solipsism of my condition, I discovered that King David's Psalms described depression with beauty and accuracy, and I found some solace there. I ate only cereal, and that with effort. I could not bear the sun and prayed for rain. Nights were marginally better, when I did not have to confront the light. In the wooded park where I walked my dogs, I found the darkest places and the least-trod paths. On one bend of a trail I'd never seen before, I discovered the hanging tree. Like a car wreck, it drew me back again and again. I didn't want to study it, to want what it promised, but I was defenseless against its allure. Every afternoon I walked around the old oak, admiring its solid, sturdy arm under which I believed I would achieve my final rest, like a bird, nesting. As school was out, I did not teach and had no daily obligations. I was six months pregnant—six months off my meds.

Friends worried, though I only hinted at the nature of That Place, where I was once again residing, a familiar neighborhood to me during a lifetime lasting—hard for me to believe—39 years so far, though I felt sure I couldn't breathe that toxic air much longer. Six months earlier, ecstatic, the proverbial biological clock inside my body suddenly wound and humming after years of desire, I thanked all the powers, gods, and spirits as I read the results of my blood test. A hitherto unknown sensation of peace flooded through my veins as I walked alone across the OB/GYN waiting room in which, with my gray hair, I appeared 20 years older than all the other women, expectantly awaiting news alongside husbands, boyfriends, and mothers.

Despite a decade of therapy and medication, depression inevitably followed elation, as pride goeth ineluctably before a fall, but my brand new condition seemed somehow outside the parameters of that lifelong template. Proverbially, I glowed. Never once experiencing morning sickness, I gloated, considering myself of stronger stuff than a friend who puked every morning for the first three months. Wanting a healthy, natural child, I stopped taking anything that might harm Helen/Isaiah—I chose to be surprised by my child's sex— including alcohol, tobacco, aspirin, refined sugar, and antidepressants.

Only many months later did I recall a psychopharmacologist, whom I'd once consulted when it seemed my ordinary medications (Prozac and Trazodone) and excellent therapist were not helping me extend my stays long enough outside That Place. After testing me, the doctor decided I'd been misdiagnosed and really my problem was Obsessive-Compulsive Disorder, which often masqueraded as depression. Obsessive thought and behavior described my siblings and me perfectly; Dr. H. had healed me with a new description, or so I wanted to believe. He prescribed Luvox, and for a while all was rosy, with my spanking new label and a medication that sounded like love. Should I ever become pregnant, he insisted, I would need to return for help in getting through pregnancy, as Luvox would not be appropriate. Perhaps I filed that information in the need-to-know folder I imagined I kept at the ready in the back of my brain, beside other memories I deemed not especially useful. Or perhaps, even then, I thought I knew better; pregnancy itself, I presumed, would be the medicine for what ailed me, and medication superfluous.

Initially, it was. Pregnant, I felt gleeful and generous. Knowing my reputation for tough, no-nonsense instruction, my students were perhaps surprised to confront this jolly, roly-poly silver-haired professor quite unlike the unflappable, take-no-bullshit teacher of college lore. As I didn't disclose my pregnancy until safely past the common miscarriage timeline, and the results of my amniocentesis were in without initiating a struggle over keeping or aborting a child with Down syndrome, students and colleagues alike must have assumed a change in my spirit that came with approaching 40.

"Lighten up," was advice I'd heard all my life and always found banal, inappropriate to a world smeared in suffering, a darkness I assumed veiled the lives of most human beings, for how could it not?

In the summer of 1999, abruptly battened inside That Place, I blamed the Columbine Massacre for such rude transport, its fusillade of child-inspired violence restoring the veil, obscuring the light I had come to trust, foolishly, as my new abode. Columbine murdered my apparently fragile optimism. The Colorado high school, which I'd driven past many times, was a few minutes from an old friend's home; her daughters would attend that school some day. As immediate as if it were the school down the block from me, to which my child would one day go, Columbine's particular horror reemphasized—because I had indeed forgotten—the true nature of existence. What had I been thinking to bring a child into a world of Columbines? Ever a news junkie, I devoured the papers and kept the radio on all day, suffusing myself in terror. For the first time, added to familiar depression was a previously unknown anxiety; I felt anxious every minute of consciousness. Hoping for a simple solution, I eliminated all caffeine; I took baths and drank Calming Tea, but with prodigious time to fill, no longer able to concentrate on the small print of *David Copperfield* or *New Grub Street*, I worried.

I worried about everything I had not worried about before: I couldn't afford a child, I thought. I couldn't provide the support Helen/Isaiah would need from a single parent. Most importantly and obviously, I didn't have the mental stamina to be a parent, just as I had always believed to be true about myself until the biological clock startled me with its alarm at 36, muffling previous fears and good sense.

In the most painful part of that turning from joy to sorrow, a close friend made it known she thought I would fail to be a good mother, due to my proclivity toward depression, from which she also suffered. Before the turning, I scoffed at her words, hurt but in no way destroyed. I read her many-paged, handwritten letter on legal yellow paper as I walked jauntily up a path in Forest Park, across town, in the days when I felt powerful and free, walking my two mutts with my big belly and no worries. I threw the letter away; what was the purpose of it? Did she believe her words would prompt me toward a late-term abortion because she thought I was incapable of mothering? I laughed at how wrong she was, how limited in her imagination.

After the turning, I could only agree: she knew me better than I knew myself, I thought. She knew the true me, the me who was at core a depressed and hopeless self, certainly not mother material. To help me from the pit, she called all my other friends to set up an Annie-watch, to make sure I was surviving, but the other friends detected *schadenfreude* and kept their distance from her. Later, I felt it too, when I regained an awareness of the world beyond despair. Many years passed before we were able to repair that breach of trust.

With time and perspective, I realized Columbine was merely a bad coincidence, and the less dramatic, chemical truth was that every time I'd quit my medication in the past decade—and who hasn't, feeling so much better and believing drugs wicked, for the morally weak—six months later, with a criminal calendrical efficiency, I would descend into the suicidally friendly darkness of That Place in a kind of homecoming. However, I found peculiar comfort there. It was, after all, familiar, *gemutlich*, reminding me of my childhood home, unlike the land of light, to which I was a relative stranger. At the time, Columbine and the hormones of pregnancy seemed stronger than the inexorable pull of blood, but now I see it was after all exactly like the fall of 1996, not pregnant and unprompted by any Columbines, when I walked a path outside a writers' retreat in Scotland, searching for the proper cliff from which to throw myself into a gorge. For the six months prior to that dark October, I'd experienced bliss, free of medication's stigma, writing fiction furiously, in love with Colorado light and the in-cloud lightning of summer storms.

And that episode was just like 1993, again abroad, when I found myself at Lands End, six months' gone from Prozac, in St. Ives, Cornwall, where I could glimpse Virginia Woolf's lighthouse whenever the fog failed to blot it from the horizon. In the cold rain and despair I succumbed to my truth that, unlike other people, I was not meant for this life. The ends of the earth drew me for a reason, for my own end. "There are other places which also are the world's end," writes T. S. Eliot in "Little Gidding." "Some at the sea jaws, or over a dark lake, but this is the nearest, in place and time, now and in England." Like King David, Thomas Stearns Eliot knew depression like a mother, I am sure of it.

What saved me from the hanging tree, the river gorge outside Edinburgh, and the Atlantic off the Cornish Coast were, I believed at the time, piddling details. In the first case, I worried what would happen to my dogs. And, more importantly, what if some child found me bulbous-eyed, hanging on a red dog leash as she raced along the path, thrilled to be flying on her new two-wheeler? No. I would never involve a stranger—especially a child—in my demise. In Scotland, I wondered what would happen to my body, fearing to involve my parents with an overseas casket-transport, and in the last case, in the relentless rain near Woolf's summer home, I discovered that the waistband of my silk trousers had lost its elastic, and during my walk, unbeknownst to me, the gold harem pants had descended to my knees, blaring my long underwear to the world. Of course, no one else was walking in the downpour that afternoon at Lands End, so my shame was all my own. Only later could I see the humor in it, the slapstick quality of a suicidal woman diverted from the deed by her golden fancy pants' dysfunction, but at the time it was a terrible humiliation from which I had to flee.

In my premedicated years, in the early 1980s, not six months past the serotonin deadline but an entire lifetime, I roamed another Lands End at the western edge of San Francisco, thinking the same despairing thoughts, wanting to die. The Pacific Ocean would be a wistful name for my unmarked grave. In those days I discovered a temporary solace in alcohol. In therapy but before the days of minimal side effect antidepressants, I abhorred the notion of drugs, remembering my mother on Valium, tranquilized into nothingness. Better depressed than empty, I concluded, better suicidal than a zombie.

When I was 12, my mother tried to kill herself, and every moment after that middle-of-the-night, dreamlike event darkened my life with despair, ordinary problems twisted by the possibility of a suicidal solution. Only in my early twenties, with a good therapist, did I begin to understand this distortion of my adolescence, the way I had shouldered my mother's depression in the hope of saving her, to prove my love and loyalty. But understanding did not enlighten me. To the contrary, I found such new awareness more frightening than my vague, pre-analysis unknowingness, so I drank to keep it at bay.

During my early- to mid-twenties, a friend and I visited bars together and drank until we could hardly see, often winding up in strangers' beds, behaving in what was to us unconsciously but to anyone else obviously suicidal behavior. Four o'clock in the morning with a group of guys in a car next to a park in the heart of the city—what exactly did we think would happen?

At 39, however, I believed myself beyond such self-destructive acts. Hadn't I spent many years and thousands of dollars on the psychiatrist's couch? Hadn't I pushed beyond my fear of medication's disrepute and tried most every pharmaceutical manufactured to facilitate recovery? Wasn't I completely in charge of a life that appeared to outsiders accomplished and full? And finally, wasn't I fantastically lucky to get pregnant so easily at such a late date when many women of my age were struggling to do so? No longer the caricature of an unhappy post-adolescent roaming San Francisco at night, an A-student binge drinking on weekends and sleeping with men I couldn't remember, I was a professor, published and sober. Not only did I see myself as too sophisticated for a black-and-white worldview, but it was selfish for a woman in the upper-middle-class tax bracket to imagine she was suffering. So much of the world lived in misery; I had no right to my despair.

The most helpful thing a doctor ever told me was the following: on scans of severely depressed people, whole sections of their brains remained unilluminated, completely out of service.

In the dusk of my suicidal depression and the seventh month of my pregnancy, after trying to hang myself with the red dog leash—too short—on a rafter in the basement—too flimsy for my bulk—I ended up on the Kaiser psychiatrist's couch. My OB/GYN nurse practitioner had sent me there after requiring weekly visits to her office, simply to make me appear for appointments, and witnessing, at the start of my last trimester, a sudden failure to thrive. Instead of gaining, I lost weight, and, despite the apparent health of my fetus, I was inquiring about how to "adopt out" the child who would shortly be born to me. After the inadequate rafter experience, and an afternoon with a purposely broken glass in the bathtub, I concluded that I needed to kill myself *after* the birth. For an adult of sound mind—which I believed myself to possess—to commit suicide was a right in a world in which one had control of one's destiny—a privilege on a planet where most had no such agency. But to murder another— akin to including the hypothetical bike-riding girl in the park—was unconscionable. After all, I did have standards.

So I decided to live—for a while, at any rate, until my due date of September first—and to see the doctor who, according to my nurse practitioner, had lots of experience with depressed pregnant women. Having only heard of *post*-partum depression, I considered myself an anomaly, typically, depressed at the wrong time, an asshole to be wanting to die while a friend my age in another city had been trying for years to conceive and failing.

Why did the doctor's description of a depressed brain's malfunction perforate my darkness? Despite all my reading, education, and therapy, there remained inside me enough of my German father's stoicism to deplore my condition as symptomatic of weakness, an indicator of a feeble will. After all, my father had escaped the Nazis and hadn't succumbed to depression. He'd lost his mother at 12, most of his family had been exterminated in his twenties, his first grandchild had died of an obscure, genetic Jewish disease, and he'd had to commit his wife and son to psychiatric wards more than once, but he'd never been depressed, or so I told myself. What was my failing, if not weakness? As the smart daughter, the accomplished child most like my father, I could not admit, much less demonstrate to the world, likeness to my pathetic, crazy mother.

Whole sections of my brain, said Doctor O, were either operating at sub-par levels or not functioning at all. Like the outer world, the inside of my brain had slowed itself to crawl in darkness. Studies had proved that the eyes of severely depressed people could not recognize all the colors in the spectrum, he told me. It was as if the patient had suffered a head injury in a motorcycle accident, or fallen from a height onto concrete. This scientific fact, something empirical that even my steely, brilliant father could not deny, managed to penetrate the veil of my despair. To my mind, his likening of a mental state to a physical one reduced the stigma, making my condition seem less a question of will than of chemistry in one's brain. Certain medications, Doctor O insisted, could help me while not harming Helen/Isaiah. Because my due date was so close, and I knew babies could be born at seven or eight months without long-term, life-damaging results, I decided to accept his counsel. If I could live long enough to deliver the baby safely, to hand him or her over to a loving stranger, it would be enough.

A few days later, my pregnant self, my father, and brother were drifting down the Willamette River on a faux steamboat, the recorded info-spiel too loud in our ears. In the group of tourists by the bar stood a very pregnant young blonde, drinking beer and smoking a cigarette with what looked like extended family and partner/husband. People stared, but no one said anything. What an irresponsible mother, everyone was surely thinking. Completely unselfconscious, she seemed to be having a wonderful time, chatting and laughing. I marveled at her brazen flaunting of the unwritten law that now prohibits all smoking and drinking for pregnant women—at least in public. Watching the populated riverbanks diminish as we floated south, barely able to speak as depression still compressed me, I asked myself how could I condemn her nicotine and alcohol infusions when I had come so close to destroying my child in a far more drastic way?

My father had flown out from New York, and my brother up from California to check on me; when they'd made the reservations months before, I'd anticipated an interesting parental/filial/sibling relation "learning lab"—my old therapist's phrase for family visits—but nothing dire. After the turning, I pleaded with them not to come, but my sudden resistance-without-a-reason affirmed their resolve to see me.

Each day of the new med regime and regular appointments with Doctor O, I struggled to feel a millimeter better, to detect an iota of improvement. Did the light hurt less today? Did I feel a trifle less unhinged as I managed to eat a meal out with Steve and Baba, my close, quasi-parental friends? At the diner I managed a milkshake, and afterward, window-shopping on the way to Ben & Jerry's for Baba's lemon sherbet, I ducked into an upscale hardware store's entryway and began to cry. Steve had been telling a story and stopped, mid-sidewalk, to find me gone. In the alcove, when I told them I wanted to give my baby away, they didn't raise their voices in shock, or tell me I was absurd. "You're feeling that bad, huh," Steve said, rubbing my back as I wiped my eyes, leaning incongruously against the display of gardening tools speckled with packages of heirloom tomato seeds.

"Oh honey," said Barbara, hugging me, "it's not going to be like this always."

After all, they had raised children and helped with grandchildren, had their own extensive histories with depression and anxiety. It was Baba who had recommended the renowned psychopharmacologist Dr. H. to me years back, after he'd helped alter her days from troubled to tolerable to terrific. In her fifties, she said, she was finally enjoying daily life. Steve was one of many colleagues with whom I could talk antidepressant dosages along with how to teach Modernism—a number of us English professor–types knew similar darkness.

My father was staying at the Hilton downtown, my brother with me, and in my little Honda I was driving us all over town, with or without the two dogs' accompaniment. The two male members of my family of origin tended to argue often. Although we were all now old, gray, balding, or bald, it seemed to me the discourse hadn't change much between my brother and father from the days of the younger screaming "Fuck you!" at the dining room table, blaming my father for all his ills. At 20, my brother had descended into another genre of pit, diagnosed first as schizophrenic, then manic depressive. Was his version of the family pathology more typically male? Instead of self-destructing in the female fashion, he struck out, testosterone fueling a brief stay in jail after punching a Mercedes Benz that nearly hit his dog; another time, he drove a car onto our lawn and yelled expletives at all of us, then wrenched the screen door from its hinges. My parents called the police. After running away from various psyche wards, the chi-chi private ones as well as bare-bones state ones, he ended up sojourning in his bedroom for many months, eating cereal and watching television, a zombie on Thorazine. I never knew who he was, nor did I try, as his over-the-top illness terrified me. First Mom, now big brother—surely I would be next if I didn't take considerable care. My big sister had apparently escaped the morass by marrying young and exiting the family manse. One day, my brother left for California, poised by the highway with his thumb pointing west, and never returned.

Nevertheless, a couple of decades hadn't much diminished the tension, my father seeing my brother as a now middle-aged failure and my brother charging my father with his own shortcomings. Nowadays, however, we were more polite and did not use epithets. My position as the fucked up kid was novel for everyone—in its nakedness, at any rate—and such strangeness elicited their generosity, sublimating their age-old battle, at least temporarily. At dinner, my brother very sensibly deconstructed all obvious distresses. My father reassured me not to worry about money. Neither understood how my former thrilled optimism about impending motherhood had metamorphosed into its opposite of constant dread. Over salmon at a chic restaurant downtown, they tried to talk me into hopefulness. I didn't disclose the particulars of my recent descent into the pit, but I did admit to suffering from depression in the past, and it was again upon me like a curse.

"See a doctor!" my father commanded in his brusque, Berliner way.

"I have," I told him.

"Good."

In my twenties and thirties, when I'd asked him to pay, he'd resented my seeing shrinks, as though his youngest child's regular trips to the therapist condemned him somehow. His wife and son had resided in crazy wards, while I had, to all appearances, avoided them, climbing the white-collar ladder to higher and higher education until, like him, I had a doctor degree. My sister became a secretary and stay-home Mom like my mother, and my brother lived in his van, working when he worked at all for a delivery service. I was the professor, the one who liked to travel, who could speak other languages. Together, we had visited Brussels, Telluride, Taxco, and St. Petersburg.

So what on earth did I need to see a psychiatrist for? "Freud ruined civilization," my father liked to say. Freud wasn't the only culprit, however. Perhaps it was being born into privilege that had harmed us, our lack of struggle. Not only did we have every financial opportunity for advancement, but we were American citizens, growing up unafraid of persecution, tyranny, and impending war at home. During the World War I embargo of German ports, my father's teeth turned brown from scurvy. His mother died of pernicious anemia when he was still a child, and his father had struggled to make a living during the Weimar Republic, and lost his job in Hitler's 1935 decree. They survived as well as they could, relying on the income of the Gentile stepmother librarian.

In response to these troubles, my father did not crumple, did not self-destruct with anxiety and/or depression. Instead, he worked harder. With a shrewd finesse of the rules, he managed to continue studying law despite the edict prohibiting Jews from doing so. In 1936, he wrote a book on the expanding number of anti-Semitic laws and found a publisher for it. In 1939, he finagled his way onto the last boat out of Genoa, bound for Shanghai. Under threat to his very life, he thrived.

Like the children of many such refugees to the United States, his offspring had known nothing of comparable struggle. My teeth were orthodontically straightened and healthy—at least until I fell on my face at 25 in another suicidal moment, drunk on a bicycle alone in the night, leading to a trip to the emergency ward and years at the prosthodontist. In the U.S., no one in government or business demanded our jobs, our homes, or our lives due to our Jewishness. My father never blamed us for these circumstances, but I couldn't help my guilt at failing to thrive, though I'd spent a lifetime covering up these failures. Succeeding, for the most part, until now.

After their departure, for reasons I couldn't quite pinpoint, I felt slightly better. At the end of July, my birthing classes scheduled for the following weekend, I began to read in preparation for what I was determined would be an entirely natural, drug-free birth. Although I still felt strange everywhere I went, a depressed alien in the land of happy Portlanders, happy because it was summer and therefore sunny while I worked hard to avoid the light and couldn't remember how to smile, the impending end of pregnancy encouraged me. While I was no longer 100 percent sure of my adoption-then-suicide plan, I remained in a holding pattern, reserving judgment.

On Friday, Baba and I went shopping for a bassinette, the last big purchase I had yet to make. (Evidently, I didn't foresee giving up the baby until after I had made use of the perfect bassinette.) It was hot, my car had no air conditioning, and we stopped for something cold before heading to the baked flatlands of the outer avenues where Babies-R-Us had its outlet. Sitting in the drive-through lane at Burgerville, U.S.A., I discovered one could get shots of espresso in a mocha milkshake. A former coffee junkie, I'd been without caffeine for months, and I still don't know what possessed me to ask for a double, but I did.

In short order, I began to feel better, more like the self I remembered. In the back of a horrid warehouse-like emporium, I found The Bassinette—unpainted wicker and Victorian, with wheels to move it from room to room. The cushion and pillow were soft white cotton, trimmed with eyelets, and I could picture my baby inside it, resting peacefully. The price was more than I'd planned on spending, but I bought it anyway, encouraged by Baba to trust my instinct—a certainty I hadn't felt for months. It wouldn't fit in the Honda, so Steve promised to pick it up in his truck the next day. All afternoon I yakked and even laughed. In the morning was my first birthing class, and I was looking forward to it. That night, I never fell asleep, reading *The Birth Partner*, feeling so alive I couldn't shut my eyes. Though I blamed the caffeine for my inability to rest, I was simultaneously grateful, as that double-espresso mocha milkshake appeared to have reset my clock, springing me back into the land of the living.

When N picked me up at 8:30 a.m. for the class, weird sensations pulsed inside me, brand new ones. While she drove, I looked up my symptoms in the book, and we decided I must be experiencing false labor pains. But they wouldn't go away, and by the time of our first break at 11, I was feeling surpassing strange indeed. Are they contractions? the teacher asked me. How would I know? I'd never felt one before.

Still fueled by caffeine and wired from lack of sleep and powered by whatever else was going on inside me, I could feel another kind of turning upon me. I was given a room in the midwifery labor-and-delivery wing, and it appeared I was indeed going to deliver this baby early. After eight months and one week, perhaps catalyzed by my double espresso, Helen/Isaiah was ready to enter the world. Or perhaps s/he had sensed my turning and knew *I* was ready to give birth. I listened to Richard Burton reciting John Donne, studied *Van Gogh in Arles* and took endless showers, waiting. My midwife was a man named Tom, the only male member of the team; he reminded me of a beloved former teacher, now dead of AIDS, and I liked him at once. N left to attend to details—no one except the baby was ready for today. Somehow, I hadn't yet notified the adoption people, and this omission did not occur to me.

Happy labor stories are all alike, but every labor is astonishing in its own way.

Approximately 24 hours after being admitted to the hospital, I gave birth to Isaiah Max, 19 inches long, five and a half pounds.

Baba stayed over and Steve brought us meals. Friends arrived to marvel. When I saw the red dog leash hanging on the ladderback chair, I didn't think of the big oak in the woods, waiting for me. Instead, I hooked it to Ralph's or Pete's collar, strapped Isaiah in my Snuggly, and strolled the park with my baby and dogs, showing off to the dog-walking crowd I'd been studiously avoiding for so long. I put the psalms away.

Annie Dawid has published three volumes of fiction: And Darkness Was Under His Feet: Stories of a Family *(Litchfield Review Press),* Lily in the Desert *(Carnegie-Mellon University Press Series in Short Fiction), and* York Ferry: A Novel *(Cane Hill Press, second printing). She teaches at the Taos Summer Writers Conference at the University of New Mexico. In 2012, she won the Orlando Fall Flash Fiction Award and the Dana Award in the Essay.*

BARKING, PT. REYES

by Rafaella Del Bourgo

poetry 1st place

in the dark gloss of night
he is barking and I am awake
he's barking at raccoons fighting to get into
his food on the front porch
at the orchard
where a flock of quail with sequins for eyes
hunker down for cover
in a nest of wild grasses
and deer eat pears at dawn

barking at coyotes
yipping on the wetlands of Tomales Bay
the splintered cold
three in the morning
he is barking
at the strange man
creeping around
with the long sharp knife
trying to be quiet on the gravel driveway

at termites chewing up the foundations of the house
at the war in Afghanistan, war
in Iraq
at the financial meltdown
barking at a flock of wild turkeys
one male gobbling from his roost
at the complexity of Medicare

he is barking
at ravens
glossy and moonless
like the night of my senior prom
pale blue strapless dress
white roses at the waist

barking
another friend just died
one more name to cross out
in my address book
or because the whole east coast was splintered by cold
then sweltering sweat dripping down the back
because poisonous squid
hide deep in cracks between rocks
or because there are no poisonous squid
off the coast of California

barking at sleeping quail
bobbing head-feathers
on a moonless
three in the morning
he is barking
at coyotes chewing off the edges of Tomales Bay
100 yards west of us

San Andreas Fault
silently tearing the whole earth apart

barking
my thumb has started to hurt
I can't open jars
my friends have lines in their hair
their faces are grey
the dark gloss of night
owl nesting in the cypress
the long sharp creeper
he is barking at the knife

an empty young man
barking mad
filled with poison
fails to explode the plane
barking because there are no poisonous squid
just black ink as they disappear
black ooze of oil in the gulf of Mexico
brown pelican on a nest of dead eggs

because of the soldiers dead and alive
vanished in the mountains
of Afghanistan
the rattle of the metal can
raccoons on the front
no, because of the earthquake
Haiti broken into fragments
the mothers who grabbed their children too hard
made them cry, the mothers who couldn't rescue

he is barking at the folding of cloud upon cloud
thick shawl around the moon
in the earliest part of morning
the dark gloss still on the night
quail black sequins for eyes
hidden among cattails near the pond
late rain storm on the horizon
at the noise like a car door slamming
the strange knife
termites demolishing the foundation of this house

men and women
snow-tipped mountains
of Afghanistan
he is barking at Bedouin camels, no
at 33 miners gold dust on the tongue

barking at the still no jobs empty wallet
people with sequins for eyes
waiting in line for water
for pears
for the capsule to ascend from the bowels of hell
and all those bodies still buried under rubble
the owl shudders in the cypress

now he is asleep on his dog bed
dreaming of his walk on Limontour Beach
people stroking his ears
big black dog
beautiful dog
the strained light
wet on pink sand

I am at the window awake
because of the orchard
where deer eat succulent
in the long sharp
in the moonless
raccoons chase one another
chittering among the trees
apples and pears
and the ravens
fly invisible

Rafaella Del Bourgo's writing has appeared in The Green Hills Literary Lantern, Caveat Lector, Puerto Del Sol, Rattle, Oberon, Nimrod, Spillway, *and* The Bitter Oleanders. *Her many awards include the Lullwater Prize for Poetry, the Helen Pappas Prize in Poetry, the Paumanok Prize for Poetry, and the New River Poets Award. In 2007, 2008, and 2013, she took first place in the Maggi Meyer Poetry Competition and in 2010 she won the Alan Ginsberg Poetry Award and the Grandmother Earth Poetry Prize. Her first collection of poetry,* I Am Not Kissing You, *was published in 2003. Her chapbook,* Inexplicable Business: Poems Domestic and Wild, *will be published in February 2014 by Finishing Line Press. Rafaella has traveled the world, lived in Tasmania and Hawaii, and currently teaches college-level English and resides in Berkeley with her husband and three cats.*

SIMPLE FRACTIONS

by Margarite Landry

short fiction 2nd place

ENNIS IS DEEPLY REGRETTING HIS EDUCATION AS A COMPUTER scientist. When he sees a New Hampshire license plate in front of him that reads "Live Free or Die," he starts wondering where he can go online to buy a nice grenade launcher. He and his new girlfriend, Jill, could become survivalists, and live in a grass hut on a beach somewhere, and not pay any income tax. They could fish for their food, and wear sarongs, and he would rewrite *Das Kapital* as a graphic novel. His red string guru bracelet, a gift from his previous girlfriend, has gotten stuck on his watch, which is distracting. The car in front of him, the New Hampshire guy with the rusty pickup, is inching forward, and jams on his brakes hard, which Ennis knows is an act of hostility. Gotcha, flatlander dog from Massachusetts. Die! But Ennis's reflexes are faster.

He is stuck on Route 3 trying to get to Chelmsford, late for a conference call (do they have to call them "telenars"?) with the up-all-night software group in Bengalore, engineers with soft accents, and (he knows this from his two business trips) undriveable roads full of potholes and motorized tricycles called tuk-tuks. But is his own commute, surrounded by high-powered German cars (leased from dealerships), going four miles an hour, any better than that?

Ennis wishes he had a jelly donut.

37

As his girlfriend Jill tells him, he really ought to eat healthy. And she's right, of course, but possibly part of that half-pound of beef jerky he bought yesterday is still in the back seat. Emergency rations he can eat in case of a breakdown, he'd tell Jill, or in case Route 3 some day totally becomes a solid line of cars welded together, and there's some horrible existential meltdown into a different dimension, and he will need the beef jerky, even though it's full of nitrates, to trade with the alien life forms, or roving postapocalyptic gangs not held in check by police.

"Fuck," he says, reaching over the headrest and winnowing through the pockets of the sweatshirt he'd thrown into the back seat after his last pick-up basketball game. No beef jerky. He does find a package of sugarless gum designed to prevent cavities, and that will have to do. He opens four pieces, puts some of the wrappers in the cup holder, and throws the rest in the back.

The CD player has been broken since somebody in his band (no one will admit to this) accidentally dropped a cigarette on a CD as they were shoving it into the player, and fried it. At least, that's how Ennis reconstructed it when he took apart the CD player last Saturday and found melted plastic in the middle of Volume II of the Delta Blues, welded into the mechanism. Guilt and sabotage. No one confessed, so it was probably their ex-drummer, Duane, who comes from the Midwest and is still therefore embarrassed by his failures.

The New Hampshire pickup has gunned suddenly into an empty space in a neighboring lane, startling a woman talking on her cell phone in a Lexus. She blows the horn. The truck flips her the bird. Ennis chews harder.

Human beings are numberless, Ennis chants in his head. I vow to save them.

You can tell the Land Rover ahead is a leased car, because the driver is afraid to apply bumper stickers.

* * *

On Tuesday Ennis is driving his girlfriend's son, Tyler, to soccer practice when he notices Tyler is crying.

"What's up?" Ennis asks him, refraining from calling him buddy. Tyler, as some other man's child, and evidence of someone else's grown-up life, with his small, blond head, soccer uniform, and tendency to blurt out in public that Ennis is not his real father, actually intimidates him.

"Nothing," Tyler says. "I hate everybody."

"Is it soccer?"

Tyler shakes his head. Ennis suspects this may have to do with Tyler's recently rearranged custody visits, and the fact that his father is moving to San Diego with his new wife, Sondra, an insufferable (in Ennis's opinion) real estate agent with overly white teeth, and obviously cool feelings about Tyler himself, who is a good kid. Sondra is (Jill has said) unhappy because Tyler admittedly is evidence that Tyler's father has had sex at least once with Tyler's mother, Jill. A fact that doesn't bother Ennis, but then he's not a woman, and as Jill has told him more than once, women feel differently about these things.

"You want to blow off soccer?" he says to Tyler.

"No."

"I can take you to my work afterwards," Ennis says. "You can use the cafeteria."

"I don't care," Tyler says.

"We have a satellite link to anywhere in the world. We can Skype Lapland, or Russia."

"I don't know anyone," Tyler says.

"They have soft-serve in the cafeteria."

"I don't care about junk food, Ennis. I wish my mom would drive me."

"She has to work until eleven. Come on, I'm not that boring."

Tyler looks at him dolefully.

A BMW cuts in front of Ennis, because he's paying attention to Tyler, and Ennis says, "Capitalist twit."

Ennis puts his big paw of a hand on Tyler's shoulder, which is small and boney because he is eight and thin for his age. Time to negotiate, Ennis thinks, and arrive at a good solution, which involves, as most good solutions do, a distraction and something slightly illegal or dangerous.

He tells Tyler he can skip his homework after practice and come to Ennis's band rehearsal, if he promises not to tell his mother until after they get home.

* * *

The garage where Ennis and his band practice (it is a garage band, after all) contains about a hundred and fifty thousand dollars' worth of musical electronics, because it's a bunch of programmers, skilled thinkers, and logicians, and they know how to make things sound good. Ennis tunes his Fender, and Tyler, after being introduced to the other beer drinkers, sits on the seat of a 1987 Honda 500cc that has been put up for the winter, and picks at the last of the French fries from Burger King. He is not doing his homework, obviously, but Ennis will find a way to explain this to his mother. He wonders if, in Tyler's eyes, the band guys look cool, or if they look like highly paid and educated software engineers who are reliving their high school, when they were anything but hip.

"Tyler," Raj, the lead guitarist says, "don't kick the bike, man."

"He's not kicking it," Ennis says.

"He's rapping his foot against it," Raj says.

"Don't be so OCD, man," Ennis says, feeling that Axl Rose wouldn't give a shit, but none of these guys is stoned, after all, they have to go to work tomorrow. "Tyler," he says, "you want to sit on my speaker?" Tyler gets up grudgingly.

"I should be doing my homework," he says. "You know that."

"You don't need it," Lenny the drummer says, tapping triple beat on the snare. "I never did homework, and look where I am now."

Tyler meets Lenny's overly eyebrowed stare head on. Lenny's blond hair, which he wears to work in a pigtail, is now flowing down his back in crinkles. He looks like someone out of the Bible if it was shot as a low-budget film. Tyler looks at Ennis as if for translation. Lenny is from the Bronx, and he radiates Eastern Europe even though his family has been in the U.S. for three generations. Tyler says, "My mother will kill me."

Ratta-*tap*, Lenny goes on the drum. "Mama's boy, still?"

"He's still into that mode," Ennis says, wishing Lenny would shut up.

"You know what my mother says to me about my music?" Lenny says. Ratta-*tap*.

"No," Tyler says. "I don't care, either."

It suddenly strikes Ennis that Tyler is in a room with four fathers, if you count David, who is coming through the door now, with his new guitar case, which still has the price stickers on it. A roomful of fathers who are as unsatisfactory as Tyler's own father, the highly paid migrant worker (dermatologist) who has bought a three-million-dollar house in San Diego (Ennis has been cyberstalking, no harm in that) and taken off. Skyping won't cut it. Who is there that Tyler can rely on?

Ennis volunteers David to help Tyler play the bass line for their first song, if David will let him. "It's a simple line," he says. "Tyler can do it."

David, who is utterly tractable because he is thinking about numbers all the time, and code sequences, and because life seems to swirl and eddy around him while he watches it, amused, says it's fine with him, does Tyler want to learn the fingering? David has two children of his own, which makes him more compassionate than Raj, who is trying to get pregnant, and therefore thinks his children when they are born will all outpace everyone else's, and both David and Raj are more compassionate than Lenny, whose life is mostly channeled through his pigtail, and is otherwise an out-of-body experience. Jill has said that Lenny is a good example of spectrum disorder, but Ennis knows that he is from a long tradition of biblical scholars, and that's what they act like.

Tyler is happy to play the rhythm, and actually shows aptitude. They play fourteen covers from Metallica, and Raj and David sing, with sweat flying off their faces toward the end. Ennis joins in with vocals sometimes. Tyler, hunched against David, plucks the strings with his face crunched up, and eventually bellows like the rest of them, horrifyingly sincere in his expressions of hate and outrage.

Surely, Ennis thinks, this is better than doing your math problems. The kid is a ringer.

* * *

By the time they leave to go home, Ennis's ears are ringing, probably terminal tinnitus, and Tyler is hoarse when he asks if they really have to stop now. The band is closing up, guitars into cases, a long, mournful final rattle of the drums, the shifting and dragging of sound equipment to one side of the garage, where David tells Raj to avoid leaving the amp in the oil stain on the floor. There were cars here, once, obviously, with compromised oil pans or hoses. Ennis is slightly depressed, as usual after music, but Tyler is smiling. Ennis rests his hand on Tyler's shoulder, as if Tyler was his own. The band makes plans to meet again, which, Ennis knows, will be totally rearranged by email several times in the next few weeks before they actually get together.

* * *

When Tyler and Ennis get home, Jill is waiting with the psychic equivalent of a rolling pin at the kitchen table, where she is pretending to pay bills.

"I played in a band," Tyler says.

"What about your homework?" she answers.

"The kid's got talent," Ennis says. "He's a natural."

"What about the pages of fractions and the sevens tables?" Jill has beautiful, red hair that falls down her back under the harsh kitchen light, and Ennis runs his hand down the back of her head, and her shoulder, to feel its smoothness.

"Go," Jill points to Tyler's bedroom. "Where's your backpack?"

Ennis is holding it. When Tyler has gone down the hall, and slammed his door, Ennis cracks a beer and stands leaning on the open refrigerator door, which he knows drives Jill crazy.

Ennis knows this and he does it anyway. "He's upset about his father," Ennis says.

"I know," Jill says. "It makes me sick to my stomach."

"You didn't do it," Ennis says, knowing that he's lying, because "irreconcilable differences" means they (the parents) both failed in some desperate and fundamental way to take care of their kid. Jill lays her forehead on her arm on the table and says to her bills, "He'll probably lose his hearing."

"I hope he comes again," Ennis says. "I'll get him some of those noise-cancelling headphones."

"Door," Jill says, waggling her hand.

He shuts the refrigerator door, a source of chilliness he was unaware of. It seems to Ennis that the kitchen has sunk into a peculiar light, with his ringing ears, and his post-musical let down. He dreads sitting in his cubicle tomorrow, even if they are paying him six figures. He can feel the presence of the boy down the hall as if it is a melody line, a fragrant little hint of camaraderie. Of asking. He sits down across from Jill and takes her hands. "You're a good mother," he says.

* * *

Fifteen minutes later, he's sitting next to Tyler at his undersized desk, the top of which is killing Ennis's knees. Tyler is hyperventilating, as he does when he concentrates, trying to explain to Ennis the denominators of three similar fractions. Ennis's beer, getting warm, sits on the desk under the lamp shaped like a football. Tyler's fingers strike Ennis, as they hold the pencil, as surprisingly small fingers. He notes that they are red on the ends, probably from the playing. The harsh strings. Metal and flesh. He wants to interrupt Tyler to ask if his fingers are sore, but he doesn't do it. It's part of toughening up, he decides. Tyler can do that, too. He doesn't know how long it will be until Tyler's next screaming fit at Stop & Shop about Ennis not being his father, and having no right to decree broccoli over canned ravioli, and Ennis's other food choices made to curry favor with Jill. Probably those fits will be less embarrassing the more he (Ennis) gets used to them.

Tyler's fingers are looking redder by the minute. After the fraction decision (correct on Tyler's part) is made, Ennis says, "You want to soak them in cold water? That's what we do. But you want to keep the calluses. If you get any."

In a minute, he and Tyler are sitting on the side of the bathtub and the toilet lid, respectively, and soaking their hands in a washbasin full of cold water. Ennis's hands are big, and Tyler's are small. Ennis's red string bracelet, which he got from the old girlfriend two years ago, before he met Jill, suddenly pops off, and floats in the water, as if some voice from the Great Beyond has made a point of something he doesn't quite grok.

"You want to play with us again when we get together?" Ennis says suddenly, not even sure why he's saying it.

"The guitars?"

Ennis nods. Tyler is swishing his hands, like fish. Which seems tentatively affirmative. "You've got a knack, man," Ennis says. "I actually think that."

"You aren't my father."

"I know that. But I like you."

"My mother won't want me to," Tyler says, carving the water.

"I can fix that."

"Swish," Tyler says. "Swish, man."

Ennis winks at him, and Tyler, surprisingly enough, winks back. Now Ennis, while he examines Tyler's beet-red fingertips, is making plans. Maybe on Saturday he and Jill and Tyler can go get Tyler a guitar at Big Daddy's Guitar Emporium. Excellent name.

Margarite Landry's short stories have appeared in Nimrod, Bellingham Review, The Baltimore Review, Tampa Review, Pisgah Review, Provincetown Arts, Wordstock Ten 2012 Anthology *(first prize), and numerous other publications. Her novel-in-progress received the James Jones First Novel Fellowship in 2008. She holds an MFA from Vermont College of Fine Arts. Living near Rte. 128 in Massachusetts, she has been able to observe many software engineers in their native habitat.*

BACK TO NATURE BOY

by Vyvyan Brunst

personal essay/creative nonfiction 2nd place

WHEN I JOINED THE POUDRE WILDERNESS VOLUNTEERS I DID IT THE way we do everything on the Internet. Softly and privately, with the back-of the-brain sense that we can reel it in and no one would know. I'm not even sure of the order of events. Did I fill out a form on a Web site? Where was that site; how did I get there?

I remember expressing an interest. And it strikes me—it struck me even then—that what I had done and how I had done it was at exact odds with the thing itself.

Poudre Wilderness Volunteers help out the U.S. Forest Service by patrolling the back country of the Roosevelt National Forest and Pawnee National Grasslands, a vast stretch of north-central Colorado that comprises four wilderness areas, three national recreation trails, two historic districts, and Colorado's only Wild and Scenic River, the great trout stream of my hometown, the Cache la Poudre.

Sometimes they go on six-hour day hikes. Sometimes they camp and do back-to-back eight-hour hikes. Poudre Wilderness Volunteers talk to people, often hundreds of people a day. Sometimes we and they chat and we all go on our way; sometimes we tell trail users they are in a wilderness area and that their dogs should be on a leash, or that their horses should have weed-free hay, and sometimes they don't like that.

PWV rangers don't carry guns. They have no enforcement authority beyond what they call the Authority of the Resource. The Authority of the Resource is the notion that the wilderness—that all of what we glibly refer to as the Great Outdoors—has needs, a particular set of requirements if you like, and if we ignore them, the land suffers. The job of Poudre Wilderness Volunteers is to speak for the resource. But if someone tells us to stick it up our ass, we smile and say, "Have a great day out there!" and walk on.

The difference between the Internet and the trail is wider than the 650,000 acres of the Canyon Lakes Ranger District. It is the difference between thought and action; between the keystroke and the footfall; and between living within yourself and living outside yourself.

I have never been very good at living outside myself, being open and confident in public, having a clear idea of the intrinsic blessedness of social interaction. In elementary school I was a smart aleck. Sixth-grade teachers routinely put me in a corner for a shouted comment—"Okay Vyv, that's enough from you!"—and until my late teens I carried, like a warm stone on a cold night, the impression that somehow I was an extrovert.

Girls turned in their chairs and rolled their eyes. The broad-shouldered guy kicked out of class would glance back at me, a kindred spirit, a fellow Marine. Fuck them, right? But I wasn't a kindred spirit; I wasn't a class clown or a rebel. I was a social sniper. I acted in borrowed camouflage, softly, privately. But when the lights were on me I froze, bewildered and scared. I was not the broad-shouldered guy; I was not the Marine.

After class I walked home alone, along a network of streets in the northeast suburbs of Los Angeles, in the beauty of the foothills of the San Gabriel Mountains. First there was road and asphalt, the red-brick factory of our school, a wax paper cup, broken glass, a condom, and then the street would turn onto Baseline Avenue and I found myself walking against the eucalyptus, the path in shade, the glass gone and the cars few. I waited for them. Sometimes a convertible passed; its breeze lifted me up into the wild oil of the wood, the throb of insects, the shade of the path home. On the weekends I hid in the wood, and the dark ineluctable smell of geraniums reached out into my tent of piñon boughs, into the damp earth.

When they discovered me, unadvertised, and thought fixed in their minds as it does, the neighbors began to call me Nature Boy. They smiled when I joined the group: "Hi Nature Boy, where are you headed today?" There was none of the penalty of class, none of the confusion of being bold or quiet. And it was almost as good as being on the damp earth and smelling the bright red flowers from the hill, except that here there were people.

In the months after I filled out whatever form it was to become a Poudre Wilderness Volunteer, and for whatever reason I did it, on whatever Web site, I heard nothing. After a while you begin to think you will hear nothing. Sometimes you do: sometimes you hear nothing.

And then the emails began. It was late winter. The first messages were unintelligible bursts. From the Forest Service: "Here is the correct link for Patrol Scheduling Preferences (I had an extra 's' at the end by mistake)."

It was as though I had crawled into the attic and found an old radio.

"The link to the Scheduling Questionnaire in the Recruit Welcome Letter 2013 that you've received today is incorrect. Please use the corrected link in the letter attached in this email instead, or click on the link below. Sorry for the inconvenience."

Then: "Hello Future PWV Member, We received notice that you were interested in joining PWV. We are pleased that you want to help us with the good work we do for the Forest Service. The next step is to complete our application . . ."

I had established contact, but I wasn't sure with what. There was a get-together in May. Would you be able to make it? Interviews began. And then a sketch of order. There were the interviews; after that, a kick-off meeting; after the kick-off meeting, Spring Training. They were mandatory, the kick-off meeting and Spring Training, a whole weekend at the Cub Scout Camp at Red Feather Lakes. Here is a list of what to bring.

"Please understand it may be cold and wet during the weekend and on the hike. Know what you need to be comfortable. Please sign and return."

I know what I need to be comfortable. I need to stay at home. I need anonymity, camouflage, a place alone in the piñon pine on the damp earth. I don't need Forest Service rangers asking questions about my hiking habits, a roomful of strangers with felt-tip name badges, introductions, potluck dinners, bad coffee in the morning, and a lot of awkward, sleepy small talk. But at 53, if I had wanted to be comfortable I wouldn't have done whatever it was I did when I filled out that form.

* * *

My parents must have signed me up for the Boy Scouts. And that was another difference. When you are 53 you make a choice to embarrass yourself. You don't need anybody's help. When you are 11, your parents do it for you. And, of course, when you're 11, you don't think about the terror of meeting a full-bodied adult wearing Hitler Youth khaki in a fluorescent-lit schoolroom for bizarre ritualistic role-playing, but you do remember going to the store to buy the knife.

My mother also had been given a list, the sort that in those days would have come in the mailbox, with a pale blue cancellation mark and a cheery "Scouts Über Alles!" sticker. At the grocery store she was a picture of efficiency: she glided down the aisles, grabbing milk and Fruit Loops off the shelves with practiced confidence. And there were times, even then, when we pulled into the parking lot of a nondescript building and she fished out her booklet of green stamps, the one I sometimes saw them pasting late at night at the kitchen table, and leaving us in the car, she popped in and returned, putting the package in the back and giving us a strained smile, a proud Cornish girl.

At the Claremont sporting goods store she was nervous. She had never been there before. She held the letter in her hand when she approached the glass-topped desk. Everything smelled old, oddly out-of-date, but in their peculiar local agreement with the Boy Scouts of America, anointed.

"My son is just joining. The Scouts."

He looked over the reflecting glass, smiling. There exist a few photographs of me at that age. We grew quickly after the Summer of Love, and given the fact that it was 1970, in an LA suburb, and that our family had immigrant quirks every Ellis Island passenger also had known and regretted, I was probably dressed in a skin-tight long-sleeved t-shirt with blue and red horizontal stripes, pale blue corduroy pants that belonged to my brother, and six-inch dark blue velvet bell-bottoms that made up for the length of what we once had been and now were.

For the sporting goods manager with the thinning hair it must have been as though Sonny Bono had walked into the recruiting office unasked. You know, lady, I think we can do something.

I wasn't much interested in the slacks, the belt, and the shirt. The Manual held promise: it seemed to offer up secrets in matte-green and black. But the knife was different. It came in a raw leather sheath, brass rivets, a thick brass pommel guard, and a five-inch steel blade, arced back extravagantly to a pin-point tip. I heard, as every boy had heard before in a similar situation, the dull voices of whichever committee had approved this precious gift:

"Hearing no objection, be it moved that pursuant to the rules every prepubescent child with anything resembling a penis should, if his mother has the list, be allowed to carry, wield, or otherwise display, a fully functional heart-stabbing steel blade of such length that woodland creatures should cower, and notwithstanding the throat-gripping fear of his scout leader, be accorded etc. etc." And around the table, yea and yea.

And so I marched out of the Claremont sporting goods store with a bunch of dust-colored clothes, which in an inexplicable way had caused my mother shame, and a knife, which did not, and which I do not recall her ever asking about again.

Before the mid-90s the Red Feather and Estes-Poudre Ranger Districts were doing pretty well. They had 30 seasonal employees and three full-time forest service staff members working on wilderness trails. By 1995 they had been combined into a single ranger district and the seasonal employees reduced from 30 to 2. For one of those two remaining seasonal employees that seemed inadequate, and so he founded the Poudre Wilderness Volunteers.

The PWV don't replace United States Forest Service rangers, they just shadow them, the way a roadie shadows a rock star, or the way a studio apprentice shadowed a master painter in the Renaissance. While the Forest Service Web site will tell you that more than 30,000 serve in career positions in the Forest Service, many who contribute are temporary workers. If you want to get into the highly competitive Forest Service as a forester, technician, civil engineer, botanist, or researcher you might take forestry, forest management, ecology, botany, biology, wildlife or fisheries management as a college student.

On the other hand, the members who fill the ranks of the Poudre Wilderness Volunteers are very often older folks: retirees with the time to spend a weekday on the trail in the summer months; kidless older couples with the weekends free; software moguls with backpacking obsessions. Fifty- and sixty-year-olds who already have a career—often for many times the 30 to 40K paid by the government—and who want to give back, or who hear faint whispers of something that was important, insistent, and small, from a time when they were not very much responsible, to have the whisper eclipsed by a time when they were very much responsible, when they had reduced doubt the way a prospector reduces gold from stone, and when in the end they weren't talking to counselors about career paths but standing on the wooden decks of their rural houses, the mortgage paid, the weeds growing, the deer eating the sour cherry, the Audubon subscription and the water bill.

"Hi, I'm Vyvyan," I said to the pretty girl in the chair to my right. I hadn't waited until the MC at the PWV kick-off meeting had urged us to turn to the person on our right and introduce ourselves. "I'm Kelly," she said, and pointed to the felt-tip name badge already on her chest.

"I guess you're a recruit, too?" Of course we were recruits. "Are you a CSU student?"

"Yeah, I'm doing wildlife biology."

"Hmm," I said, thoughtfully. I eyed the buffet table, where my oatmeal raisin cookies were going fast. Kelly eyed the only other person of her age, a boy with a drift of beard and a messenger bag. When he approached I took the opportunity to study my field guide.

* * *

Not long after I joined the Boy Scouts I climbed Mount Baldy in a blizzard. Mt. Baldy is the highest peak of the San Gabriel Mountains, at something just over 10,000 feet, which for residents of Northern Colorado puts it in the "Jeez, I tripped over that shoe box you brought home last night, fell on my ass, and almost slipped down to 10,000 feet" category. Be careful next time. Jeez.

But for those in Los Angeles County, scoutmasters in particular, the real draw was you could get there in an hour. Even if you hadn't studied the weather report.

It was probably the fact that we all wore those knives with laminated leather and wood grips that gave our leaders the confidence they could take a group of children with no wilderness training up Mount Baldy in early spring, when the average high is about 48°F and the average low is 28°F. And then the weather can turn. It did when we reached the snow, along an unmarked ridge with the summit in view.

"Now listen to me good, guys," the scoutmaster shouted through the blowing snow. "If you fall off this side, the side that goes down, I want you to Spread Eagle! Can you do that? Show me you can spread your arms like an eagle! Good! That's great, Todd!" He seemed a little wacky. When we took a break I noticed the assistant scoutmaster had wandered off, so I followed him. He disappeared around a thin ledge on the mountain. Maybe the guys who hadn't caught the snow fever were leaving.

I found him standing on a lip overlooking a steep drop, holding his dick. A stream of pee arced into the void, falling far below on those who had been sensible enough to stay around the television, test the beach, or go to Disneyland.

He turned when he caught movement. "Heh, kid. Just taking a peeton. Whee!" I went back to the group, we climbed to the summit, and went home. The next weekend we played Capture the Flag outside some church and I hit my shin on a rock.

* * *

The interview at the Forest Service headquarters was a half-hour drive from our house. It had snowed. We had two cars but I drove the older one, a 1999 Mitsubishi Mirage sports coupe we had bought when we had no money. It had been designed for and was driven by college girls whose parents couldn't afford a Hyundai, and it had a safety rating a notch above Suicidal with good tires, of which I hadn't any.

Still, I took it down the hill to get the paper. That part was good. On the way up I stuck it in a ditch and slid backwards, carving a good groove in the shoulder. There was no going forward or back. Worse, I blocked the one road to our hill so effectively that when a hill-dweller I had never seen before turned up the road in his truck I could only make small talk.

"Out early?" I started.

"I went into Old Town for breakfast. The Silver Grill."

His truck still had the keys in it; it was puffing smoke.

"They make a good breakfast," I said. He glared.

Some time later a new resident of Red Cedar Drive turned up with a winch, pulled out my car, and disappeared back down the street. I had never seen him before, nor have I seen the sour Silver Grill breakfast guy since. Craig, across the street, after we walked up the hill together, said, "It takes all kinds."

With that thought I nervously entered the Forest Service headquarters on Center Street for my interview. It was a beautiful building. Everything seemed cantilevered: the heavy door swinging open, the gray-haired lady pushing it, perfectly cantilevered, her smile perfectly cantilevered, the rough wood beams of the foyer, the tumbling slate waterfall and the competent mural of rushing water, the diverse and happy fauna of a Diego Rivera on USFS Prozac. I couldn't help grinning at the woman holding the door. She wore her Poudre Wilderness Volunteer shirt with the two patches—the Forest Service Volunteer patch and the PWV patch that had been approved unanimously for its being almost but not quite a Forest Service patch—and I grinned at her and everyone I met in the room as though I was president of the Kiwanis Club.

I was ushered to the reception counter, where this evening, instead of Forest Service guards asking pointed questions—What exactly brings you to our forest? And you heard of this forest where?—two perfectly coifed, dulcet-toned though unnaturally short women pointed to first one and then another sheet of paper. "Please sign in. If you could write your name as you want it to be spelled on your name tag. And then this one . . . check if you want a hat and a badge kit."

I checked. What size are you? they asked. I understood, as a ragged-haired six-footer, that I was not necessarily from their planet. They offered a sample shirt. I tried it on. Extra-large—usually a sure bet—was actually a little too large, an impossibility given the diminutive handmaiden behind the counter, and there ensued a mental Adventures in Wonderland exercise in which I judged the shirt to grow in reverse proportion to the stature of the women.

"I guess large will do for you," said one of the women sweetly.

I grabbed a hat from the counter.

"Whuup!" the lady twittered. "That's a sample. You'll get yours when you graduate."

I hadn't been interviewed, but already I felt as though I had been measured for my casket at my birth.

"Well, it's not exactly an interview," said the docent from the first inner sanctum. "It's more like a meet'n greet. We get to know you; you get to know us. I was a recruit last year, and I don't do well talking to people. Actually, I was real nervous! I'm going to show you a movie about the PWV. It has a lot of John Denver songs in it."

"I love John Denver," said the woman on my left.

In fact, there were only the two of us. However many recruits were interviewed, we were apparently meeted and greeted two by two. The ark leaves at nine. John Denver's "Rocky Mountain High" was already playing. The video explained the origins and mission of the Poudre Wilderness Volunteers, and the craggy-faced gent on the screen kept using the phrase Authority of the Resource. I had no idea what it meant. Are we the resource—fifty-something John Denver lovers? What authority is that? Is it the Forest Service, stamped down to a powder few by budget cuts? Where is the authority; what is the resource?

The term was coined by George Wallace, a Colorado State University professor. Wild nature, he explained, can be said to have its own authority. Nature has its own rules, operates in certain ways, and has certain laws. There are consequences when those laws are violated. Nature is the Resource. When you articulate it, the Resource speaks through you. You speak for it. Red flowers. Damp earth.

* * *

One of the few times my family ever went to the Yosemite, that caldera of right-thinking national park environmentalism, it rained the whole trip. We camped in the valley. It rained. My father, no stranger to rain being an Englishman, but apparently a stranger to Yosemite rain, took off his boots and put them in the campfire grate. They burned and we retrieved them, smoking.

The next morning, in the planned highlight of the trip, my brothers and I packed lunches and took horses on a day ride. It rained and it kept on raining. In the end, with our sandwiches soaked through despite plastic bags, we slumped home, bent over our horses like a sentimental Western bronze of an Indian holocaust.

The day after, no longer expecting to see the sun, we hiked to Bridal Veil Falls. Today, the Yosemite Web site cautions you to expect spray in spring and early summer at the base of the falls, but the hike is an easy half-mile. I am convinced that we climbed to the top of it, a torrent of rain mixing with the spray. My clear memory is of grasping a slick steel rail, jointed along the length and green with moss, and seeing my father's burnt boot for the last time ascending the rubber-slick rock, and the image in my head at the time was an engraving of Sherlock Holmes and Professor Moriarty cartwheeling through the mist of the Reichenbach, tumbling irretrievably down, and my father years later, with a sad look, saying, "I almost saved him—my boy!—but my burnt boots split as I turned and his hand slipped out of mine and he cartwheeled irretrievably down!"

Memory or fact, I gave my life to the water. If we were to tumble against the rocks, would I also be lit by the small sun that lanced into the valley, would I be equal to the damp duff of the valley floor, would the trees smell still brighter going down?

* * *

The male broad-tailed hummingbird has a green back and a red throat. While most people know it for drinking at trumpet-shaped flowers it is one of the wild's great showmen, with its soaring courtship dives, its incredible memory, and its ruthless aggression.

When Jane and I bought our house in Bellvue, in the low foothills of the Rocky Mountains just outside Fort Collins, Colorado, we bought it for the view. Or at least that 260-degree panorama to the east—straight ahead, downtown Fort Collins, over the Horsetooth Reservoir, that miracle of 1940s WPA ambition; to the right, Loveland, 21 miles to the south; behind that, Greeley, 43 miles south-southeast; to the north, the ranches of Waverley and Wellington, with the towers of the Anheuser-Busch plant picked out by late evening sun; far north, Soapstone Prairie, a 28-square-mile patch of shortgrass prairie that includes the Lindenmeier Site, the largest Folsom culture campsite yet found, dating to the ninth century BC. Just beyond that, Wyoming. It was all visible.

In the evening of a good day, at 5,600 feet, mourning doves fly each way below the redwood deck, and the clouds, highlit pink and white, hang within reach in the impossible blue of late evening Colorado sky. After we had lived there a year I told my wife that when I went out on the east deck in the evening of a summer's day I thought I was in heaven. It was no hyperbole. The simplest man knows heaven when he sees it.

In heaven, apparently, there is a bird with a green back and a red throat that through the late spring and all through the summer, in the late evening, climbs 60 feet into the air, against the impossible blue of the Colorado sky and then turns—flips, really—toward the ground like one of those air show disasters in Ohio or California. The split second between mouth agape at the boldness, and then stunned by the horror. Except that with the broad-tailed hummingbird there is no disaster.

He sweeps toward the ground just slowly enough that you comprehend the action, but too fast to fix it, so that when he resurfaces again against the paste, pink-frosted cloud, and starts down again, you favor the sound, unable to rely on sight, and the sound is, now that I think about it, like the zip of the zipper of a tent when the day is finished and you are at the end of a day in a campsite somewhere. It might be the Yosemite; it might be in New England, or in Barstow, or in Montana. The sound is the same.

But it is not all love. I once saw a hummingbird go through the motions of his courtship dive, but there was no female in the lilacs. A rival stood where the incumbent usually stood before the dive—on one of the Austrian Pines out front. He still rose, and flipped, and raced to the ground, but his target this time was a still, mirror form at the top of the pine. He did that a couple of times, and his rival flew off. Hummingbirds have been known to chest-bump in mid-air when threatened by another male.

A photograph shows me at 10 years old presenting a family friend, a Bangalore-born teacher named Ramsey Harris, with a coat of arms I had drawn for him. Each side of the shield was a hummingbird. Ramsey made sick birds better. Students in Claremont brought him injured sparrows, sometimes larger birds, and he nursed them, fed them ground beef and water from an eyedropper, and his house hung with sugar water and the zip of hummingbirds. He taught me to bury the dead ones and dig them up months later, to know their bones. When I gave him the coat of arms he squeezed my hand and said, "Thanks, Nature Boy."

So I gave my life to the hummingbird. If I could fight and love and hate and do it all in beauty, and know and not know, that was for him.

* * *

Spring Training came. It was at the Cub Scout Camp in Red Feather. I arrived late on the first day because I was working. It was a Friday. I had spent some time packing, and then taken an hour to read the field guide; packed a little; read the chapter on noxious weeds, or the Ten Essentials of backcountry camping. But when I climbed into the 1999 Mitsubishi Mirage for the hour-long drive to the camp I felt like an undergraduate who had spent the night before the exam watching *Star Trek* and getting stoned. How could I possibly pass?

We had been put into animal groups at the kick-off meeting. My group was Coyote. Ky-Yoat, most PWV veterans pronounced it, and I tried to follow the pronunciation, although all my life I had said Ky-Yoat-Ti. I wheeled my gear up to the registration table. They gave me a schedule, a map, my patch kit, and my hat.

"Which group are you in?" one of them said.

"Ky-Yoat-Ti," I said.

She looked to the other Hobbit girl for agreement.

"Ky-Yoats are next to Badgers," she said, pointing at the map.

My group leader helped me put up my tent. I apologized for it.

"I'm getting a new one this year," I said. Another Coyote had smelled blood and joined the tent-raising. He fiddled with a broken pole.

"Don't worry about that. I'll finesse that later. I'm getting a new tent this year!" I assured him. He pawed the ground in frustration. "It's okay," I said.

The only thing I remember from the orientation that night, other than the fact that when you are 53 and not 11 you can have a brewer for a major sponsor, was the Forest Service liaison saying we should put all our food into our cars before we hit the hay.

"This is bear country," he said. "You should expect them to come around."

Just as I had when I was a kid, at the Boy Scout camporee and on the high school road trips, I expected them to come around. At nine o'clock when I turned in; at one o'clock, after several hours of fitful sleep; at three o'clock when the wind—or was it a bear?—tugged at the tent and distant voices said, "He brushed his teeth before he went to sleep, can you believe that? The bear ate his lips!" And again, at bear breakfast, with the sky getting light.

But then, with the sky getting light, I gave my life to the bear. If he let me sleep, wake in the morning to the familiar zip of mosquito netting, to the boots at the foot of the bag, and the bad coffee, that was for him. That was our joke. And I slept.

My first mentor patrol was also at Red Feather Lakes. It was the week after Spring Training, Memorial Day weekend. An easy six-hour hike in national forest. No leash laws, no stringent fire and campsite regulations. I had been given a high fastball to hit. Still, barely half a mile up the trail Sherri, my mentor, pushed me forward in front of an approaching couple: "You take this."

They were some of the easiest words I ever spoke:

"Hi there, folks, where are you headed today?"

Vyvyan Brunst was born in Reading, England in 1959. A naturalized Canadian, a permanent resident of the U.S., and the husband of a New Jersey girl, he is the author of four books of poems, the last two, Weather *and* Ur Skin: The Poems of Kat Couch, *published by Lilibug Publishing, LLC of Bellvue, CO.* Panic Water: More Poems by Kat Couch *is due out at the end of 2013, also from Lilibug Publishing. He is currently completing the novels* Herringbone *and* Slider.

ALAIN

by Sara Blazevic

poetry 2nd place

We have our bandannas up
to keep out hay dust
like bank robbers
or Alain at Nanterre in 1968,
throwing rocks from the barricades.

There are so many machines to learn:
the one that cuts grass in meter-long swaths
the one that whips it into long rows
the one that rolls and compresses the bales.

In ragged bathrobe he rests his
hand on the donkey's haunch
and feels his sightless way
through the yard.
He tells me about the revolution
and falling in love:
Our heads were floating
in the same cloud.
The rooster gets
underfoot and Valtz,
the last horse he birthed,
cranes her thick slick neck
across the electric fence

to nose-bump his chest
like an infant trying
to breastfeed.

The hawks circle down
diving for mice
between fat spirals of hay.
Something catches the tines
of whatever we're hitched to
too hard, and we spend hours tinkering.
Alain works without eyes
and I follow instructions mechanically
not knowing the words for a single thing
I touch, up to my elbows in machine.

Sara Blazevic is a Croatian New Yorker. Her poems and photography have appeared in the Newport Review, Thrush, Apiary, We Are Wild, *and* Szu Magazine.

WHAT THE TREE SAW

by Jennifer Shepard

short fiction 3rd place

NOW IT'S COMMON KNOWLEDGE THAT A TOWN OF A CERTAIN SIZE will have a witch, if only for the purpose of eating disobedient children and thereby keeping the population at manageable levels. My grandma said that mothers of naughty boys and girls offered up more prayers on behalf of their offspring than mothers of obedient kids. To keep down the praying, witches started eating up the troublemakers who were giving their mothers extra reason for heavenly correspondence.

"Didn't their mamas pray even more when their kids were et up?" I'd ask. Sometimes I'd get as much as a huff out of her, but mostly her answer'd be that their mothers forgot about them quicker than a girl my age would care to dwell on.

I believed her, because my grandma was one of those witches.

She lived at the edge of town—the edge of town that seemed to be downhill or at least downstream for where the wind would pile up the worst looking dead leaves—in a large gray house that backed up to the only creek in the county. That house had stood through the war. Rumor had it that a Yankee general had tried to burn it, but it wouldn't light. He tried again and half an oak tree fell on him and his horse and smashed him dead for his effort. The part of the story that most people left out, cause it made the house and the town a whole lot less special, was that this general was burning houses in the middle of a near monsoon. It was too wet to burn a can of gas. The storm and some wind knocked that branch down on his head. Nothing more than bad luck.

It was at the base of that very tree that my friends and I congregated today. The weeds grew high in the yards around us, so we were free from the watchful eyes of adults. We'd been hunting toads all morning along the banks of the drainage ditch that ran behind the house, and once again, the sun had gotten high without us even sighting a single one. We slumped in the shade. There were five of us: me; Ray; the Treemont brothers, Finn and Buck; and my little brother, William. I was the newest to the gang and Will didn't even count he was so little, so we were getting the least amounts of shade, but not complaining.

"'Genia, how big'd God's gun be?" Will asked as he poked the cracked ground with a stick. He'd just turned five and always asked the oddest questions. But the rest of the boys hushed and looked around sort of furtive-like, maybe sensing that the conversation had just veered toward the deeper secrets of the universe and more importantly, that we were all bound to get in trouble for it.

Ray was the oldest of the gang and seemed to feel it his duty to field this query. "Gotta be the opposite of a toad's."

William laughed. "Toad with a gun," he sort of sang and the Treemont brothers chuckled too.

This made Ray mad and he stood up, getting his face right in Will's. "What would you know about it anyway, yer dumb baby bastard."

I wedged between the boys, shoving Ray back. "You talk to him like that again and you'll be doin' it with a whole lot less teeth."

Ray reclaimed his spot in the shade glaring at me in a way that proclaimed me as more crazy than tough. But he backed down and that's all I cared about. During the tussle, Will's mouth had fallen slack, but he managed to clamp it shut like a bulldog that had just learned the world could kick. He looked 50 years old. I didn't like it—seeing him in these moments when he was forced to grow up. Will's education 'bout society had seemed to be in a race against time ever since we'd moved here to Jackson.

Back in Missouri, people were used to us not having no daddy. I don't think Will even realized he was missing one. But here it was hot news. Made me feel out of control, all tippy, having people I'd just met know all about my business and be mean about it; made me treasure all the more, the privacy I still had. For one, these dumb boys had brought us out to the *witch's* house, telling us stories—trying to scare us—not having any idea she was our grandma. My own mother was probably in that house, visiting, right this very minute. Ma had gotten sick lately. We'd moved into town to be walking distance from her ma.

"We gonna do this or not?" Finn, asked. "If Eugenia's fixin' to box Ray, then I reckon she man enough to make a potion."

Ray shrugged. "Voodoo works better with a odd number anyway." He held out the pie pan he'd nicked from his ma's pantry. The dish was full of mud and a stick to stir it with.

Buck threw in a handful of sand from the base of the tree. "Good thing, cause we'll be needin' a *girl* to pick the flowers."

I shot him a look but he was sneering toward Ray. "That looks like it'll be you, *Ray*chel."

Ray snatched back the pan. "Hell, on'y reason you're here not wettin' yourself is cause it's still daylight."

"I got flowers." Will, always helpful, held out a fistful of dandelions, roots and all, to Ray. "What are we doin?"

Finn took the wilting weeds from Will's chubby hand and began to tear them to shreds as he explained, "We're making a potion for gettin' our toads back. This here tree is where the leprechaun lives. Tiny little sprite devil, on'y comes out at night to do the witch's bidding." Finn's eyes glinted on his last words and I noticed, with some satisfaction, that once again he was quite confused as to why neither of us new kids seemed to care a hide about this witch. Finn continued, "Leprechaun's the reason we ain't seen no toads. See, he's wrangled'em all."

Buck chucked a rock toward his brother's head, but spoke to Ray and me. "Finn just watched *Shane*. Thinks he can talk like a cowboy now."

None of us paid any attention to Buck. Finn was the brains of the outfit and whether his daft brother realized it or not, we all wanted to hear how we were gonna get the toads back.

"What's he wrangled them for?" Will asked as his fingers slowed over the yellow petals. Finn put his arm around Will and began filling him in on the finer points of leprechaun culture. They don't have cars. Of course they don't, they're too short to reach the pedals. Leprechauns travel by toadback through underground passageways that connect their trees to the trees of other witches.

I looked at the oak's trunk all gnarled and lumpy. Low down at the base, where the roots grabbed into the earth, the wrinkles in the bark are so deep that I could stick my fingers halfway up before my nails come out dirty. "Can I add the flowers now?" I asked.

"Sure. But slowly, so you can stop if the potion gets chunky."

We add pinecones and bits of string, spit from each of us and even some mashed up worms, until it smells rank. The theory behind the potion seems to be, that if a good child sprinkles some around a leprechaun's door at night, then that leprechaun will come to investigate and when he opens the door, all the toads will leap out. I picture an old woman in her bathrobe and curlers peering out her porch door after being ding-dong-ditched and the dag-nabbed cat slipping away.

"I've mashed the berries and he's gonna love this," Ray adds. All five of us huddled around the bucket of swirling brown, alternately stirring and adding precise extractions from our pockets. At one point, Buck had to use the bathroom—he tried to convince us all that he should be allowed to relive himself into the potion—but then realized that I was there watching, and all of a sudden remembered he had something to do at home. When he returned, he came with a carton of moldy cottage cheese and some ambrosia that'd gone round the bend. We stirred it in.

"Now all we have to do is wait till nightfall," Finn directed and a few of the boys looked around like they was already getting spooked about hanging around in the witch's yard after dark.

"I nominate Ray," Finn and Buck say in unison, and I can tell that this two-against-one stunt is something they pull frequently. Ray curses toward his feet.

"I'll do it with ya, Ray." Will grins. And before he even finishes the last word, I know that these boys won't see his offer as a kindness. Ray glares at my baby brother and something mean passes behind his eyes.

"How bout ya do it yourself? I'll make it real easy for ya—I'll dump the potion right now." Ray was quick and grabbed the pie tin of stinking slop and made to dump it on Will's blond head. I knocked the tin away. The potion we'd been working on all afternoon sloshed all over the base of the tree.

"Back off a him!" I'd begun to growl, but Ray plowed headfirst into my gut like a charging bull. Knocked me into the ground with him on top. I went down hard and I guess he thought I'd stay there. He gives me this cocky grin and that's when I punch him in the jaw. And then just keep punching. Believe me, he punched back and the two of us tussled like two tangled-up tumbleweeds in a tornado. Ray left crying.

I felt like bawling, but was too in shock for tears to roll just yet. Finn helped me up and kinda chuckled, but not cruel-like. More like he was trying to get my mind off my hurts. He said, "You rolled in worm guts, Genia. And 'sides that, you're not supposed to dump the potion till nightfall. Maybe that leprechaun put a spell a clumsiness on you in order to protect his wrangled toads."

I swiped at my nose and pointed Will toward home. "Or maybe the Great Smiter didn't like us talkin' bout his gun collection."

That was the first fistfight I'd ever been in. When I came banging in through the screen porch of our house, I wasn't really hurt, exactly, but I just felt like bawling. Momma took me into her bathroom and cleaned me off; treated me real tender and just talked to me like we was two kids that got in fights every day.

"They hate me, Momma," I cried into the lap of her soft cotton nighty. "Why'd we have to move here, anyway?"

Momma glanced down. She sighed, and I thought for a moment that she might cry. "They don't hate you, Eugenia. They're just boys. Takes their kind a bit more effort to not be cavemen." She pressed a cool rag to the hot spot on my cheek. "You understand that we came here cause your momma's sick, right? Doctor says I've got a lot of tired days ahead of me until I beat it." I watched her face, the way her lips pulled tight at the end of her words like she was holding in other words that wanted to spill out. She smiled, real easy at me, like we were them kids again—the ones used to fights—and said, "Your brother wears me out when I'm *full* a vim and vigor. If I'm gone be getting tired, I'm gone need your grandma's help. 'Sides, it'll be nice for the two of you to grow up near some family."

I groaned. "Everybody thinks she's a witch, Momma." I pointed my swelling eye toward her so she'd be sure to get a good look. "What you think they gonna do to me when they find out I'm kin to a witch?"

"My! I forgot how delicate these wonderful boys are and how careful we must be around their opinions of us all. Pardon me!" Then her face became sober and she held up my punching hand and sort of surveyed the knuckles that were already purpling. She made sure I saw her doing it before she looked me straight in the eye. "Eugenia Francis, you made me real proud today. You took a lickin' to save your brother, but you also gave one cause you knew you deserved better."

Three months later, my ma was dead. A whole lot a days passed after that that I don't clearly remember. Neighbors with casseroles showed up all the time. Grandma said we had to come live with her, but I wouldn't leave the house that Momma had picked out for us. Said I couldn't, just yet. And so Grandma looked in on us and saw that we took baths and got to school. She practically set up residence on our sofa a good number a days, but I could tell she was giving me my time. There was a For Sale sign put up in the front yard, and as patient as my grandma was being, I knew that sign didn't care about me.

Then one Sunday evening, my daddy showed up. The crickets were singing. Grandma opened the door and her face took on a look like she'd just smelled something rotten.

"Eugenia. William. This is your father," she said, and at those words, a little something bloomed inside of me. The man that stood in the twilight was tall with short-cropped blond hair—a shade identical to Will's. Daddy was real, and he'd come for us.

"You've gone and gotten big," Daddy said in a voice too loud for the small entry. He stepped over the threshold to get a better look at us. I tried to stand up taller.

"I'll be goin' now," Grandma said, her lips pursed like she'd just been forced to swallow the rotten smell. I heard her pause just outside the front door and let out a curse before the porch steps creaked her descent.

Daddy seemed to know what she was cursing about; his eyes took on this faraway look like he could just imagine what she was seeing and couldn't wait for her to get out. "Your ma's gone. They tell you that?"

Will and I nodded. Daddy's eyes flashed to mine and he surveyed me up and down, like he was trying to place where he knew me from.

"You have the look a your mother," he finally said.

His gaze switched to Will. "How old a you?"

Will's voice shook a bit as he answered, "Five, Sir."

At the "*Sir,*" Daddy blinked like he'd just heard a snatch of something humorous. "Good boy. Well, then I brought you an older sister." He glanced lazily in my direction. "And you, a younger one."

Daddy turned and bellowed through our still-open front screen door, "Del! Get in here. Bring yer stuff."

The little something that had bloomed inside of me only a minute ago got prickly and angry, as a girl, no bigger than Will, crept in and stood in my daddy's shadow. My daddy. I didn't like her. I couldn't imagine how I'd suddenly gotten a sister. As I stared at her, her tiny hands fumbled at the handle of a worn out carpet bag, the kind vagrants carried. She was brown—the color of something that had been left on the stovetop too long. Her darkness was only enhanced by the way she seemed to hug the shadow. Her eyes never lifted from the floor, so I got a real good look at the top of her head. It was an ugly head. I hadn't had my daddy for more than two minutes and here she was, standing closer to him than I ever had. It made something angry crawl up my throat to realize that she'd at least traveled with him, and at most, had him for her entire life.

Daddy was talking. He sent us to bed and Del was directed to join Will and me in our room.

Will was aquiver with questions for our new sister and wouldn't lay still in the bed. "You gonna live here, too?"

I glared at my brother, but he didn't notice in the dim light.

The girl seemed to be hardly breathing, almost like a fish tossed out onto the bank now that she didn't have a shadow to cower in.

"And yer colored—how'd ya get colored?" Will asked.

Days passed, then months, and I guess I got a year older. Daddy slept a lot and smelled like liquor most of the time. Slowly, Will and I started to spend more time at Grandma's. I didn't speak to Del and she seemed to understand that she shouldn't speak to me, either. Every once in a while she'd answer one of Will's thousand questions, and I listened. Her mother was colored. She'd died like ours. Del'd lived with Daddy for the past year. Getting these measly questions answered represented months of Will's questioning and still, I wouldn't be able to tell you the color of Del's eyes, but I had every hair on the top of her head memorized. Daddy yelled at her a lot. Which was fine by me. But his yelling got so bad that Grandma came to have us live with her for a spell.

I was doing well in school. I wanted Daddy to see how smart both Will and I were, so we studied every night, and every day on the walk home from school, I'd drop off my papers for Daddy to see when he woke up. I knew sooner or later Daddy'd want to ask me a bunch a questions bout myself and I wanted to be ready. Del didn't go to school. She was silent and blended into the backdrop of my old house and my new father.

Grandma asked about her frequently, or else I'd have forgotten about her altogether.

"She's fine, Grandma," I'd answer and always get the eye like I was being dishonest. The truth was, I didn't want to see that my daddy was mean. But it wasn't many days more that I was able to go on pretending. One evening Daddy yelled at Del real bad; smacked her up against the peeling floral wallpaper of the kitchen just cause she'd dropped a orange.

Red blood fell from Del's nose and she sniffed and tugged at her dress like she was trying to make it cover more of her.

"You're my age aren't ya?" I whispered to her and cleaned up a pot of grits that had splattered along the leg of the table. She nodded.

"Turned ten las' week."

Del's eyes were brown.

After that day, things were better between Del and me. Since the colored school was a bus ride away, Daddy'd said she couldn't go. Said it would interfere too much with her housekeeping chores. Del missed learning, and one night she showed me all my old school papers. The one's I'd been dropping off for Daddy. She'd erased my marks and redone the work on her own. She showed me the table she'd made into her desk and this sad nub of a pencil she used—said she'd found it in my old room. To keep it sharp, she used a funny little pocketknife with yellow daisies painted on the pearl handle. That knife was a gift from her momma. Del confessed that sometimes, on quiet nights, she'd do the schoolwork twice. I told her that if she admitted this to anyone 'sides me, she'd be doing her arithmetic in the sanitarium before next term. Del had laughed and laughed.

Word had gotten out around town by now that I lived at the witch's house. The old gang wasn't near as accepting of me, and one evening, after an exceptionally rough day at school, I plunked down at the base of the leprechaun tree and stared out across the crick. It was just a trickle now. In a few weeks the storms would come and its water's would rise up high and wavy. Maybe I'd climb in there after the first big rain and let the tides take me away. Then they'd all be sorry.

Across the bank, a rustle of scrub brush and a smudge of brown and pink caught my attention. I recognized the faded pink potato sack dress Del always wore.

I called to her, but she put a finger to her lips. "Hush, Genia, I'm just goin to the Piggly Wiggly."

"Why don't you use the road like normal people, then?"

"There's boys, friends a yourn—chase me, throw rocks." This was news to me. I didn't know people were mean to Del. I actually hadn't given a thought to her ever leaving the living room of my old house any more than I'd pictured the coffee table leaving. I felt dumb for not realizing sooner that Del would be the one getting food.

"Wanna eat at my Grandma's tonight?" I asked her retreating back.

"Cain't." She answered without turning.

Then for no good reason, I followed her. I snaked along the squashed weeds of the creek bank that made the scant path Del walked. I hung back and slunk low in the cattails so she wouldn't see me. While she did her shopping, I waited. And when she emerged from the Piggly Wiggly with a bag, I followed her home. When the screen door banged shut leaving me out in the dark front yard of where I used to live, I wished I was Del, and at the same time, knew I was lucky not to be. Those two warring feelings set up a tug of war in my throat that nearly choked me on my long walk home.

Autumn came and I convinced Del that she could come to the church's Halloween festival with us. Daddy was so drunk most nights that he wouldn't notice if she took up tuba practice on his pillow, so sneaking out should be easy. Del wasn't so sure. When I promised her I'd take care of Daddy, she moved on to worrying 'bout being seen by the townsfolk. But I had that covered. The week before, Grandma had thrown out a set of sheets. The festival was a costume affair and the two of us would go as ghosts.

Only thing I didn't count on was the weather. On the day of the party, Will and I swung by the church early to plan our attack on the pumpkin pies and apple tarts that were being delivered by the women of the Junior League. They had twice the tables they'd had last year!

The rain had just begun to fall outside, when the pastor burst into the hall calling everyone to attention. He said a dam had burst up North; that a storm was on its way; flooding was imminent, and worst of all, that the party was canceled. Then he made all us kids milling about sandbag the perimeter of the church. And then sandbag his own house, too. Instead of getting dizzy on sugar, we slung sand until our arms were saggy jelly. The pastor's wife recognized Will and I and gave us two pies as a thank you. She said we better get home fast before the storm hit.

I sent Will ahead with the peach pie because it was Grandma's favorite and I went to let Del know that I hadn't forgotten her. I carried with me a pumpkin praline, and imagined that maybe Daddy, Del, and I could enjoy it together.

By the time I got to the old yellow house, it was late. All the lights were off. I whispered for Del, pressing my face up against the screens to get my voice into the house, but she didn't answer. I crawled up onto the trashcan to peer into the kitchen window over the sink. That's when I saw the blood.

It had spread across the gray linoleum like someone had gone and painted a lazy-edged shiny rug where I'd cleaned up the grits a few months ago. And in the middle of all that blood, facedown and not moving, was my daddy with the hilt of a tiny pocketknife jutting out of the side of his neck. It was the shine on that puddle that sort of froze me in place at the window; the way the moonlight glinted off the pool in a way that proved that liquid was too thick. And it was the little daisies on the handle of that pocketknife that froze the terror in my heart so that I thought I'd never move again.

But then Daddy did.

He rolled up on his knees and by the time I bowled through the kitchen door to be at his side, he was struggling to his feet, grabbing for his gun and cussing that he'd kill her. He grabbed at me without even looking, but his hand was so slick with his own blood that he couldn't hold me. I'd never seen my daddy so scary. Blood covered him; that baby knife handle poked out where his neck shoulda been smooth; but it was his eyes, burning with hate, that made me run.

I turned my tail to my own daddy and I ran.

Outside the streets had been abandoned to the rain that was beginning to pound the clapboard houses and the wind that had begun whipping the branches of every tree. I ran blindly like the Devil himself was chasing me and only slowed when I heard Daddy bellowing Del's name. His enraged voice was far away. Not chasing me like I'd feared. He was going after Del; going to kill Del, and suddenly I knew where she'd be.

When I reached the edge of the drainage creek, angry, swirling water grabbed at my ankles. The creek, grown fat from the rainwater of the entire county, had swollen higher than I'd ever seen it. Dirty water clawed up the banks to overtake Del's trail. I made it to the edge of Grandma's property by half wading and half crawling.

I yelled for Del as soon as the leprechaun tree was in sight. I kept yelling and I kept running. The rain had soaked me to the skin.

"Genia." A soft, weak plea came from a pile of flood debris near the choppy creek. I could make out the pink floral of Del's dress. She was curled up, her arm hanging at a unnatural angle and her face already swollen and blackened. She'd surely taken a beating before turning on Daddy, but I hadn't expected her to look this bad.

"My grandma'll fix ya up fine," I soothed as I hitched her good arm around my shoulders and hefted her up the bank toward the old oak and the lights of the big gray house. I kept talking to her as we climbed, but the thunder wouldn't let up long enough for me to see if she would answer back. When we reached the crest of the hill, Daddy was waiting.

His face, mottled with rage and hurt and drink, was a mean, twisted version of the one that had come for me a year ago. He was hardly more than a dozen paces away and he was pointing a revolver at us. I heard the click of the hammer pulling back.

"She tried to kill me, Eugenia. Step away from'er or I'll have to shoot ya both. She don' matter. They'll hang her for what she did—she hurt your Daddy."

Thunder rolled again and a smattering of sodden leaves dropped from the overhanging branches of the leprechaun tree and slapped onto Daddy's extended arm. I'd made it to Grandma's yard. I was standing in the exact spot where I'd had my first fight, and right then—shivering with fear and wet and hurt beneath that tree, while my daddy prepared to kill a girl that coulda been me—well, right then, wondered if God or the witch or the leprechaun had brought me here to fight again. As rain poured down on all our heads, I pulled

Del closer to my side and took another step toward the lighta my grandma's house.

"Eugenia. I'm gonna—"

And that's all he got out. Those were the last words Daddy ever said, cause right at that moment, half a tree fell and crushed him dead. The tree we were all clustered beneath—that tree that decades earlier had broke and killed a Yankee general; the same tree that'd been splashed with potion and witnessed my first fight; the tree infested with a greedy leprechaun and a whole town's worth of toads; a tree that had endured countless storms—gave up its fight against this one.

That oak cracked somewhere deep down inside. It fell and crushed my daddy. Nothing more than bad luck.

Jennifer Shepard lives in Eden Prairie, MN. She spends her time renovating houses with her husband and three adventure-loving children. While her days consist of attempting to make buildings more beautiful, her real love is for beautiful words. This is her first publication.

Easy Journey to Other Planets

by Barry Maxwell

personal essay/creative nonfiction 3rd place

FIVE WINTERS AGO, CARTER MACLAINE'S OLDER COUSIN TRUSSED him wrist-to-ankle behind his back and slammed him into the trunk of the family car. He drove to the dark roads beyond the glare of the city, beat Carter with fists and a tire tool, and left him.

After his cousin—his blood kin—drove away, Carter struggled back to the lighted places and survived. His body was broken, but not fatally. He was damaged, and permanently altered, but he lived.

I've never tried to extract any more details from Carter— there are layers of calamity he hasn't unbandaged, and a beating like his doesn't come from nowhere, after all. But his secrets are his to keep. If he decides to tell me more, he will.

Carter's life snapped that night like a brittle bone, and the fragments have been slow to knit. That he didn't die is what counts, and I'm glad of it, because Carter MacLaine is my friend.

We met like most friends do, at a lucky intersection of time, accident, and geography.

I had suffered a beating, too, but mine was self-inflicted. A harsh cocktail of pride, guilt, and shame had left me homeless and hung-over, as poor in cash as I was existentially penniless. Help from family was out of the question—I hadn't seen them in years, and the collateral damage from decades of heavy drinking had exhausted the sympathy and goodwill of any lingering friends. As a refuge of last resort, I took loose root in the ground of Austin's overburdened homeless shelter, on the books as client number 113-119.

The shelter was packed the morning Carter and I met, as it always is when the temperature drops, and in spite of months in and out the doors, I never felt part of the tribe. I'd come back from the men's room to find my scavenged copy of *The Accidental Tourist* had "got disappeared" from my chair, where I left it to mark my place. I'd closed my eyes and rested too long behind the locked restroom door, insulated from the roar of the lobby, ignoring the filth and the smell for the sake of the calm. Someone pounded for their turn and shattered the quiet, and meanwhile, a literate thief had liberated my book. I was too green then to realize you can't expect anything to stay where you leave it, not even an Anne Tyler novel in a room full of rough men.

The din in the common area rose with the body count, rising ceiling high in layers of human noise. It filled the glass-walled space like an ominous, operatic sediment; the overture based on a rumbling *ostinato*, stacked with minor chord threats of "Hey Motherfucker! Don't be touching my shit!"

Little Rosa, the asphalt-voiced cigarette girl, hustled counterpoint through the noise. "Roll-ups two for a quarter!" she shouted. "Marlboro Reds, fifty cents!" Rosa hawked her smokes like a crackhead evangelist, louder by a trick of will or acoustics than the raucous congregation she bullhorned through. The cold-weather crowds were like Black Friday for Rosa's business—her pockets bulged with spare change.

The staff clung bravely to a tenuous illusion of control. Bright young emissaries waded in, armed against indifference with nothing more than clipboards and optimism, their idealism stretched thin as Bible pages.

"Has anybody seen Rodney?" a 20-something intern asked, scanning the milling bodies. "His case manager's on the way," she said. Overhead, contradiction barked from the loudspeakers: "Attention, gentlemen! Today's case management meetings are canceled due to icy road conditions. I repeat, *canceled* . . ."

With no pages left to turn, I grubbed through my bag and tried to wish up enough change for a smoke, but no such luck. I slumped over in the folding chair and wondered what to do next—or if anything at all could be worth the doing. My senses shut down in the claustrophobic maelstrom, and I nodded out, overwhelmed.

I heard Carter before I saw him, and I only saw him because he stepped on my foot.

His voice broke through the clamor as he shouted into his cell phone, "Yea, we'll talk, man. Between the Web pages and the furniture hook-up, we're gonna see some serious bank!" He rummaged through the crowd like a rickety little coat rack, his wiry body overloaded with worn-out gym bags, a pair of sagging backpacks, and tangled, dangling ear buds. His belongings were the only ballast holding his Mad Hatter energy to the ground.

"Pardon me," and "Sorry, bro," punctuated his conversation as he shouldered through the rabble, his words sporadically choked by a dry, asthmatic hack.

I looked up when he apologized to the old man next to me for stepping on *my* foot. Too tired to be annoyed, I folded up tighter inside my space to make way.

"We need somebody building these Web sites," he complained. "We should be closing deals already!"

His words fluttered to my feet like loose dollar bills, waiting for me to snatch them up. I could *do* Web sites. I'd been damned good at it, back in the day. Showing up sober to client meetings had been problematic, but Web design I could handle.

I had to stop him, but it's best to avoid putting your hands on anyone in that room—especially a stranger, and never on purpose—shit will start, for sure. But Carter didn't look like the type to cop an attitude, so before he gathered himself to scurry off, I risked a quick nudge to his elbow.

"You need some Web work done?" I asked, clearing my throat. "I heard you saying . . ."

Sirens and the blasting horn of an ambulance interrupted, knocking the volume of the room from intolerable to excruciating. It was only the second 911 call of the day, and no one paid any mind. The EMTs gathered their equipment and headed for the doors.

Carter drifted for an instant, his attention fixed by the commotion on the street. He looked as if his ride had just arrived. I wondered if he'd heard me.

"Shit. I'm late," he said. "Meeting a money guy for coffee at the Hideout ten minutes ago." With barely a once-over glance my direction, he pocketed his phone and started laying out a business plan. "I need somebody that knows HTML, and somebody to write ad copy for Craigslist. It's a win-win, dollar-wise." He stabbed his palm with an index finger, running item by item through an internal to-do list. "The furniture is drop-shipped—all quality stuff, major manufacturers. We name our price. Undercut everybody and still make a nice percentage on every sale."

A smear on his glasses distracted him, and he wiped them on his sleeve, holding out the bent frames and squinting for missed spots, then stepped back into pitchman mode: "Do you know there's a five-billion dollar market out there that nobody's touching?"

His nails were dirty, but he was friendly. Civilized.

"I used to design Web sites," I told him. "And I can do okay with sales copy."

My résumé, served neat, in fifteen words or less.

"I've got a laptop." I offered. "at a friend's house."

I didn't mention my friend hadn't answered a call in months, but the extra incentive bought some face time. Carter inked his number on his own palm before he realized what he was doing, then shrugged and stuck it out to shake. He smiled around the gnawed pen between his teeth.

"I'm Carter. What's your name?" He hitched up his trousers without waiting for an answer, ready to move on. "We need to talk, but I gotta run."

"Look for you in line tonight?" I ventured.

Carter nodded to confirm the appointment, and trotted toward the exit, load swaying as he pulled a strap higher on his knobby shoulder. He squeezed his bags through the glass doors, bumping past the medics as if they were no more than idlers in his way.

"Make a hole, gentlemen!" a staffer yelled. "*Make a hole!*"

The EMTs hustled upstairs in the elevator and came right back down, their equipment piled on the empty gurney.

A false alarm?

I wasn't sure yet, but it felt like something might actually be *happening.*

If nothing else, Carter had apologized for stepping on me . . . sort of.

It was forgivable.

The two of us joined forces in the lottery line that evening, shuffling along with a couple hundred guys, all gambling against one another for a spot to sleep indoors. Carter and I both drew good numbers, and the next morning we dug into his plans like pigeons on a pizza crust. We became the Internet marketing wizards of the homeless set, peppering Craigslist with ads for furniture we'd never seen, determined to stockpile our earnings and get the hell out of Dodge. Carter did market research, gathering demographic stats and product info, relishing the crunch of limitless data, while I pounded away at ads, uploading our determination to the 'Net. We'd found a mission, and we had something bigger to do than stand shivering on the sidewalk, waiting for spring.

The winter weather was hard on the homeless that year—like every winter, really, even in mild-mannered Austin. Overnight lows were in the 20s, and the afternoons were just warm enough to trick drunk or unthinking streeters into a frostbitten sense of comfort.

Carter and I spent our days steaming warm in the shelter's second-floor dining room. Our main office was whatever table space we could grab amidst the litter of backpacks, greasy cloth coats, and junk-food wrappers, and we enjoyed a corner-window view of the adjacent parking lot, ringed by anonymous office buildings, St. David's Episcopal Church, and the Austin Omni Hotel.

A quieter crowd peopled the dining room than in the main hall downstairs. Movie lovers huddled elbow-to-elbow around laptop screens, craning to see the latest bootleg download of *Avatar* (dubbed English over Spanish, with Russian subtitles). Gamers hovered fascinated, cheering while a shooter fragged digital enemies in *Resident Evil* or *Assassin's Creed*. Boozy nappers stretched out on the floor around the walls beneath "NO SLEEPING!" signs, their snoring faces buried in backpacks until the staff came in on the half hour to kick their feet and rouse them.

We were too ambitious to waste time on movies or games. We hammered out ad campaigns, frittered over details, and schemed what-if scenarios of easy profit and the fine things we'd own. Some dreams were as simple as a really good bed and a door to lock at night. Other ambitions were more extravagant, like the adolescent fantasy women we swore would share those beds—hot, smart, and adoring, the girls would climb out of our wallets like strippers from a cake. We slurped soup kitchen power lunches of cabbage stew and pimiento cheese on gooey white bread, and packed our bags with stale charity pastries for emergency munchies.

The Omni Hotel teased us from the skyline with its rooftop pool and hot tub. During breaks we'd watch heads bob above the mile-high railing as guests climbed into the bubbling oasis of luxury. The top of the Omni was one of our prime motivators. We swore we'd stay there, play there, and get laid there when the money machine slipped into gear.

Carter was the idea man and corporate cheerleader, but he also had more practical skills, including a gift for scoring free bus passes. He hoarded them for barter, late-night ER visits, and desperate escapes. When his cell phone died, he handed me a day pass for a ride-along to the Cricket store.

We boarded the #3 Cap Metro, and while Carter pored over a lapful of notes and crumpled flow charts, I thumbed absently through the previous week's Sunday *Statesman* and dozed away a hangover.

Carter nudged me with a question, and I was surprised when I looked up to find we were rolling through my childhood stomping grounds. Déjà vu stunned me. I'd been a goofy little kid on these streets, and a too-big-for-his-britches teenager. Scenes from lost incarnations unfolded as the stops rolled by, and like "just right" words on the tip of my tongue, I knew they were alive somewhere, but weren't quite real. I'd left myself behind on the way to hometown exile, and somehow, I'd forgotten my own story.

Top Notch Drive-In was still flame-kissing burgers on Burnet Road. My family used to eat there on warm nights, cheeseburgers and onion rings filling the back seat of the Delta 88 with gritty salt packets and the aroma of fatty satisfaction. And there was Genie Car Wash, where me and my sixth-grade buddy, Peewee, would press our faces against the glass walls to drool over 'Vettes and Beamers gliding sudsy through the machine, following them until they emerged glistening and spotless on the other side.

We passed the decrepit Northcross Mall, most of the shops bankrupt, doors locked. I was more ancient than the washed-out mall, and felt as empty and obsolete. I had run like a wild boy there, in the open fields and hackberry thickets, years before construction began. My bare footprints were somewhere under that parking lot, buried with tangles of kite string and balsa airplanes lost in stands of Johnson grass.

The fogged-over world outside the safety glass grew more and more aloof as the blocks stretched behind us. There were no excited, finger-pointing moments of, "Look, Carter! That's where I hung out when I was just a punk-ass boy!" The #3 lumbered past a world that had given up on my friendship a long time back, and I shrank from it, gutless, like a child too roughly handled to trust any memories of security or safety. These places didn't miss me, or welcome me home. They'd forgotten who I was.

I slouched, hiding a creeping fear of boarding the wrong bus back or getting separated from Carter. I worried we'd be late for dinner at the Salvation Army. If we didn't make it to the shelter by the 6:30 lineup, we'd be locked out for the night. And it was fucking cold.

I didn't have any money, and I didn't have any booze.

I was deathly afraid of my hometown.

As underhanded as any 6th Street hustler, homelessness had become my home, and I was so frightened of the world I'd run out on that I panicked. It was an act of will to stay planted in my seat and white-knuckle it through the trip. I needed desperately to pull the bus over and rush back to the seething concrete womb of the shelter.

Carter was all business across the aisle, making notes of furniture stores we should visit. "Product knowledge, man. Product knowledge," he declared between scribbles. "What's a good word for soft?"

"Sumptuous, plush, luxurious, cushy, comfortable," I reeled off synonyms and random associations in a preoccupied monotone. "Downy, tender, gentle, giving."

Weak, I thought. *Pointless. Ineffectual. Spineless. Lost.*

"And don't forget plain old soft," I added.

I was growing numb to Carter's chatter, and I think he knew it.

I needed a drink.

Alcohol never held any appeal for Carter. Outside of hospitals and illness, he'd never done a drug stronger than his inhaler. He understood my alcoholism from a sober distance, letting drop an occasional hint about my stopping into an AA meeting, or suggesting things might go easier if I lightened up on the liquor. He understood though. He knew I'd only fight if pushed.

Like Rosa hawking her roll-ups, vodka spoke louder then than any other voice in the mob, and despite our enthusiasm, the work Carter and I poured ourselves into hadn't produced anything more than Xs on the calendar. Scooping ground-score change from the sidewalk was more profitable. I didn't care much for high profit margins anymore. I just needed four bucks for a bottom shelf pint of Kamchatka.

That afternoon on the #3 marked a tipping point in my mind-set, and my connection to Carter lost out to the urge for accelerated self-destruction. Chasing a buzz took precedence over friendship and sanctuary. I took to sleeping outdoors, or crashing in vacant apartments. There were still times in and out of the shelter, avoiding people I knew, passing through between binges for a shower, a meal, or a mat for the night. My days were too busy for Carter. There was serious drinking to do, and my priorities didn't necessarily involve being human anymore.

I left Carter and our dreams of fat wallets and trophy girls to fend for themselves.

That was over three years ago, and I was still a year away from putting down the bottle. Once the weight of it was gone, I managed to hit escape velocity, up and away from my identity as number 113-119. Like *The Accidental Tourist*, I disappeared myself from that world.

When I was a teenager, living two blocks off the #3 bus route, I had a book entitled *Easy Journey to Other Planets*, by His Divine Grace Abhay Charanaravinda Bhaktivedanta Swami Prabhupada. I never read beyond the back cover, but I'm sure it's as profound as the author's title is long. His Divine Grace's jacket blurb claims that to travel the universe as an enlightened day-tripper is a simple matter of stepping beyond our conditioned beliefs. On the planet where most of us lesser souls live, though, it's no simple trick to shift our weight from one universe to the next, traveling in our own skins, winging it without guidance through this particular life.

There is no *easy* travel between the shifting boundaries of our inner worlds. There are barbed-wire borders to cross, with roadside searches and indefinite detainment, and the inhabitants of neighboring lands often find themselves misunderstood, their once common language faded and forgotten.

Our eyes open from every sleep to an alien landscape, puzzled to find ourselves cast as the outlaw or the community pillar, the lost-cause alcoholic become sober, or waking from the dreams of a younger self in different dress, moving blindly toward the disasters and triumphs ahead. We all live somewhere between what we were and what we're becoming—we should be used to it. But when you awaken to the realization that your image of self no longer applies, when you find yourself standing in the chaos of neither *this*, nor *that* . . . it's during those nowhere times that the fear sets in.

Our fragile personae exist like colliding galaxies, and when they clash, lives collapse, universes crumble or explode. Sure, you might take the metaphor further and plead that new suns are born from the destruction, that new worlds emerge from the detritus of the old. I believe that's ultimately true, but when you're flying in pieces from the center of the blast, call me then, and tell me how star-like you're feeling at that instant.

Some of the dust clouds of my personal implosions have settled, but not all of them. There will always be unfinished business, a drawer full of unwritten endings and thank you notes. And there's a sky filled with star-bright moments to look back on—I can show you the scars.

Since my years in the shelter, my addictive affections have turned from alcohol to nicotine and caffeine, and I'm secure in a place of my own. The apartment would be beneath most people's standards, but it's above the street, and the funkiness suits me. Today my desk sits by the window, ostensibly so I'll blow the smoke outdoors, but the window seat is most important to sit and stare down from.

Occasionally a homeless person wanders by, carrying their burdens on their back, or pushing an overloaded H.E.B. cart clattering with cans for the recycler. I turn from the monitor while I'm working and watch them pass. The cops don't come through here much, so sometimes the wanderers sit on the curb for a rest, glad to hold still for a minute without any hassle. They go about their business without knowing I see them, and I presume to understand what they're about and what they might be thinking. I feel as if I'm spying from up here, but really, they wouldn't give a damn about one more set of eyes judging them.

I'm like a weekend sailor now, with one foot on the dock and the other on the gunwale, straddling self-definitions as they drift apart. I've weaned myself from soup kitchens and food stamps, but find there's reliable and mysterious safety in a bellyful of cabbage and noodles. And a smear of pimiento cheese on white is a gummy delicacy I never acknowledged in my less grateful years. To this day, I scan the ground for change, and peek over the side of dumpsters as I pass. I get excited when I spot a long cigarette butt on the ground, though I don't usually pick them up anymore. And if anyone spied on me, they'd see a tendency to travel via alleys and across parking lots rather than open sidewalks.

There's still a comfort in the option of hiding, and I always notice the secret places, the holes in the façade where, if needed, a night could be passed unseen.

I remind myself I have plenty to eat, and a door to lock at night.

Some rules still apply, and probably always will: Don't keep your smokes in your shirt pocket. Don't let on you've got *anything*, however trivial or insubstantial, or someone will plot to take it. If you have trouble with the word "No," or aren't willing to lie and say, "Sorry, buddy; not a good day for cash," you'll wind up giving too much away. If anyone asks for a cigarette, tell them, "Fresh out, bro. Maybe next time." The one you're lighting is always your last.

Sometimes when I pass the panhandlers on the street I'll make eye contact and say hello or nod, but most often, I find myself keeping my eyes to the ground.

And I used to wonder how people could so completely ignore another human being.

Carter and I talked a couple of weeks ago, and he sent over email archives of all the ads we'd posted that winter downtown. He saved everything we'd produced.

The furniture project still exists, but on a far back burner. He's got a deal in the works to sell high-end Koozies and water bottles emblazoned with brass, leather, and wood, laser-engraved custom logos. Everybody's going to want one. "It's a win-win," he told me. "Huge per-unit profit, and if we move as few as six a day, the bank's going to pile up just selling on the street." I could hear the bullet points. "This'll kick ass on the Web!"

Carter is still in the shelter, while I'm two years into a new life. He's trying to pull himself up, but I think if he weren't held tight by some internal binding, he would be out here and happy. He lives in a world much larger than mine, as confined by circumstance as he may seem. He's not missing the forest for the trees; he's flying over the canopy, missing both the forest *and* the trees, his eyes on horizons I worry he may overshoot.

Why I worry, I don't know. He'll land on his feet when the time comes. He'll be grinning down from the Omni rooftop, his skinny arms draped around a trophy gal or two, cell phone in one hand, inhaler in the other.

We talked about getting together and I instinctively deflected him from my door.

"Yeah, I'd love to see you," I said. "Let's meet up at the Hideout for a coffee."

We didn't set a date or a time. I didn't even tell him what street I live on.

Boundaries aren't meant to be unbreakable, but I fear mine have grown overly defensive and inflexible. The old life might have claws I can't see, and it may have strength to scratch its way through a crack in the walls of the new. My house is built of Popsicle sticks and Elmer's glue. It could all come apart any second.

I've let myself walk away from more than one good life in the past, stumbling straight off into the worst of shit without even noticing I'd tripped. Am I aware enough now to watch my step? Am I planted firmly enough in this new soil to stand on my own? I think so, but only cautiously. And while caution may keep a lot of valuables locked away in the past, the potential gain may not be worth the risk. I hold my own confidence in suspicion.

Carter must have wondered why I didn't invite him over.

If he did, I hope he knows, as the old saw goes, that it's not him, it's me.

I can't guess what I'd do if I looked out to see Carter marching down the sidewalk, holding last year's Obama phone to his ear and conducting business as usual.

It placates my egoism to imagine inviting him up to hang out and pitch his latest escape strategy. I'd feel beneficent and oh-so-charitable, as if I were holier than my history, but I would worry that Carter might become part of the furniture, or install himself quietly on the shelf like an unread book. It would be a concern that he'd knock unannounced when the days got cold, and if I didn't answer, he'd slip his world under the door into mine.

My selfishness and high-horse arrogance astonish me. If I were to let Carter walk by while I quietly closed the shutters, I might be willing to ride out the guilt for leaving him outdoors, but facing my indifference to a friend burns in my gut like cruelty. I like to think I'm better, at least, than his murderous cousin. I like to believe I'm above rolling away as if he never existed, leaving the battered friendship for dead. But still, I've lied to myself before and swallowed the bullshit whole.

It's my shameful hope that with patient denial, this crisis of conscience will pass and no one will have to notice. Sweeping my callousness back into the past would be an awful relief, like the near miss of an errant asteroid, or hearing news of disaster in a nearby town. But that hope is inescapably and unacceptably selfish. It's the bitter sentiment of "Better him than me."

It's a finer hope that I aspire to—the hope that Carter will fight himself back to the brighter lights of the world, put down his bags, and call me up from *his* new space. He'll either outshine his secrets or come to accept them, and we'll speak the same language again. I think that then I could tell him why I never asked him over, or how I might have even watched without a word as he passed below my window. He might understand well enough then to forgive my failure, and I might understand well enough to forgive myself.

Barry Maxwell is a native of Austin, Texas, and a student at Austin Community College. His work has been published in ACC's The Rio Review *and he is currently hip-deep in life as a 53-year-old schoolboy. Barry strives to approach each day with authenticity, audacity, and humility—his hope is to bring those qualities to the page, along with equal proportions of grace and grunge.*

WITHOUT POLISH

by Sandra McGarry

poetry 3rd place

*"If we only have love / We can melt all the guns / then
give the new world / to our daughters and sons."*
—Jacques Brel Is Alive and Well and Living in Paris

They move toward a camp on a bus
carrying whatever is themselves,
other small packages at their sides.

Screams, rubble, remains for this day
whether it was Tuesday or Sunday, no matter.
A missile rides on a finger's command.

The boy, nine or ten, repeats
into the newsman's recorder what he couldn't
hold onto, as if said even *it* might go away.

*From next door, the man's head,
nothing else,
was on our kitchen floor.*

His mother gathers him,
in a wing-like way women do,
wordless, astonished that

someone in the crowd gasped.

As if the only thing that happened
was the vase cracked, flowers seared,
and water pooled.

Sandra McGarry grew up in Boston, MA, and moved to New Jersey to attend college. She is a retired New Jersey elementary school educator who has lived in Fort Collins for seven years to be near her family. Her dream would be to have the ocean alongside the mountains. Her hobbies include reading, writing, and finding money.

TALL TREES

by Nathan Ferguson

short fiction honorable mention

I WAS HIGH ENOUGH IN THE REDWOOD TREE THAT THE COPS couldn't reach me. I'd counted 10 trespassing tickets tacked to the lower trunk. The rain had ceased, but big drops were rolling off the leaves 200 feet higher and hitting the tarp above the recycled wood platform. Northern California could be so cold.

The things I'd do for Trevor. He was probably back at our apartment half-drunk, half-stoned, or half-crazy. How many times had I written his college papers? Or lied to the police about his whereabouts?

Tomorrow was Election Day and Trevor wanted to vote. He could have voted absentee like I did, but he didn't have his shit together enough to send in the form. So he passed the duty on to me, the rookie tree-sitter, to protect the tree that he'd named Athena. Trevor figured the logging company would slay her the minute he came down.

It was now 8 p.m. and the fog had moved in to the delight of the big trees. I'd been studying Athena's bark patterns since noon. I owed something to Trevor for getting me out of the apartment and onto the cliffs near Mount Shasta last summer. I avoided most risks anymore with a bad leg, which I shattered in a motorcycle accident when I was 18, but I soon became a decent enough climbing partner, not that I

97

had overcome all of my fears. Trevor was different. On rock his lanky frame moved with the confidence of a lizard.

Fear of falling 10 stories had sapped my energy. I was dozing off when I heard howling penetrate the fog. It was high pitched and female. Tree-sitters greeted each other that way in the forest, but without practice, I thought I'd embarrass myself by howling back. I waited for the flickering light to come closer.

She/it howled again.

"Hello," I said.

"Is that the best you can do for me, Palmer?"

It was Calliope, Trevor's girlfriend. She was aiming her headlamp up the tree trunk and asked if she could come up. I lowered the rope. In the light I could see her putting on her climbing harness. She connected her ascenders to the rope and started working her way toward the forest canopy. Girls back in Upstate New York couldn't climb like she could.

I helped her swing over to the platform and clipped the back of her harness to some nylon webbing with a climbing carabiner.

"Thanks, Palmer," she said, as if I had opened a door for her. She slid off her backpack and let it thud on the platform. "I brought you some goodies. Green tea. Those granola thingies you like. Dried fruit. Chocolate. You gotta have chocolate if you're spending a night in a tree."

I thanked her. "How's Trevor?"

"How should I know?" She took off her headlamp.

I always loved Calliope's personality. She was the stabilizing factor within the Incredibly Round Earth Society, the cool head among burning torches. She came from a farm family in flat, humid Bakersfield. As the public relations chief, she gathered newspaper clippings and Web postings of the movement's exploits, and rallied everybody when Trevor decided it was time to protest. She was in her sophomore year at the university. I was a senior.

Trevor, on the other hand, was the son of a San Francisco shipping magnate. I remember the day we went to the bank, him all stinking of booze, salt water, and sex. The teller must have thought he was homeless until she saw how much he had in his account. Trevor thought it was cool to act poor. He had gone to several colleges in Northern California but, at 25, failed to complete a degree. He liked to lead without responsibility, provide the lightning without thunder. I sensed the movement was beginning to fracture, with some saying he was in it all for himself.

Calliope looked up at me with a confident smile, her dark hair pulled back in a ponytail. My memory filled in the hazel in her eyes under the dim light from the battery-powered lantern. That's how she must have looked to the judges when she was a high school gymnast. She had that petite, well-proportioned frame, packing plenty of power, and never wore much makeup. Calliope would make us breakfast in nothing more than a long T-shirt. That was until Trevor began the marathon tree-sit a month ago to save Athena. I missed Calliope's smile hovering above the stove.

"Not much room to dance up here," she said. "What've you been doing?"

"Counting squirrels."

"And you're up to?"

"Twelve, counting you."

She puffed up her cheeks. "I guess I'll take that as a compliment."

"You should. Squirrels are extremely cute."

She slapped my shoulder. "Been reading?" Calliope knew I liked to read. She had borrowed books from our apartment.

"Mostly I've been dozing off. I'm glad I can't see the ground anymore."

"I'm here," she said, putting her hands around my waist in a kind of half-hug. "I'll keep you safe."

I could never tell if she was interested in me. One morning when Trevor was off somewhere, we sat at the kitchen table and talked about our families. She reached over the table and held my hand in hers, warmed by a mug of tea. Calliope wanted to know why I hadn't been around much, and I told her I was trotting along the beach for therapy. Truth be told, I was afraid to be in the house when they were most likely to have sex. Calliope didn't make much noise in the past, but a creak of the bed lately was enough to tear away at my dreams of being with a woman like her.

At the same time, I knew Trevor was leading a double life; steamy sex with other women, sometimes in trees. As long as the coastal redwoods were around, Trevor would have a steady source of groupies and an element of danger to turn them on. But how could he do it behind Calliope's back?

Athena held us up now with her hundreds of years of patience. I sat on a foam pad with my back up against the tree trunk. Calliope sat between my legs with her back to me as if we were about to go sledding off into oblivion. We listened to the redwoods shedding water. Calliope was wearing fleece pants. She leaned back to unzip her insulated parka and I took in her mango-scented shampoo. She'd left a bottle of it in our shower. Underneath was a turtleneck. She reached in her backpack and pulled out the thermos of tea. She poured a cup, took a drink, then carefully handed it back to me.

"I know about the women," she said, as I was about to take a drink.

"The women?"

"Trevor's little sluts."

"How'd you find out?"

"A woman journalist, oddly enough."

"I'm sorry. That's a horrible way to find out."

"Especially because I helped build Trevor into whatever he is now. How do you think he got on all those magazine covers?"

Trevor was, after all, a marked man ever since he chained himself to the bumper of a car, which happened to be owned by a logging company president, and fasted for three days. Though weak, he shoved the police when they cut him free. With the long hair and gyrating hips, people compared him to Jim Morrison of The Doors. Thanks to the national publicity, blondes with dreadlocks started showing up at our apartment at all hours with fake handcuffs and flowers, making offerings to a god who subsisted on Fruit Loops and popcorn.

"That's why you're here? The women?"

"I'm here to see you. I didn't think either of us would be sleeping well tonight."

"I wanted to tell you."

"You couldn't. I know. I respect that."

I handed the cup back to her. I reached for my down sleeping bag and pulled it around the two of us. "I'm glad you turned out to be a squirrel instead of a wolf."

"I didn't think I was good at howling."

"Scared the hell out of me."

Her head drooped. "You know, I see you as a family man someday."

"Really? Now I feel boring."

"No, you're not. We're high in a tree on a flimsy platform built by my cheating so-called boyfriend."

My mind locked on the "so-called" part. She'd never put it that way.

We finished the rest of the tea and she stowed the thermos in her pack. She reached back and grabbed my wrists and placed them on her little knees. I instinctively rubbed her thighs and her head fell back on my shoulder. Her legs were as smooth and firm as the arm rests on a velvet wingback chair we used to have.

"That feels so good. You have strong hands. Sure you weren't a farm boy?"

"I aim to please."

"Oh, you do," she said.

More drops hit the tarp.

"So what's your deal? You've always been on the periphery of the group. It's almost like you've been studying us."

"I moved in with Trevor mainly because the apartment was cheap. Besides, his circle seemed entertaining. Then I got sucked in, at least partially."

"It's easy to do."

"Unlike Trevor, I want to finish my degrees and get out of school." I was majoring in environmental science and economics and wanted to find ways to make environmental policy profitable. They nicknamed me Wall Street for the budget work I did for the movement.

Calliope leaned forward. "Now do my shoulders."

She rolled her head side to side as I rubbed. When her head stopped moving, I hugged her waist tightly and she pressed back into me.

"Who do you admire?" she asked.

"Besides you for bringing me chocolate?"

"Yes," she laughed, "besides me."

"Teddy Roosevelt."

"That's an interesting choice."

"He created Yellowstone and overcame tragedy. He lost his wife and mother on the same day in the same house."

"Same day?" she asked.

"Valentine's Day."

"Oh, that's sad. So sad."

"I read about him when I was all messed up in the hospital."

"How's your leg? Is it this one?" She guessed left, which was correct.

"It hurts when it's cold and damp, but you took my mind off it."

"Score one for me. So you didn't know it was cold and damp when you moved here?"

"I had no idea what I was getting myself into. I read about Roosevelt going out West to rebuild his life. That's what inspired me."

"That's beautiful. I like that."

I hugged her again. "Are you warm enough?" On the North Coast, it was either 55 degrees and rainy or 65 degrees and sunny, mostly the former, year-round.

"Oh yeah, Palmer," she said. "I feel great."

I put my hands back on her thighs and slowly worked my way up, expecting to find my limits. I felt her turtleneck and she wasn't wearing a bra. I caressed her breasts and she rolled her head on my shoulder. I moved back down. The harness left open the crotch area and I felt moisture work its way through her tights.

"Definitely not a farm boy," she said. "You've got the soft touch."

Just as she was getting excited, she rolled over and kissed me. Again and again. Long ones and short ones. She stopped to remove her jacket.

"Oh," she said, flicking some strands of hair over her ear. She unzipped her jacket pocket and pulled out a condom. The wrapper trembled in her fingertips.

She stared into my eyes and must have seen my own nervousness, but the darkness and the great trees and our lust for skin made us behave drunkenly as we started undoing our waist belts. If the platform collapsed now, we'd be yanked out of our leg straps and fall headfirst. I made a pillow out of our jackets and slid down while she climbed on top. The lantern had dimmed, but I could still see the lines of her little face. More rain hit the tarp. Our pants were partway down in a confused mess of softness and sweat.

"Damn this climbing equipment," she said, before landing on my chest.

It was a good excuse for us to stop and come to our senses. Maybe this was impossible. Maybe we weren't willing to completely let go. I pulled the sleeping bag back around us and formed a cocoon.

I asked her to stay for a while.

"Lovely." She put her arm around my neck. "You know what they're going to say, don't you?"

I shook my head.

"Palmer and Calliope, sitting in a tree, K-I-S-S-I-N-G."

"How will they find out?"

"The trees talk."

We dozed for a bit until one of us must have moved. We slept some more, but this time for a couple of hours. We awoke at the same time. More rain. Our eyes met and we immediately started kissing again. Our minds were still out in the land of dreams where you could fall but not actually die. She reached down and, with her eyes still focused on mine, started removing her harness. I followed her lead and we pulled off our pants. She climbed on top of me and we worked ourselves into an ancient ritual under trees that had been around for centuries. We didn't bother looking for the condom. We were animals now. Whether or not we were still dreaming, as the platform creaked and groaned, we were depending on Trevor's carpentry skills to protect us from gravity.

We restored our pants and harnesses and slept until dawn, although dawn came later in the darkness of the redwood forest. She had awakened once in the night to laughingly pee in a bucket.

"Time for your little squirrel to get to class. That was a nice night."

"That was a perfect night." The oddness of it all still hadn't sunken in.

"Are you staying up here all day?"

"Until tonight. That's what I promised."

"You don't need to make promises. I think this tree will be safe for a few hours."

She stretched, put on her backpack, and gave the coil of climbing rope a kick. The rope became taut, dangling from the loop of webbing around the trunk above us. She ran her figure-eight rappelling device through the rope.

"This should be a fun commute," she said. "Call me when you come back to Earth."

As we were kissing good-bye, she fell away with a playful smirk. She zipped down the rope about 10 feet and stopped. I peeked out over the platform.

"Hey," she said. "You're a generous lover."

"That's the nicest thing you could have said."

I watched her turn into a yellow dot. Calliope ran up the trail and disappeared into the fog's clutches.

By blowing off a class or two, I had the rest of the day to think about her. Was she just getting back at Trevor? Would she return to him? Would this become some awkward event that we would never talk about again? Or was she, in fact, my little squirrel? Whatever happened with her, I decided to tell Trevor. I couldn't live under the same roof in a fog of deceit. I'd pack my things and move out, whatever happened.

I held up my end of the deal anyway and stayed up in the tree until evening. This was more out of respect for Athena than Trevor. I rappelled to the ground and patted her on the bark.

* * *

I found the apartment full of marijuana stink, and it would have been dark if it weren't for the disco ball shooting a too-perfect universe on the walls and ceiling as if God himself had been stoned. There was a forest of cannabis with red Christmas ornaments hanging from their leaves. Trevor didn't think highly of the police, especially federal agents, and thought he could fool them into thinking they were tomato plants.

I took a shower and saw that Calliope's shampoo bottle was half empty. For the first time, I took a little. Would anyone notice?

I grabbed some pizza from the refrigerator then jumped in my beat-up Toyota truck. Members of the movement were probably at The Nest on the peninsula. Our headquarters was about the only place in California where poor people in windblown bungalows and shanties could live near the ocean. Trevor had bought a two-room house complete with flower boxes and a white picket fence. If it weren't for the giant banners on either side of the slanted roofs that read, "No More Clear-Cutting" and "Take Action, End Greed," my grandmother could have moved in. A home inspection had revealed that the house, like many other older ones in the area, had been built with genuine redwood beams and siding. Trevor wasn't bothered by it. He said we were merely recycling. He laughed when I questioned whether it was a good investment.

"It's just money," he said. "It never loved me so why should I love it?"

The home inspector looked at us askance while he was taking notes. "Don't let this place catch fire," he said. "This shit burns fast."

Trevor just smiled. The house was consistent with his hot-headed personality.

When I pulled up outside The Nest, there were four other cars, including Trevor's VW bus. The surfboards had blown over on the porch and two of the sea kayaks were probably out on the bay. Our bearded and always-oblivious webmaster, Bytes, was grilling vegan burgers in the side yard.

He raised his water bottle to me. "Hey, Wall Street."

The front door had a giant padlock attached to it but it was never locked. The Nest was always occupied. Inside I was met with the sounds of bongo drums. I didn't recognize two of the people, but they acted like they knew me. We always had a fresh supply of new students or people who came from all over to be in Trevor's presence.

Logging plans were tacked to the walls and there were pictures of coho salmon, northern spotted owls, pileated woodpeckers, and flying squirrels scattered about. Signup sheets for upcoming workshops on banner painting, road blockading, and tree climbing were partially filled out.

I asked about Trevor and a girl with a beaded headband pointed toward the back room. I stuck my head in and heard the sliding of heavy-duty zippers, the clank of aluminum pans, and the rustling of nylon.

"Man, what the fuck happened to the beer?" he asked.

"I don't know."

"Of course you don't know. You're too goody-goody for half the shit around here," he said, as he was throwing bags of rice into his backpack.

I asked him where he was headed.

"Just taking the show to Oregon. There's a big protest up there. Maybe the biggest. As soon as I get my shit together, that is."

"They want some celebrity?"

"All they can get." He smirked as he stomped back into the main room, not noticing that he'd hit me on the shoulder, Calliope's pillow, with his backpack.

"How long this time?"

"I don't know, eternity."

He always said that, although I was hoping for a straight answer for once. I was beginning to lose my nerve.

He carried his pack and a duffle bag out to the VW bus and came back for a couple of stolen milk crates.

"Dude, thanks for handling Athena last night. I think we took care of that rat bag running for office. I got somebody else taking over for you. I know you like your studies. Have you seen Calliope? We need to get a press release out there. I can't keep track of that fucking broad."

Fucking broad? Since when did she become that? I was irritated now. "I saw her last night," I said.

"In the tree?"

I nodded.

He tried to read more from my face, which must have been blank, then took the milk crates out to the bus. I heard him slam the side door many times like a spray of gunshots in the ghetto, shades of my last apartment. I wasn't sure if the door latch was failing again or he was angry. It was obvious that he'd come down from his latest high.

He came back in, grabbed his keys, and pulled his jacket from the cushions on the sofa. Popcorn flew out. He stopped in the doorway with his back facing me, his head cocked.

"Did you fuck her?"

"Yeah," I said.

He nodded a few times and tried to act like he didn't care. But I could see the jealousy rising in his shoulders, the muscles tensing in his jaw.

"Stop the fucking drums." He glared at the man in a knit fisherman's hat. The man's eyes were closed as if he were in a Havana bar and charming serpentine dancers. "Stop the fucking drums," Trevor said again.

Before the man could yank them away, Trevor was turning them into kindling with his hiking boots.

Trevor stomped out and I felt stares on my back from what remained of the dance floor.

As I followed, I heard him slam the driver's side door. The windows were always halfway open, despite the rain. He started up the engine as if the rumbling of mistuned valves and pistons could speak for him. For a second I thought Trevor had made it so easy for me and that was that. He slammed on the brakes and his hair flowed over his shoulders.

"Hey," he said, the hair whipping back. "Fuck you."

From his pointy eyes and focused brow, I knew it was the first time since I had known him that he wasn't kidding.

* * *

With a wave from Bytes, I headed back to the apartment. When I dialed the phone, I was surprised to get Calliope's chipper voicemail. I figured she must have been in the shower or at the library, so I hung up. I came up with more excuses as the evening went on and dialed two more times, finally leaving a message, but she didn't call back. More excuses. Days went by and still nothing.

I sent an email to Bytes to see if he knew anything.

"Comrade," he wrote back quickly. "She lit out. She went to Oregon."

I stared at the screen, byte by byte. My stomach turned. So she's back with him? And she didn't have the decency to tell me?

* * *

For the next two weeks I was careful where I went on campus. I stuck to routes that were safe from Calliope, never in such a hurry to graduate.

Then one night there was a pounding. Calliope? My sleepy brain, I learned, could be forgiving. As I made my way to the door, I knew it wasn't her because it was too masculine.

"Man, did you hear?" Bytes's eyes were burning red and he was breathing hard. It wasn't like him to make house calls.

I couldn't react.

"Trevor, man, Trevor," Bytes went on. "He's dead."

I immediately thought of a car accident for some reason. I saw a smashed up VW. "Dead?"

"He fell, man. He fucking fell."

* * *

As the shock was setting in, some members of the movement went on a media rampage. They were posting items on the blog, calling Trevor's death a murder. They claimed that there was a yelling match going on between protesters and loggers, which had distracted Trevor. They also were checking into some potential climbing gear failures. Mainstream media reports quoted the police as saying that Trevor had fallen after the protest had disbursed and that he wasn't roped in.

I had a different view. Maybe he was distracted by the betrayal of his own roommate, friend, and climbing partner. I didn't want to go near The Nest.

The funeral took days to pull together as Trevor's father was returning from the Middle East on business. While it was taking shape, the movement circulated a postmortem picture of Trevor on the Internet. They'd converted it to black and white, but with some novel photo editing, had left his eyes blue. His face was perfectly preserved and he had this peaceful look as if he were back in our apartment on his favorite chair. He was an instant martyr and the movement knew he would live on as long as the redwoods in some digital form.

Guilt was already nibbling away at me in the quiet ash heap of our apartment. Members of the movement came by to collect Trevor's belongings. As soon as everything was gone, including the beer and pot plants, I went on an all-night cleaning frenzy. I washed the walls, waxed the floors, and vacuumed every fiber of the carpet. I'd forgotten what season it was until Christmas lights started popping out on Victorian homes.

* * *

I was walking along the beach one morning, a week before Christmas. I was about to hop on a plane that afternoon for New York to exchange brown sand for brown snow. The beach was never crowded, not with the cold water and unreliable sunshine. A few surfers in wetsuits had packed it in and were walking with slumped shoulders to the north toward Oregon.

The tide had gone out and the sand was hard enough for running, but I didn't feel like it today. The ocean had drawn me here by its own accord. Once the surfers had disappeared, I noticed something else moving about a quarter of a mile away. At first I thought it was a large bird or a trash bag washed up, but then it stood up. From the movement, I knew it was Calliope in a navy barn coat and blowing hair.

Clutching a sand dollar, she turned toward me.

"You're picking up the broken ones?" I asked.

"I used to think that's what I did best," she said. "I thought you'd be out here somewhere."

"So I guess this qualifies as somewhere. Shouldn't you be in Bakersfield for the holidays?"

"I'm leaving soon. I would assume that you're returning to the Arctic."

I nodded.

"Winter is nice, but not totally necessary. I'm such a wimp." She dropped the sand dollar. "Mind if we sit down over there?"

We found a spot on a redwood trunk. I was about to express sadness for the way some giant trees end up this way, but I couldn't do that. I was still mad at Calliope and didn't want to mask my pain. We looked out at the ocean and there wasn't much to see, except more water and mist creeping around the point.

"I think I killed him," I said.

"That's a helluva a way to break the silence."

"No, really. He was distraught when I told him about our night in the tree. He wanted to run me over."

She cradled her head in her hands for a moment. "There was a lot more to it than that," she said.

"I heard you went to Oregon."

She let her hands fall and looked over at me. "I did and it was a disaster," she said, dabbing her eyes with her scarf.

"You saw Trevor?"

"I found him easily enough. We had a big fight in the woods. I knew I'd hurt him and I guess I wanted him to show it in some sincere, nonexplosive sort of way. But he wasn't capable of that."

I shook my head. "So you just left?"

"Not before resigning as his so-called PR chief. He didn't seem to care."

"Did you go to the funeral?"

She shook her head.

"Me neither," I said. "I felt as if I'd been kicked out of the movement. It went off in some strange direction."

"It's not our fault. Trevor was a great climber. How do you think he managed so many affairs?"

"That's true. He had incredible focus. I saw it when we went rock climbing. Except he had that death wish, which made me nervous. But he used to say, 'Not today, partner, not today.'"

"Jesus. What a way to live."

"So I guess he got what he wanted," I said. "How about you?"

She smirked. "Not entirely. I've made a big mess of things."

"I'm sorry I contributed to the mess."

"No, no. You don't need to apologize for anything."

We watched a seagull hover above the waves.

"I think you're addicted to drama."

"That's insightful," she said. "Have you been doing some thinking out here?"

"Mostly tearing up the sand. I run a couple of miles each way. It gets tough at high tide."

"I think you're right about me. But I don't want this craziness in my personal life anymore. I think I got my passions mixed up. I'm sorry Trevor had to die for me to realize that."

"And I think you're right about me. This is a good place to think."

"I bet you're in the best shape of your life."

I nodded to her as well as the seagull who probably recognized me.

"Look, I'm sorry for disappearing," she said. "I didn't mean to hurt you."

"I know," I said, which of course I didn't.

A misty rain flicked our faces and provided an easy escape for either of us, but we stayed and watched the waves destroy themselves. It was getting colder.

"This might turn into snow," I said.

"Oh, great."

"No, really. Snow on redwoods is the most beautiful thing you'll ever see."

"That does sound beautiful."

"At least Athena is doing okay," I said.

"Yeah, she's quite all right."

I realized now that we were every bit as alone as we were that night in the tree, except there was nothing left to explore.

Nathan A. Ferguson is a writer, editor, and photographer who began his career in publishing as a newspaper reporter. He's presently finishing his first novel. "Tall Trees" is the beginning of a collection of nature-inspired short stories. He lives in Denver, Colorado, with his wife, Sonia, and two dogs.

SÖYLEYELIM

by Delaney Nolan

personal essay/creative nonfiction honorable mention

I WAS NAKED WITH ONLY ONE MAN FOR A LONG TIME AND THEN I moved to Istanbul, and now, here, I cannot be naked the same way. Back in Louisiana, I used to walk around my hot house in just my underwear. I used to sit on the balcony, pants off, feet up, and holler at the tennis players across the way. The one man and I would stay undressed all Sunday long, the church bells next door tolling off-key, and there was the afternoon I got him naked in the yard, stripping off his shirt in the sunlight, the priest's house next door the only one with a view. I took off my clothes when I wanted to; I showed skin or I didn't. I took it for granted. Here, I'm learning the value of the body.

When I first arrive in Istanbul, taking a bus across the border in the blue pre-dawn, the call to prayer is echoing from every hill at once. I don't know what it is, and I stand still to listen. Different mosques begin the song at different times, and so the same call comes repeated, repeated, repeated. Nearby, someone turns off a car radio because you aren't supposed to drown out the call to prayer. I bow my head, but I don't know if I should bow my head.

I am in Istanbul to teach or because I'm confused or because that third arrest is making it difficult to find an American job. I teach English at a private K–12 school. I lied about my teaching experience. I have no idea what I'm doing.

115

On my first day, I stand in front of a class of high schoolers, thinking, *we are practically the same age, I know nothing,* trying to find something helpful to say.

My students ask me about my home, my hair, my cell phone. They ask if I know celebrities. They ask me if I'm Muslim. They ask me what I worship, and I shrug. Then I apologize, like maybe I've offended them, but they're just interested; they're excited. They raise their hands again. They ask me if I'm married.

I ask my students what they'll do on Friday. They tell me *pray, pray.* I nod like I understand; I press my hands together in a steeple. They shake their heads, they laugh, no, I'm doing it wrong. They hold their hands up and apart, palms in, bent at the elbow. *Pray,* they repeat, shaking their arms, *pray.*

There are things that I learn from my students, such as: the Golden Horn is glass-clear but no good for swimming. And: the grounds of Turkish coffee will tell your future (flip the cup; put a coin on top). And I learn that around seventh grade girls start wearing headscarves: blue silk, red silk, silk with patterns, folded and swooped about the neck. And I learn that I do not know how to be a woman in a foreign country. I don't know when to cover up. I don't know what to wear, how to move, whose eyes I am supposed to meet. There are women with only their dark eyes showing, and there are women who wear the tiniest skirts, and there are men who hiss and holler when I walk alone, and there is me, balancing.

I can't wear my short dresses, and I can't wear a headscarf. The headscarves are technically banned in school, but the girls wear them anyway. And the girls who wear them aren't quiet or shy—they smile and laugh and talk too much in class. In the morning, in the women's bathroom, I stand next to them in the mirror, putting lipstick on and dabbing it off again, while they carefully pin the cloth to their hair.

In the evening, I walk the residential district of Ortaköy. Men pull fishing nets from bed-sized boats. Vendors deal fruit from stands, kumquat branches thin and long; they snap like wrists. The women around me are excruciatingly pretty and exquisitely dressed. They are done up in high heels, gold bracelets, dark eye shadow. The women in *hijabs* have designer purses that match their headscarves.

The Galata Bridge lights up in the distance, the massive freighters slide along the water, and children with air rifles shoot candy-colored balloons floating on the Bosphorus. Glass-eyed cats roost in piles of pillows and jeweled lanterns, women in *burkas* buy candy waffles from booths of electric light, and I walk and look and I walk and I look. Everything is pretty. In the morning, the air is clear. Between the buildings, colored *hijabs* hang on laundry lines; they snap like flags. At night, when I hear the Turkish fishermen pull their low horns, I think of the Mississippi: its dirty shore, the buried tires on the bank.

Back in New Orleans, the one man and I would sit on his stoop, pants-less, smoking cigarettes in the evening while handsome old neighbors strolled by. On Sundays, we danced in second lines, the neighborhood parades, following the floats and brass bands down the avenue, and bought bottles from the backs of trucks in the Lower Ninth, trumpets sounding in the rain.

Orleans is the murder capital of the country—its murder rate exceeds Detroit's by around 20 percent—but, as a woman, I never felt unsafe. In America, I knew all the places to be afraid. In Istanbul, I don't know when to feel afraid, when to feel safe. Because here, women are helped and protected. Men offer me their seat. Men walk me home when I get lost. Men give me discounts and free, honey-soaked baklava. But this is the kind of protectiveness that develops in a culture where women are vulnerable.

Recently, Turkish Prime Minister Recep Tayyip Erdoğan said that he didn't know whether a woman arrested during a violent protest was a *kız*, meaning maiden or young virgin, or a *kadın*, meaning an older, sexually experienced woman. Meaning: these are the only two roles women are given.

One night, I make the mistake of walking home alone. In these small morning hours, the sidewalk is empty. I see others only occasionally, and I see no women.

I hear a hissing, and a car slows down on the dark road. It's crawling alongside me. Two men with closed-off faces stare at me somberly. They are serious and unreadable. They take me in with their eyes, very hungry, like I take the city in.

One calls something in Turkish.

I mumble, "Leave me alone," and I turn my face away.

The car crawls along next to me for another minute. Then, it pulls ahead and parks at the side of the road. It sits there while I keep walking, coming up next to it again. I have my keys between my knuckles, ready to stab, to gouge, to sprint off screaming. As I pass the car again, though, it finally shoots off.

This harassment happens again and again. Sometimes more than one car is crawling alongside me, staring and yelling, sometimes opening the door to invite me in or maybe for a passenger to jump out. I am terrified and I feel foolish, utterly stupid, for choosing to walk alone at night. I am the Dumb American. I feel that I have offended people in some way. I have lost night-walk territory in moving to this new city. I never knew it was a land I could leave so suddenly.

Sexual harassment and sexual shame aren't keeping with Islam. Sexual intimacy is part of the religion's lessons. There are *hadiths*, sayings attributed to the prophet, that encourage a man to move slowly and kindly in sex, passages that prescribe foreplay. One reads, "When anyone of you has sex with his wife, then he should not go to them like birds; instead he should be slow and delaying." To be close to one another: this is holy too.

I go into a mosque for the first time over the summer. It is hot, and I am wearing blue short shorts and a red tank top, sweating at my scalp. I stand in a long line to enter the Sultanahmet Camii. At the end, at the entrance, a volunteer hands me a long skirt and a scarf to cover my hair. I step through the elastic waist and pull it up to be snug around my hips. I try to tie the headscarf in the way that the women around me are wearing it, but I can't figure out the knots— over and over I twist it around the nape of my neck. The women around me stepping in to worship look graceful, polished. I look like a turnip in a napkin.

I step inside and it is hushed, hushed. A wide low room hung with small electric lights that imitate candles, the carpet soft and plush, the acoustics muted, and in the clear open space towards the front where worshipers can kneel in prayer, children running back and forth yelling and playing. I sit on my heels, and I am quiet. The screened-off section behind me is for women only, and I can hear them whispering. They are covered, closing their eyes in concentration. Men in long *thawbs* sit in pairs, talking softly.

We are all of us sitting on the floor. I tuck my legs underneath me. I could curl up there; I could sleep. It is a place of shelter. With my head covered that way, I am my own secret. I think about kneeling on the harsh wooden pews of my Episcopalian church back home; I think of the statues of a nailed man hanging on the wall. A little girl nearby crawls across the rug to smile at me. My headscarf comes undone. I try to make it stay, but it just slips right off.

After a couple weeks in the city, I start sleeping with a friend of a friend, an Irishman. He's got too many ex-girlfriends, and he thinks of other women when we're together. We decide to keep it simple, sex alone; skin on skin is a comfort in a strange new country. He's got a chipped tooth, which cuts when he bites my lip. When he moans, I hear his accent.

This is the Western thing I'm used to: When I come to the front door, we don't kiss hello. When I go into his room, I take my clothes off myself. In the morning, with the pale washed-clean light coming through long curtains, I forget where I am for minutes at a time. I turn and put my mouth to what's next to me. New skin. I keep my eyes closed. And I turn back to the wall. I miss my best friend I miss my best friend I miss my best friend, the man back in Orleans. He used to pull me towards him in his sleep. But he is far away.

And so I give the Irish boy head. Afterwards I borrow baggy, clown-like pants to walk to the bus stop because I cannot be a woman, alone, walking in a skirt. There are too many strangers in cars. I don't want to be bothered; I don't want to be looked at that way; I cannot be sexual outside.

I get a different job, teaching English in a kindergarten. All day I play with children and try to get them to speak English. We play games and sing songs and build things with blocks. I watch them solve puzzles. When they speak Turkish, saying *merhaba, merhaba, hello, hello,* I scold them, as if their very language is a mistake they make on purpose. When I leave the school, I whisper *merhaba, merhaba* under my breath, greeting no one.

My first day at the kindergarten, I have to attend a seminar that has something to do with our feelings. We have to do Tai Chi and watch an Italian music video and then draw pictures with colored markers on a big piece of butcher paper. After dark, exhausted and angry that I had to doodle those rainbows, I start the two-hour commute home. I'm wearing a blue dress that goes to my knees.

On the tram, near the end of my journey, I sit next to a man whose face I now don't remember. I'm staring into my lap. My eyes wander left where I see his hand working, the knuckles flexing, that pink pinch of skin there in his lap. The man next to me is masturbating, pressed close on the crowded tram, while staring at my knees. I jump up and spin towards the back of the car. Nobody else moves. I flush hot all over. The man gets off at the next stop while I stare at the back of his head. I pull down the hem of my dress while I watch him stand up for the next stop, hunch at the shoulders, make a small movement which I know is him zippering his fly. And I am ashamed, I am disgusting, and I want to explain to him that he is the one who should be ashamed, he is disgusting, him, him. However, I don't speak the language, and already he's gone.

Every weekend night, friends and I drink Turkish Rakia; we drink gin. We go to clubs where suddenly I can wear whatever I want and blend right in. I rub skin on skin, I pay too much for beer and liquor and we listen to American pop music and I jump up and down and yell English words with the other people yelling English words that they don't understand.

Men put their hands on my back. Men step up behind me and press their legs to my legs. Strange tall men with serious faces. The girls dance in tight circles, and I think, *yes, this is like America; we huddle there too.*

I jump up and down and I yell nonsense and I do the sprinkler, I do the shopping cart, I do the lawnmower because in this city nobody knows who I am and I want to look stupid. I want to scare them all away.

There in the noise and the lights and the heat, I'm thinking of the one man back home. I'm thinking of Louisiana and the power going out. When the air conditioner whirred to a still, we went walking through the murky house to the table set with candles in tinfoil cups. There was jambalaya made in a pan on the still-living stove. There were the two of us sitting on the front steps while the thunder shouldered over us again, and again, and still again. That pink electricity at a distance. All the streetlamps off. Some faraway shouting. Nodding to neighbors. And the earliest fireworks. Me and the one man sitting on the steps, some jambalaya, a jar of whiskey-water, a happy dog trotting by his lonesome down the sidewalk, and explosions in a far-off place that we cannot see. Groups of bicycles happy-shouting over the thunder noise, and always the wind drawing cool through sweat-damp scalp. Too hot to live indoors. There was darkness when it gets dark. And me leaning into the heat of him.

In the middle of the crowd, gin-struck, dazed and ready to leave, there is suddenly a face swooping down towards me and a strange man in the crowd leans across other people to kiss me, once, on the lips.

"What the actual fuck!" yells a girl who's with us. "Did that guy just kiss you?" I just nod. I'm too surprised to get angry.

We leave the club and head down a nearby main road. We pass prostitutes; we pass transvestite prostitutes. I have not seen any cross-dressing or gay couples anywhere in Istanbul during the three months I've been here, but suddenly there is a man in a skirt getting on the back of another man's motorcycle. And they are smiling, they are laughing. Another prostitute tiptoes up to touch the shiny bike. She cries out happily and runs away. As we pass the man in the skirt, he is still smiling. I want to give him a high five or a hug or tell him *I'm sorry if life is difficult for you here sometimes*, but maybe he does not need a high five or a hug or if he does, he would not understand my English. Now it is too late, because we have already passed him, and they are on the motorcycle speeding away.

In November the Irishman and I stop sleeping together because he is sleeping with somebody new. In December, I try to cut his hair, lunging at him with the scissors. I only end up cutting my hand. That night I enter his room, lie on his bed to talk, and I see a used condom on the floor. We laugh, and I give him shit about his dirty room, like haha funny, like haha it is only sex and we had it and now we don't, haha. I am thinking: he did not use condoms with me, and I am thinking: that will stain the floor, and I am thinking: I used to wake up here in the gray wash of early morning and open my eyes, he is throwing the condom away, I used to wake up here, naked, and now it is another body naked waking, he's throwing the condom away and I used to wake up rising, here. I am thinking: this is another way to cover the body. It is not shelter.

The next morning, on the sofa, I wake up to the call to prayer, a wail I love the sound of. It is a long and solitary call, but soon I hear the songs of other mosques echo on behind, voices more distant. I open my hung-over eyes and think *dış*, the Turkish word for *outside*. The imam's voice is coming through the minarets in long minor notes, and I think I can make out *söyleyelim, let us sing*. And it is a sweet song, this call you hear when you wake, alone, in a pre-dawn room. It is sweet. It's a sweetness sung for you.

There are many new and beautiful things in Istanbul. I try to explain them to people back home, and I can't. I eat fruits I don't know the names of, pulling the seeds from the flesh. I watch men on the bridge cutting open the bellies of tiny fish, feeding the cats. When it snows in December, I take the bus to the mosque nearby, past the shining *çiçek* flower shops, the bus nesting its own dun light. When we get to my stop, I step out of the heat and the heat doesn't follow me. I watch families play in the courtyard. A woman in a *burka* throws a snowball at her child, and they're laughing. I start to learn some Turkish words: *bayan*, woman, *adam*, man, *eve*, homewards.

Back in Louisiana, I slept with my best friend, a man who worked in construction and nursed electrical burns on both his hands. He lived in the 9th ward, and we were broke as hell. We slept naked under his big white window. In the morning, with the gulf breezes blowing through and the freighters moaning on the river we smoked spliffs in bed and ate food stamp toast and a there was warm breath on the back of my neck and this was the One Safe Place.

We bought bottles, and we brought flasks to bars. We danced in second lines and we climbed tipped oil rigs. There was tomato sauce on a blue dress, the smell of coffee on the stained paper, those last days in a small living room, tobacco and early mornings and mirrors that reflected no face, only light and the bells of the church next door. There was an understanding. There was a risk we both took. There was one night, lying on our bellies on my red-quilted bed, smoking out the window like children, like criminals, and the rain going, and the huge shape of thunder rolling always towards us and our clothes still on, and how he stayed with me and no anger. How we slept and his arm around me and we didn't do anything. We didn't do anything. We didn't even take our clothes off. We only slept.

This, this, this is what makes sex holy. Real intimacy. To know that a body is not shameful or dirty or evil, and is not cheap and is not meaningless. To be unafraid. To undress in the daylight. This is the sacred thing I've known.

Delaney Nolan's fiction and nonfiction have appeared in Oxford American, Guernica, The Chattahoochee Review, The South Carolina Review, The Rumpus *and elsewhere. She currently lives in Istanbul.*

U.S. Marine Aid Station at Landing Zone Baldy

by Robert Robeson

poetry honorable mention

"Pain Builds Character," the sign said.
It was the first thing wounded saw
after helicopters arrived
and unloaded their bloody burdens

at the aid station landing pad.
"Pain Builds Character." The sign said
wounds distinguish injured soldiers
and promote distinctive features.

Perhaps they should not have nailed it
above the door to emphasize *that*
"Pain. Builds Character," the sign said,
like being shot was a grand event

that warriors should accept
as a beneficial gift to
make them better human beings.
"Pain Builds Character," the sign said.

*Robert B. Robeson flew 987 combat medical evacuation
missions in South Vietnam in 1969–1970. He had seven*

126

helicopters shot up by enemy fire and was twice shot down while evacuating 2,533 patients from both sides of the action. He was commander and operations officer during his tour with the 236th Medical Detachment (helicopter ambulance) in Da Nang. He's been published more than 825 times in 290 publications in 130 countries, which include Reader's Digest, Official Karate, Vietnam Combat, Frontier Airline Magazine, *and* Newsday, *among others. His writing has also been featured in 30 book anthologies. Robeson is a life member of the National Writers Association and the Military Writers Society of America. He retired from the U.S. Army, as a lieutenant colonel, after 27-1/2 years of military service on three continents.*

LEAVING PERDITION

by Rebekah Shardy

short fiction honorable mention

MY NAME IS BLAZE MCCARTNEY. I GREW UP WITH MY LITTLE SISTER Glory in Perdition, a high and lonesome town in the crooked shadow of Blue Mountain.

Indians have another name for it. When they said it they'd look at us as if we had no sense at all. They talked about mountains the way most folks refer to relatives. A few men I've known went Indian, starting to even look like them, staying up in wild places to trap and hunt with no care of normal things.

I think my mother loved and feared them kind the most.

She said my father was one. He was big and rode a horse bigger than most, coming into town only to buy supplies, hunting outlaws for bounty money before riding back up the ridge to a home fit for a bear. She made him coffee and he asked for hot pepper instead of sugar in it. He liked to drink it with a fist of bacon fat. She said he never touched bread or any cooked food she could remember. Living like an animal made him smarter on how to find and kill them, I guess.

He died when I was too small to remember. He was riding down the middle of Black Indian Creek so no one could track him on his way home; someone he owed gambling money shot him from a bluff. Tumbled into the dark water like a cottonwood struck by lightning.

My sister Glory was everything I wish I was then: sweet-faced and kind to strangers, laughter like silk and skin the color of milk. Her eyes were blue like Mama's, not rabbitbrush brown like mine. I thought she was weak but I see now she was better than any of us put together.

She had a different father, pale as gooseflesh, skinny and mean as a weasel. He lived in Perdition and pretended not to know us. Mother made us cross the street when she saw him. Other folk crossed the street at the sight of us—a woman never married with two daughters, the 12-year-old dressed like a boy.

Since our kind didn't go to school, I was determined to be a bounty hunter. I wore a man's clothes I found in my mother's closet. I could throw a knife dead aim at 50 paces. I'd shoot squirrels from dawn to noon. Even drove mules once.

When I told her what I'd be when grown, and how I'd take care of her, she looked faraway and talked about how the walls needed more chinking or how the cow, Abigail, wanted more hay.

I took that to mean she wouldn't stand in my way.

* * *

Most folks want you to think they're better than they are and their conscience is smooth as a pearl when it's more like a prickly pear.

I will tell you right off the two bad things I done.

I stole a gun off a dead man. He was rich, stiff-legged old, and lying in the street where someone robbed and left him to die, I guess. Seemed he was about to use that gun but never did, and it wasn't helping him now. The pistol was pretty with a white shiny handle, nothing I ever seen before, and fit real nice inside my waistband. I ran home and showed it to Glory who was so scared of it she hid herself.

I'm not making excuses but I always felt a fierce need for guns. When I was no bigger than a baby, I told my mother I wanted to wear guns in the street to keep bad men off her. She'd bring a scruffy lot of men home in those days. Some even bothered me.

The second thing was more from curiosity but willful bad too.

I seen from a young age what men did with my mother and wondered about it so much I tried it on my sister. I crept up on her like a tomcat and we rubbed bellies until a warm, silky feeling fell over me, like when I saw the picture of a naked woman in the saloon window. Anything that felt that nice couldn't be decent.

One morning mother caught me. She pulled me up by my hair and I ran into the yard, bare feet slipping on the frosty earth. She picked up the only thing nearby, a plank of wood, and made to hit my behind with it, but I was scrambling so it struck the back of my legs and down I went on my face. I still have a little scar above one eyebrow from the rock my face smashed. Glory was screaming for her to stop, and she did— just to curse me.

The air got knocked out of me, and something else too.

* * *

Christmas was hard in Perdition. Everything was frozen as a stone and warmth was hard to come by. Not many trees; firewood was dear to get, fast to use.

Folks who went to church usually feasted on a roast bird, maybe mince pie. We never did and no one asked us to join them either.

Mother worked so hard, going out late to make money that might buy us ginger candy or new long underwear. She tried making soap of grease and ashes and speckled with cinnamon; nobody would buy from her. So a few nights before Christmas one year, she came home with Gervy, a man famous in town for being a pig, bigheaded and drunk, bad smelling as he was bad-natured. If there was a dog running about, Gervy was the man who would kick it.

Our instruction was to hide in the closet while she entertained, and there we were: Glory playing with a Cat's Cradle string, and me with my ear against the door trying to hear them.

"What is that? What are you going to do with that?"

"Shut up."

"No, don't, I don't want that in me."

"Come on now!" Panting.

"No, please . . ."

I couldn't bear to hear my mother beg. It seemed wrong as the moon square dancing. I burst out the closet, grabbed one of my guns and charged into her room.

Gervy was standing over my mother with an empty whiskey bottle. She was trying to cover herself, face shocked to see me. He never turned or seen me coming. I shot him clean in the back.

The bullet seemed to wake him from his drunken stupor. He reached for his hat and weaved out the door, as if he had at least the good sense to not bleed on our floor. Three steps off the porch he fell backwards quiet as a feather.

Every night that winter coyotes were sniffing and crying about the place. I told mother it seemed fitting to leave Gervy for those wild dogs. None of us could sleep. Sure enough we heard them find their prize. In the morning, what was left we pushed into the ravine a few yards past our property.

No one missed him being gone.

Glory cried for fear I was going to hell. But mother kissed me on the forehead, the first time I could remember. She said he meant to cut her where she'd never be right.

Later I dreamt he came back all cleaned up, hair combed, in a new suit of clothes. He brought a bunch of yellow flowers for my mother and sat at the table, humbled and ashamed. I told him she wasn't there and would never see him again.

I felt almost sorry for the look in his eyes.

* * *

Guess that was the end of my career as a bounty hunter. Three years after I killed a man, I was up on the side of Blue Mountain, dazzled by butterflies, song birds, and the bulging baskets of food the Berringers brought with us on a sweet white mule they let me ride. It was nothing like Perdition, a pen of dirt shaken by wind without trees.

"Poor child," I heard Mrs. Berringer whisper to her distracted husband. "Never been on a picnic before. Never been in the mountains! And so close she could touch them!"

It was true. The mountains seemed to me like a faraway worry or rainstorm. I hardly thought of them as a place I could go as easy as a hawk or a cloud. To take time away from home and work was a waste surely.

The ruddy woman tried to get me to splash her in the icy creek like she was doing to me, and I half-heartedly played along, but it was such a strange thing, and between smiles my eyes watered with tears at the thought of Glory.

They took her. Away. From me.

How could I be carefree thinking of my sister in the hold of a strange man trailing God knows where? Was she scared? Was she fed? Who would comfort her?

What happened was Mama got sick. Some said it was that disease that turns loose women blind and crazy. I don't know about that, but I know she didn't want to leave us poor and alone in the world. All her money was hid in a dusty hatbox under a floorboard but the people who came for her body searched until they found it and took it.

They took all the fine things she kept on our sitting room table, gifts given by men as payment, booty of gambling I suspect: French perfume, ivory figurines, boxes with inlaid mother of pearl, a diamond brooch, and a white ostrich feather fan with real gold in the handle. That was our future. They took that too.

The preacher was one of them, saying he needed compensation to care for us orphans. Not a month passed after his thievery that he didn't pass me to the Berringers, a childless couple nearing old age. He offered Glory for a price to a traveling salesman who said he needed someone to keep his clothes mended for him.

I will never forget how Glory looked when she held her hand out to mine that wasn't there as that scowling man's wagon shrunk down the hill. It was the one thing more terrible than losing Mama, and my poor heart couldn't hold both sorrows at the same time.

"Eat child; eat your fill," Mrs. Berringer coaxed. She didn't have to ask long. Soon I was stuffing my mouth with every sweet in the house that wasn't nailed, even sneaking sips of the brandy the Mister kept in a low drawer. Food and wine swallowed up my sorrows and my slender shape took the form of a young bear too fat to climb a tree.

The Mister ignored both of us mostly. He spent hours locked in a library, mooning over picture books of women in bloomers and such. Mrs. Berringer was desperate for human company, even that of a half-grown girl dressed like a boy. Maybe she got to pretending I was a young man come courting her.

She made me sit beside her as she played her Hurdy Gurdy, fat leg pressed against mine, nodding whenever I should move the pages of her music book. When I had to turn the page she'd move closer to my face. I kissed her. I don't think I wanted to as I felt it was what she wanted and needed me to do. I didn't want to go back to the preacher, or to a beetle-eyed salesman who would pay for a girl-wife.

The Mister happened to leave his study that very moment and saw it. Lord, you would have thought I had shot someone all over again. He took me personally to the sheriff and said I was incorrigibly indecent like my mother. "She's Amadine's little whore," was the exact words he used. "Plum trees don't sprout cherries."

I was there a long time as I remember. I thought Mrs. Berringer would come get me, at least visit with a basket of food, but she stayed away. She didn't love me, really, except the way she loved her Hurdy Gurdy: something to make her feel a little better for a little while.

Mr. Tooker came and promised the sheriff to teach me a trade—being an innkeeper. That sounded nice enough and I went gamely with him. The inn was hardly a house, more of a hovel. The floors were slanted and the windows dirty and the fireplace unusable. But people did come to stay one night or so. All men. And with only two bedrooms—Mr. Tooker's and mine—they slept with me.

It was a trade all right.

Mr. Tooker said I had a natural talent for it, even though I cried and yelled and fought it at first. He said I came from generations of women who released men from their carnal aggravation—"a worthy profession"—and I hated every part of it.

Sometimes as some stinking Joe moved on me, my mind drifted away. I saw myself on the big sandy horse my father rode. I was moving down Black Indian Creek towards home where a loving wife and warming fire awaited me. I wore big guns; no one dare stop me. The trees on every side chattered with blue birds. The moon, like a nail print on someone's flesh, bent sideways, fading in the pale morning sky.

* * *

Some things change, some don't.

I did get good at what I had to do.

Customers in time changed from miners black as tar to the bald-headed mayor, his flesh more hairless and delicate than his wife's. They had a photographer come in to take a picture of the three of us to memorialize their night of shameful pleasures.

I had myself a daughter, little Rose Belinda. I never did learn to want the love of a man, but took innocent comfort feeling her warm body close to mine as we slept, listening to her breath, touching her soft hair. That was a prayer come true and peace of a kind.

Mr. Tooker died of the tuberculosis. He left all he had to me and Rosey, having no kin of his own. I guess even a house of ill repute can be family to some.

Money and comfort came in spades then. So much I sometimes wept to think of my mother worrying at night over the last few dried beans in the cupboard to feed us.

Despite all the changes, what stayed the same was this: missing my sister. And wondering what it would have been like if I had never lived in Perdition.

Sometimes I dream both. I see myself climbing Blue Mountain with my sister to look over the other side. Above us a hawk floats in protection. A feather, like the one my father was said to wear in his hatband, falls into my waiting hand. He's there though I can't see him.

"Come on," I say to her. My sister is going to make it. She's going to grow up, become a seamstress, something respectful and ladylike.

I'm running now to the top, despite the loose dirt, the slippery gravel, the shift of earth. I'm going to make it too, but to what, I never can imagine.

Almost there and I look over the edge, that line between me and joy—but it's an uncrossable boundary. I never do.

I open my eyes and sigh to see my sleeping little girl, wishing for her all that's fine and noble, what could have been and never was for me.

Maybe what I missed will come to her as easy as the green canary I bought her, bouncing and bobbing on her fat little finger to make her laugh. When I hear that music from her lips I remember something good survives us, something grand like the Blue Mountain.

I bet the Indians even have a name for it.

"Some disappeared, some changed into curious songs, and some of them changed slowly into beautiful mountains."
    —Thomas Hornsby Ferril and the American West

Rebekah Shardy won first place for short fiction at the 2009 Authorfest of the Rockies and was nominated for Excellence in Poetry by the Pikes Peak Arts Council in 2012. She is also author of 98 Things a Woman Should Do in Her Lifetime *(Andrews McMeel, 2003), a hospice manager, and trainer on holistic aging and caregiving.*

EVACUATION

by Sonya Whitesell

short fiction honorable mention

I DRIVE PAST THE WHITE PLASTIC SAWHORSES AND WAVE AT THE national guardsman manning the roadblock. He looks young and unsure, as if he would prefer a battlefield to a subdivision in the path of a wildfire. I pull up next to the emergency services trucks parked in the meadow. A gust of wind rocks my pickup and sends dust devils spinning towards the stringers of pines and homes dotting the valley. Smoke blots out the horizon to the south, hanging on the mountain like burning clouds.

Flecks of white ash land on the windshield and I roll up the window so embers can't land on the seat. I toss my keys on the dash out of habit—you always leave your keys with your rig so someone can move it if the fire turns and comes your way—and grab a roll of black and yellow caution tape. The wind almost blows the door out of my grasp as I hop out of the truck. I slam the door behind me and walk over to the group of people gathering around the hood of a patrol car.

"Hey," I say as I edge into the loose circle of deputies and firefighters. I slap my palm against the subdivision plat map threatening to launch into the air.

"Hey girl, how've you been?" Hank leans in next to me, grabbing the rest of the map. Hank is the deputy for this part of the county, and he looks every bit the rural lawman—tall and lean, with mirror sunglasses sitting flush against the weathered planes of his face and a demeanor that makes you want to stand up straight and say *sir*. All he needs is a leather vest with a star on the chest, but it's way too hot for that.

"Pretty good. Busy. You know," My bangs blow in my eyes and I lose my reflection in Hank's glasses as I try to push my straw-dry hair off my face. "This wind sucks. Got a ponytail holder?"

Hank laughs. "Can't say I do."

"No hair accessories with your guns?" I tease. Hank rides with an arsenal in the back of his pickup. The last time I saw Hank he went after a couple of drunken college kids that were hassling me over a campfire ticket. I'd called him for help when one of the kids came towards me with a double fisted grip on a hatchet. "Well he can take a double fisted grip on my AR if he wants to be like that," Hank said, before he hauled the kids off to jail. Good guy to have on your side.

Hank pulls a rubber band off his ticket book and hands it to me. "How's this?"

"Perfect. Thanks." I pull my hair back as Phil, the local wildlife officer, joins our group. Even with the blue jeans, khaki shirt, and cowboy hat, Phil still looks like a husky country kid. With a gun. I look past Phil to where the wind is thrashing the tops of the beetle-kill trees on the ridge. The dead pines lost all their needles this year, leaving only bare grey skeletons behind. Ghost trees. From a distance the grey trees look like new smokes.

"Wildlife 5-1. Heard you've been busy chasing bears," Hank says.

"Yeah." Phil shakes his head. "They're getting into the fire camps."

"Shoot any?"

"Yeah, shot two yesterday. Been getting called out at all hours for those damn things. My wife is about to divorce me."

A bluejay scolds us from a spindly pine.

"I hear you," I say. "My son wants a new mom and dad that don't fight fire." I watch the bird hop amongst branches laden with a stress crop of cones.

This morning, as I woke my son to say good-bye, again, he clung to me and cried and begged me not to leave. As I pried his fingers from my uniform, he told me he hated fire, and hates being the kid of firefighters. "I never know who is going to watch me," he said.

"Honey, at least you can lie in your own bed and make that wish. There are many boys and girls who don't even have a home anymore because of the fire," I said, hating myself for moralizing his need. "This isn't just a fire, this is a natural disaster like a tornado or a hurricane that hit our town. We all have to try to help."

"I know. I just hate fire. I wish you could just put it out." He turned his face to the pillow to hide his tears.

"We're trying honey, believe me. We want it out too."

"I wish I could have put it out when it started."

"I know. I wish you could have too." I wiped tears from his cheek with my thumb and kissed his forehead, trying to draw all his sorrow away. My heart broke as I rose to stand over him, brush his hair from his forehead, then turn and walk out the door. I found a small grace in the fact my son was at least with family—my mother-in-law—who took the week off work to help.

The poor kid has bounced around for weeks now, cared for by a community of friends and family who mobilized when the beast first blew its hot rancid breath across town. People are desperate to do anything to help, even if it is just mowing my lawn or taking my son to the pool. At least my child is having a summer, even if it is not with me.

The other day, a psychologist spoke to the firefighters at the morning fire briefing. As we stood in the pre-dawn gloom, clutching our paper cups of coffee, the shrink told us to remember our families at home. "Remember, they're scared for you too."

I promise, when this fire is out I'll do something nice for my family. Maybe we can all go away together. Somewhere wet and cool.

The wind shifts, darkening the sky and blowing black smoke our way. I cough at the bitter taste and lick my lips, already cracked in the dry, dirty wind. I feel the tingle of a fever blister forming. Too much heat, too much dust, too much smoke; it's been a long summer and it's only June.

Hank turns to watch the smoke column, which is bulging on all sides now as if it is inhaling for a big blow. Flickers of orange and red reflect across Hank's shades. "This damn fire," he says. "It's making everything crazy. Saw a moose on the playground in town the other day." He pulls a bandana from his back pocket and wipes his streaming nose.

"Don't tell me that, I don't want to have to shoot the moose too," Phil says. He's squinting in the smoke, wiping at his red eyes.

"Oh, don't shoot the moose, it's not like there's any kids running around," I say. With all the smoke in town parents are acting like there's a lion or a serial killer on the loose—shutting their windows tight and locking their children inside. As they should. Smoke is bad, especially for little lungs.

I see a second column of smoke boil up just past the ridge.

"Shit. It crossed the river," I say. Helicopters trailing buckets of water swarm the new smoke, looking like gnats at this distance. They fly back and forth relentlessly but the new column rapidly turns black and defined, rising up in a twin column to the monster fire that spawned it.

The wind stops suddenly and for a moment I catch the scent of sun-warmed pines. A chickadee trills in the lull, until it is startled into flight by the ringing of a cell phone. The fire chief takes the call then hangs up, his face grim. He's a volunteer chief, unpaid, and on leave from his job at a computer manufacturing plant in town. The stress of the past weeks is evident in the deep bags under his eyes and the greying stubble across his cheeks.

"The fire jumped the highway and the river. The Sheriff just ordered an evacuation of the entire twelfth filing. Two hundred homes." The wind kicks in as he speaks, stronger now. A dog starts to bark nearby. "Evacuation is mandatory. Flag each home black and yellow tape so we know it's clear. If the residents won't leave we're not wasting time arresting them and dragging them out. Just take names and addresses so we can account for everyone we contact."

Account means cover your ass in case the homeowner stays and dies.

I partner with Hank. I know he won't leave me even with the fire coming our way. The chief hands out routes and I take a map showing streets and lots circled with a marker. Hank and I plot our route, deciding to go all the way in first and work our way out to safety.

I turn on my emergency lights as the smoke sinks into the valley. Hank flips on his siren and we drive out, flashing and wailing. I roll past a sign showing a smiling real estate agent superimposed across a pristine forest of green timber and golden streams of aspen set below clear blue skies. "Own your own piece of paradise—mountain living at its best," the sign says. The sign doesn't tell you that aspen grow in old fire scars. Fire has always been a part of this land, just the homes are new. Now the timber is on fire and the sky is filled with smoke and there will be no gold to remember this year unless you count the color of flames.

I tie a piece of flagging to the sign and head up the road as the first wave of evacuating residents head the other way along the evacuation route. The reverse 911 calls must have gone out, or the residents saw the fire boil up the hill and realized it was time to go. Paved roads, wells, and electricity have not fully erased our instinctive urge to flee.

The evacuees clutch the steering wheels of their cars and trucks and trailers with grim determination. There is also a small pride in the set of their shoulders—in the face of disaster they find they can do what must be done. All wave or mouth *thank you* to me through the windshields as they depart.

I wish I could turn and leave too. I am scared of being in the green unburned fuels ahead of the fire. I would rather be in the middle of the black, where the fuels are seared off and flames cannot get me and I do not have to think about whether my truck can outrun the flames or if the flames will starve the engine, trapping me in the path of the fire. I am scared of the long driveways ahead with no end in sight.

Please let me get to all homes before the fire arrives. I am scared when I cannot see the fire to know if I still have time to turn around. I am scared but don't tell anyone.

My gut tells me we still have time and people are still in their homes. I know Hank and I will keep an eye on each other and make sure we both get out. We've run this drill too many times this summer, as wildfires gobble through our forests of beetle-killed pines and all the subdivisions in between. The first time was a midnight surprise, the *we've never seen fire do this before* disaster. The second time we were prepared. Expect the unexpected became the norm, and assume the worst because it's coming this way.

At first the firefighters were confident but the cops were unsure. I think the cops would have been more comfortable if there was an armed gunman in the middle of the fire. Malice, they knew. Ruthless indifference was something new.

Now the cops are dialed into fire, but the firefighters are struggling with the scale of loss. Evacuations are the worst— cut and run, get everyone out of the way. I can't help but evaluate every home as I evacuate it. *Narrow one-way roads with dense vegetation—a loser, let this one go. Open clearings, room to turn around? I could make a stand here, lay down some fire, save this home. Just give me a chainsaw to knock down a few trees.*

But we can't make a stand, we don't have the people or the time. As a firefighter, I am used to direct attack—go to the fire, line it, and put it out. But I'm not on that team right now because my husband is, and we can't both be gone for the month of June. So I take the day shifts helping with evacuations—leaving before dawn and getting back after dark—but at least I am home in time to tuck the covers over our son, while my husband sleeps in the dirt.

Hank and I reach the end of the road; thank God there is a turnaround. I make the three-point turn as Hank waits. We're on a ridge and I can see the fire rage in a three-hundred-foot wall of flame, taking out the hill between the river and the homes. I watch the flames rear high in the air then charge up the hill, cresting the top in a wave that eddies over the leeward side of the mountain. In the wake of the flames a home torches like a signal beacon letting us know the enemy has arrived—but not yet on my circled part of the map. I hope the firefighters who evacuated that end of the filing did their job and got out.

"You take the left side and I'll take the right." I yell through the window as Hank pulls up next to me. His white truck reflects orange in the glow of the fire as he smiles at me, baring his teeth like an animal cornered and ready to fight.

"Lets giddy-up, girl," he says. A chipmunk bolts across the road, stopping in the middle to chirp at us, tail bobbing urgently. I drive forward, scaring the chipmunk off.

The first driveway on the right leads to a sprawling log home. I park and jog past a woodpile, and gardens fenced against the deer, to pound on the doors and windows of the home. Embers land on the porch and the wind chimes sing but no one responds. I try the door, which has a white towel tied to it—a symbol the residents use to show they are gone. The door is open so I step inside and yell just to be sure. The house is deserted and I move on, throwing a smoldering welcome mat off the porch into the gravel.

I drive past a flagpole with the American flag snapping in the dark wind. I hope the flag still flies when the residents return. Maybe the porch will be a bit singed or the house will be painted a lovely retardant pink, and they will cry with relief, and save the bit of caution flagging on their home as a souvenir.

I hope they don't return to desolation: a lone mortared stone and cement mailbox protecting the mail inside like a time capsule. *Here's your mortgage bill—for your home that burned to the ground. Oh, and the daily news marking the day your life changed.*

At the next home a middle-aged woman is closing up her house as I arrive.

"We got the calls," she says. "We're ready to go." Her car looks packed for a camping trip, rather than a last chance to grab all she owns. "The door is open if you need anything."

"I can wait here," I say, "if you need a little more time."

"It doesn't matter," she says. "It is just things. Please, may I give you a hug?"

I nod and she hugs me like a mother, giving a squeeze before she lets go. "Stay safe," she says, though I am here to save her.

A young man is parked at the end of the next driveway, looking back at the smoke and flames coming this way.

"You see that nice fire break down there?" He points to a meadow in the path of the fire. "My house is on the wrong side of that."

"I'm so sorry."

"It's okay." His serene eyes are the color of the summer sky, before the fires began. "This is not a bad day."

I nod, knowing bad days.

"Take care," the man says, and gets back into his car. The Dalai Lama gazes out at me from the hatchback window as the man drives away.

As I drive to the next house on my route I watch the glow of the fire in my rear view mirror and wonder what I would take if I ever had to choose. People leave so much behind: a telescope aimed at the stars you can see so well in the mountain sky; patio furniture set for morning coffee or sunset drinks. Cars, laundry, mail, receipts, bedding, and housewares—even the wedding china—it all stays behind. Most evacuees fill their cars with pets, and picture frames. Memories, it seems, are what people value most as they leave their dream homes behind. At every house I evacuate, I am humbled by how much they leave.

At the last house, all the trees are cut down, even the junipers under the picture window. The homeowners must have mowed the landscaping with chainsaws before they left. I get out and toss a few remaining limbs further away from the house as two dogs bark at me from the gate. Hank pulls up and we look at the dogs. One dog is a husky with light eyes and big teeth and the other a fuzzy mop that is barking like he wants a piece of me. With the concrete yard, the house might survive the fire but I don't know about the dogs. Fenced in, they can't even run.

"Is this the last house?" Hank asks.

"Yeah," I say. We've gotten all the people out.

"Let's get the dogs." Hank decides, and walks towards the gate. I am right on his heels, even though neither of us is supposed to have animals in our trucks. *Rules, you know.*

"Hey boy," Hank says and reaches out over the fence. The husky bares his teeth and snaps at Hank's hand. I'm sure Hank's going to get bit, and to my shame I hang back instead of reaching out for the dog, but Hank keeps speaking in a soothing voice until the dog relaxes and lets Hank scratch his head. I guess the "don't show fear" thing works.

"Poor guy," Hank says as he soothes the dog, "did your mom and dad leave you?" Normally pets aren't left on purpose, but sometimes people aren't home when the evacuation order goes out. The owners were probably at the roadblock right now frantically begging the guardsman to let them back in.

Hank looks at me and the wrinkles around his sunglasses crunch tighter. "Do you have any food?"

I run back to my truck. I grab my fire sack lunch and pull out the sandwich meat, then grab some parachute cord I keep on hand in case my shoelaces break or I need rope for something. Haven't touched it the five years it's been in my truck.

I return and hand Hank the bologna. We open the gate and reach out to the dogs, bologna first. I go for the big husky and Hank goes for the little fuzzy one. *Don't show fear.* I throw some meat to the dog and as he tentatively eats a piece I string the parachute cord around his neck. I try to lead the dog back to my truck but he resists, so I hold more meat a few steps ahead of him and lure him back and into the cab of the truck. As I close the door on the dog I turn back to see that Hank is having less luck with the little fuzzy dog who is still barking and ignoring the meat in Hank's hand.

The fire chief is yelling on my handheld radio, ordering everyone to finish up because the fire is exploding. Small embers are starting spot fires in the yard around us.

"Hank," I say, "we're running out of time." Hank lunges for the dog, scooping the little guy in a football hold. We run for the trucks and Hank tosses the dog into my truck, to be with his friend I guess, then gets in his car. I wave for Hank to go but he yells out the window, "I'll follow you out." I drive away as the spot fires become one and converge on the house and the big husky pushes his muzzle between the back of my neck and the seat as the little dog cowers on the floor.

I drive back to the roadblock through a deserted community—past bikes left in yards, trampolines, and garden tools scattered by a watering can. I fight the urge to speed, to find other people, to get past the roadblock, as if a piece of plastic and a young man in a camouflage uniform can keep me safe. I pet the dog pushing against me as I focus on the road and try to stay calm.

At the roadblock we meet up again with Phil and the rest of the firefighters and cops. We regroup and confirm: all resources conducting evacuations accounted for, all homes are cleared. The last few evacuees drive past us through a gauntlet of media forming behind the roadblock like hunters waiting for game flushed by the fire. Reporters and cameramen dart around hoping to catch the perfect shot of an evacuee—fear, resilience, or better yet, tears—captured in the flash of emergency lights.

One reporter protests to a deputy at the roadblock, "Someone ran over my camera gear!"

"It's your own damn fault," the deputy replies. "You got in the way." The deputy unfolds his arms from his this-will-be-a-long-night roadblock stance. "I will arrest if you don't clear out of the evacuation route. Now." The reporter starts to protest but soon becomes mute as the sky seethes with dark clouds and vortexes of flame as if a nuclear bomb detonated oh, just down the road. Maybe by the house with the flag.

Firefighter, cop, journalist, resident, we unite in the fiery destruction of our forest and community. This is the fire of our lifetime, the fire we never thought we would see—a conflagration blowing the ashes of our community into the stratosphere in a towering pyrocumulonimbus cloud. I pray that the column does not bend over or roll our way. I pray that I got everyone out and that no one dies tonight.

"I'm getting too old for this shit," Hank says, voicing our defeat for the fire—hell, for the whole summer.

I try to comfort the dogs. More firefighters arrive—crews mobilized from the other side of the fire where homes were burning too. I look around, hoping maybe it is my husband's crew, but it's not. I give the new crews my map and try to explain the layout of the homes and roads, then wish them luck and head back to my rig.

Hank is waiting for me, petting the dogs. "You want a picture of your friend? You can show your boy what his mom did today."

"Sure," I say. I hand Hank my phone, show him which buttons to press, and get in my truck—hugging the dogs as they climb on my lap. I smile for the camera because that's what you do when someone takes your picture, even if your world is on fire. I smile and hug the dogs and hope I get home in time tonight for my son to count it as me *being there*. Maybe if I show him the picture and tell him a story about the dogs he will understand. Maybe he will forgive me for a summer of being gone.

Sonya Whitesell is a Fort Collins wildland firefighter, teacher, writer, twin, wife, and mother who wants to be a warrior princess when she grows up. A native Bostonian who finds peace amongst sun-warmed pines, she alternates loyalties between Sunshine and a good seasonal Sam. Sonya admires passion, leaders, and people that shine.

THREE COYOTES

by John Noland

poetry honorable mention

They hung there
on a barbed wire fence
like something out of the bible,
ears cut off,
legs tied together

I was only nine,
but I wondered
who had hated
their calls so much,
their wildness
flowering
in the wild twilight,
who had feared
them so much
to kill
what they could not
understand

On hands and knee,
I peered
into their yellow eyes
where ants worked
to empty the sockets,
going up and down
the osage-orange
fence post
and into the earth
Peering into
those glazed,
yellow orbs,
I could see
dusky men
with feathers
in their hair,
riding black and white
Indian ponies

and I felt
how the whole grassy-brown
prairie-hide
rippled in the wind
and sent mirages
dancing,
then skulking back,
watching
and waiting

even at that age,
I wanted to do something—
take off my hat, bow—
to something bigger even
than grass or coyotes,
something I felt
answering
like shadows
of fire
in my own blood

John Noland lives on the Oregon coast, but was born and raised in the Midwest where three of his great-grandfathers homesteaded the same river valley. Winner of the Kulupi Press Poetry of Place competition for his chapbook, This Dark Land Where I Live, *he has published in many literary magazines, including* Heartlands, Laurel Review, Chicago Review, Orion Nature Quarterly, American Nature Writing, Big Muddy, Georgetown Review, *and* Seattle Review. *His Chapbook,* The Caged and the Dying, *won the Gribble Press 2012 Chapbook Contest. Finishing Line Press will be publishing his Chapbook* Midwestern Trees and Shadows *fall of 2013.*

SPIRIT OF THE PIKE

by Jim Kroepfl

short fiction honorable mention

THE LAKE LAY SILENT AND UNRIPPLED IN THE PINK MORNING LIGHT. The other learners were still asleep, but Kannihut knew the Spirit Father was up, watching him from somewhere on the hill, waiting to see if he would become a man.

He approached the water with hesitant steps. Once he went into the lake, he couldn't leave it until the beast was taken. Today, he would kill the pike and take its spirit, or be defeated and go back to the village a failed learner.

Why not a deer? Kannihut thought. I've killed many deer, and I've always honored their spirit. Why do I have to face a pike?

He gripped the spear tightly as the icy water surrounded his calves, then his knees. If he only injured the fish, he'd have to chase it all day, and maybe the next, but he would eventually succumb to the water's cold.

Enough doubt, he scolded himself. Waiting works against me. The pike will be feeding in the shallows now, but will head back to the deep water soon.

He made his way to the large boulder in the middle of the lake and set his knife on it. It would be useless in the water, and its dangling motion would only alert the fish. Standing, he lifted his spear and silently asked the spirits for their help. They were watching, too.

He glided to the edge of the weeds near the eastern shore,

153

swimming underwater for long stretches, preparing his lungs to hold more and more air. A few sunfish poked at the plants, and Kannihut watched them move through the tall shifting greens, showing no sense of a threat.

A school of perch fed in a clearing. This is where the pike will hunt, he thought. Then he corrected himself. This is where I will hunt.

He was about to surface when a perch came into the clearing, then quickly turned and flitted back into the weeds. Something spooked it, he thought, scanning the weeds.

Then he saw the pike.

It was near the bottom, lying still. The green sheen of bent sunlight made it look like a peaceful log, except for the teeth. Kannihut's eyes widened. The beast hovered there, its long mouth of pointed, grabbing teeth opening and closing almost imperceptibly. Kannihut stared at the long spikes of its dorsal fin protruding from its thick back. To grab the fish the wrong way could mean losing a hand.

Kannihut surfaced. He couldn't move on the pike without enough air. If he rushed and took a wrong thrust, it would be over. The fish would race to the deeper water where Kannihut couldn't follow, taking his future with it.

He took four long breaths, staying focused on the pike's location, then descended again as slowly as possible. He scoured the bottom but didn't see the pike anywhere. Fish always move forward, he reminded himself, and pushed himself in the direction the pike had been facing. He focused hard on the weeds in front of him, willing his heart to calm as adrenaline began pumping through his body.

The pike has to be just ahead, he thought, but which way is he facing? If he's facing away, I can't spear him true. And if he's facing me . . . Kannihut felt a chill at the thought. All animals fled from predators, but the pike had none.

Kannihut's lungs began to get heavy. He surfaced again

and took two huge breaths before descending. As he sank, he caught the muted colors of the pike's body in the weeds. It was still there, waiting for prey. Kannihut glided toward it, straining to see any part of the fish's body that told him which way it faced. Then, between the leafy stalks, he saw the tail, just over a spear length away. The beast was angled away from him, but showed enough of its side to allow for a good thrust at its gills.

He gave a short prayer to the pike's spirit and readied his body for the push. One swift motion, he told himself. One swift motion.

He kicked hard and shot forward. In the same instant, a school of perch swam in front of him. His motion exploded the orderly school into frenzy, blocking his view, but his body was committed and he surged toward the monster. Nerves fired in his arm and the spear shot forward. The pike blasted ahead, but it was an instant too late and the spear plunged into its body.

The fish lurched, ripping the spear out of Kannihut's hand and nearly breaking his wrist. The pike spasmed, its convulsions turning the spearhead in its body, tearing the flesh behind its gills and catching the spearhead's wings in its ribs.

Kannihut grabbed for the spear, but the fish surged into the weeds, bending stalks with the long shaft, ripping its body further. Kannihut kicked after it. He had sunk the spear well, but he had to catch the fish before it disappeared in the deep water. Kannihut swam furiously in pursuit, fighting the heaviness in his lungs, pushing down the panic of losing the fish.

With a strong kick, he broke into a small clearing over what appeared to be a large log, then realized he was over the pike. Without thinking, Kannihut dove and grabbed the spear with one hand and the fish's body with the other.

The beast heaved and its sharp fin gouged across Kannihut's chest. He screamed and the air rushed out of his lungs. Sucking in water, he shoved the spear hard, forcing it through the fish, then shot to the surface. Breaking out of the water, he cried out at the searing pain in his chest as it expanded to fill with air. He took two painful breaths and dove again.

He found the pike quickly, and when he grabbed the spear, the fish lurched forward and headed toward deep water, moving faster than Kannihut could swim.

Kannihut's lungs grew heavy. Now in open water, he would lose the pike for sure if he let go of the spear. The bright green water began to darken and the strength in his hand started to ebb.

Hold on, he commanded himself. Hold on. He could feel the pike slowing, but his lungs burned with violent pressure, yearning for air.

He had enough consciousness for one last effort. He tightened his grip on the spear, splayed his body against the water, and wrenched back his arm. His pull had little strength, but it was enough. The fish stopped swimming and spasmed again. Thrown off its momentum, Kannihut kicked hard for the surface, yanking the fish with him. His face broke the waterline, just as his throat gaped open to suck in air, or water, anything to fill the desperate emptiness in his lungs.

Air rushed in, but the fish lurched again, pulling him under. Kannihut let it swim, pulling him through the lake, draining its power. He needed air again and kicked to the surface. When the fish lurched, Kannihut was able to hold his head above water. He let it swim twice more. You have a powerful spirit, he thought to it. Feel your lake one last time.

He pulled at the spear and found he could maneuver the pike now. He started swimming for the rock, blood trailing from both of them. Every few strokes, the fish convulsed, but each time the struggle had less strength. The rock was more than a hundred strokes away, and the fish still struggled against him, but oxygen was returning to Kannihut's muscles, just as the lack of swimming stole it from the pike's.

When he reached the rock, the fish was spent. "You will die in the lake where you lived," Kannihut told it, reaching up for his knife. The pike lurched one last time, scraping its fin against Kannihut's chest again. Grimacing, he carefully maneuvered the fish closer to him with the spear, then took the knife with stiff, numb fingers, and sawed through the scaled throat of the beast in three quick motions. Blood blossomed in the water around them as the pike stopped struggling.

Kannihut held unto the pike's huge body. His training was over. He would be a warrior now, but the pike would never leap from the lake again. Waves of hot and cold surged through Kannihut, and his nose stung as warm tears began to fill his eyes. The pike had made him a warrior, but in the thin space between exhilaration and exhaustion, he felt an emptiness he had never known before. A hole in his feelings that would be there from now on. Whatever had filled it would stay in the lake, and was even now diffusing through the blood and water, falling to the bottom and disappearing.

Jim Kroepfl and his wife, Stephanie, write young adult stories of adventure and mystery from a cabin in the Rocky Mountains. When they're not writing, Jim is a local musician and Stephanie is an artist. They are Celtic mythology buffs and avid world travelers who seek out crop circles, obscure historical sites, and mysterious ruins.

TELL ME, LOVE

by Phil Ellsworth

poetry honorable mention

Tell me, Love, relate to me
Your epic tale, your Odyssey.
What have you been that now you are
A spirit on this circling star?
What Ithaca did you call home?
Where have your youth's companions gone?
On what blue seas, what winds of chance,
By what strange chain of circumstance
Have you come here to me and mine,
From stardust, through the mist of time?

As a mineral exploration geologist, Phil Ellsworth spent a career thinking about discovery: what it is, how it happens, and how it feels. Now he tries to find the same rewards in poetry, because each new combination of words that works is a discovery. Something new is discovered in words that were there all the time. Of course, it only works on rare occasions. Phil will be 88 this fall, so memory plays a large part in his poems: memories of the lakes and woods of southwestern Michigan and northern Indiana, a region known as Michiana; and memories of a war a lifetime ago. He lives now in western Colorado, where the hills exude poetry. But it is probably not unexpected for an old man to look back and see love as the most important thing in life, and that is what most of his poems are about.

REMEMBERED SONG

by Phil Ellsworth

poetry editor's pick

If Time should come and steal my memories,
If you look in my eyes and can not see,
If something takes away my yesterdays,
Play these my songs and know you're hearing me.

And if by chance I hear the melodies
The faithful sun may now and then break through
And I will feel the warmth that used to be
And in remembered song, remember you.

BLUE–SHADED MOUNTAINS

by Phil Ellsworth

poetry editor's pick

Dark canyons around me, and wild-running streams,
Around me blue mountains like mountains in dreams,
Around me a valley like Eden in spring.
Around all is beauty—how can I not sing?

Like snowflakes in winter the white petals fall,
The cranes circle upward—I hear their wild call.
From high in their heaven, wild, haunting, and free,
They call to the valley—they're calling to me:

"Come circle! Come circle! Come fly wing on wing!
We'll call to the valley below us to sing
Of mesas and canyons and wild-running streams
And blue-shaded mountains like mountains in dreams!"

BLACKBOX

by Tiffany Madison

short fiction editor's pick

PART I

HE COULD TASTE MORTALITY ON HIS TONGUE. THE COMPULSION TO breathe forced his lungs to retract and expand; his eyes fixed upon the spinning tread by his face. Blinking, he tried to recall what happened, remembering only a blur of action. He knew he had been shot, that his convoy was ambushed, though he couldn't lift his head to see, or feel his legs. It had all happened so fast; one second they were driving and in the next they weren't.

A rush of potent, primal endorphins coursed from his torso to his head at the reminder, nullifying bodily agony with tremors of shock, cementing his dire straits. This is it, he realized through disoriented thoughts; the understanding of his imminent death doused morbid clarity with a deluge of fear.

God forgive me for my sins, he prayed silently, urgently, knowing death was coming for him now. Nine days ago he had felt a premonition that his time was near; a sense of foreboding had hovered over his daily routine. He hadn't been sure when it would happen or how, just that his time was close.

But what if you can live through this? An errant thought of fortitude whispered. His subconscious bidding him to hold on, to stay awake and keep breathing, as painful as it was.

To survive.

Panicked courage surged, igniting his will to live and to fight back, to find his gun and shoot. But as he tried to grasp soldierly duties, a battlefield explosion shook his world so thoroughly that his teeth broke, stopping those illusions in their tracks.

"I'm sorry," he choked out to her, wishing he could have seen her face one last time.

Grasping that he would never touch his wife again, his broken hands became active, sliding through blood-soaked sand. Though acceptance of death had toyed with him, this new conclusion broke his heart anew. Would he ever see her? Be with her again?

Yes, his heart promised. With that reassurance, he spent his remaining energy on turning his head as he frantically sought color beyond the billowing smoke above, searched for Heaven prematurely, and prayed that afterlife awaited him.

Chaotic fire rang out as a tremor of fleeting life swept through his core, and he knew each second left was charity. He decided then that these final moments on Earth would be spent with her. Closing his eyes tightly, he receded to a place entirely their own as mental snapshots of wedding day memories came forward, movie-like and vivid behind fluttering lids. He whispered her name, and neither the voices of men nor the snaps of gunfire could steal him away from her laughter.

He recalled how wonderful and warm she had been in his arms, how soft her skin felt, next to his every morning spent together. As hot blood soaked his side, he could almost feel her next to him.

"You'll wait for me?" he confirmed amidst the bustle of activity. It was time to go. Kissing her again and again, he hugged her close, believing she would be good to him, wanting to be as close to her as possible. He knew that hundreds of days would pass between this moment and Iraq, each one full of the pull for her touch. She nodded as tears defeated bravery. Her fingers touched his face as she prayed he would come home to her again.

Searing pain ripped him back to reality as the forces of death slowed his heart. Still, he held on to the memory of her face, feeling regret more painful than his open wound.

He didn't want to die, didn't want to leave her.

Raging into the forgotten surrounding chaos, he wished in vain he could have fought harder for her, prayed she would be safe and happy, hoped she knew how much he loved her.

This is it, he confirmed to himself again, his vitals bowing to death's demands.

How strange it feels to die, he thought. Staring into the blue unknown, he wondered if he should close his eyes now. He succumbed then, his mind detaching from mortal determination, from reality, his last breath one of letting go.

In his final moments, as his fellow countrymen rushed to his side, those bloody, dirty fingers released the fine grains of ancient sand.

And for him, life was over.

Part II

Swallowing the lump in her throat, she stared at the box on the floor of the otherwise empty apartment; it was time to open it.

It had been so long, but the glossy black finish resurrected grieved-over memories of sitting on their bed alone, staring at the same box for hours. In it were not only the last words of her lost husband, but his confessions, his longing for a home with her—his good-bye.

During her darkest, loneliest days she had burned to read his words again, to feel him in the only way she could, to see the proof of his life.

But she never did.

Days, weeks, and months had been spent navigating expectations and obligations, existing while never quite living. Repairing herself had required locking him away to places rarely explored. For her sanity, she had refrained, believing she just needed more time.

But that was not the whole truth. Deep down she believed that after all they had shared, pretending she could say good-bye was a betrayal of his memory. Even now, standing on the edge of the very act, this conviction was so deep that she prolonged the attachment.

With a deep breath, she glanced at the new ring on her finger and repeated to herself the reason for this self-torture. It was the right thing for her future, the fair thing for both men. After tracing the glossy cardboard to delay the inevitable, she took another heavy breath and opened the lid.

At first glance the contents were seemingly insignificant, ordinary objects special only to them: ticket stubs from movie dates and a napkin with her phone number on it. He had saved her ponytail holder and a pebble from the beach where they made love for the first time.

The little pieces of the two of them were deeply sentimental to her, but these she could handle. It was the nine letters tucked in the corner that scared her, one from each month of his second deployment. She had read each one a thousand times during those days of waiting and worrying, each revealing more of the man she loved while simultaneously showing her the changes in him.

For a long minute, she stared at his writing on the envelope and his writing stared back.

"It's time," she whispered to herself, speaking her resolve aloud to prevent it from shattering.

Reaching shakily for one of the letters, the crisp paper felt like an old friend against her fingertips, but she did not relish the familiarity. In the darkest corner of her heart, she remained bitter. Instead of papers and words and all of this heartache, she still wanted the impossible. She wanted him.

Don't, she chided herself. This game would get her nowhere, stopping all movement as her chest swelled with grief. It's time, she repeated her silent mantra. And it was.

Carefully, she opened the precious envelope and unfurled his first letter from its fold, losing herself in his words immediately.

December

Your letter arrived a few days ago. When I opened the envelope, I could still smell your perfume. Thank you for that. I miss you so much.

I was going to email you, but the line was so long that I gave up. My handwriting is bad and I hate letters, but you asked and I'm doing it for you. Time is too spotty for me to jot you a long one and there's nothing good to tell, so I'll just write as things happen.

Christmas is coming in a few weeks. I feel like a kid, but I can't wait to see what you got me. I hope more pictures.

We're so bored.

My heart skips sometimes when I remember that summer we spent in your apartment. I knew then that I loved you.

It's late here and everyone is sleeping, but I can't. I think about you all the time, and how badly I want to see you. I swear that I'll make you so happy when I get home.

We got a mission and we're ready for it. Some kid that buries bombs along our routes with a small metal plate as the trigger. They're flush with the road until the Humvee presses the plate. Then all hell breaks loose. We all want to find him.

This week we hit a cold spot on Bomb Boy. So close.

Right now, I'm driving through a city thousands of years old. Older than anything we've ever seen in our entire lives. Older than anything in Europe.

I've had only two hours of sleep, and if I hear another Christmas carol I'm going to snap. None of them can sing.

I thought today would never end. We went out on mission this whole week without incident. Cooper says we're just showing presence now, and I can see what he means. Sometimes they even seem to like us.

It's almost Christmas and your package hasn't arrived yet, but I know the mail is slow. I can't wait to spend Christmas and New Years with you for once. I want a tree and decorations. We'll live it up, I promise.

Today reminded me all over again that I was born to do this. I can't help it—I want to fight. Thank you for sticking this out with me.

Merry Christmas. Do you want to know what I want? You in this tent with me right now. I miss you like crazy. I hope I get your package before New Year's. I'm sending this now. I love you—don't forget that.

Though silent tears had fallen the moment she had unfolded the paper, she cried even harder once pulled from his stream of thought, those tears insignificant responses for such great loss. All of his promises were unfulfilled; all of his dreams of their life together, of returning to her lost.

"I missed you, too," she whispered to his written words, and traced the ink with her fingertips, hoping he had meant what he said: that he was born to fight and die for what he believed in. Truly, she wanted to believe his certainty as she recalled the long months of her life spent without him, the days of pacing and daydreaming of his return, deciding it was all worth it if he had been happy.

And for several minutes she mourned harder than she had in years, the tightness in her chest straining her breath. Though it had been years since he had left her his hold on her was still deep.

But she had a dark choice then: to call the wedding off or pretend she could say good-bye.

Irrationally, she teetered on the edge of uncertainty now that her emotion was fresh, staring at the letters in the box, seeing only the one she wanted to avoid. It was his last transmission to her, a well-documented testament to the changes that contradicted her faith in his purpose; changes she wanted to pretend didn't exist.

You owe it to him; to them both; to yourself, she reminded her courage. And she was right.

Folding the paper in her hand ever so neatly, she slid it back into its envelope, fearful of what would come next, yet unable to mourn so deeply forever. With all the strength she could muster, she slowly reached for his last letter, reading his slanted script as she had a hundred times before losing him.

July

Hey. I'm sure you got the letter that I've been extended to November and if not, well surprise! When they gave me those orders, I thought I would go crazy. They're lucky I'm way out here with no way to get free. I'm better now, so don't worry. I just feel so far from you. I'm sorry about it all. At least I'll be home for Christmas.

By the way, I wrote you a whole letter last week, but it disappeared. I must have lost it somehow, but I don't understand how that happened. Sometimes I think I'm losing my mind in this heat.

The longer I'm here, the more I don't understand this place. People are so desperate for security, but they don't work with us like they could! It's all about tribe and nothing else. On some level I respect that, but, at the same time, it makes me think nothing here will ever change. That we're wasting our time and our lives for nothing.

Today was bullshit. I'm sick of the heat and the smell of people.

You should see the dirt in my knuckles. It's going to take weeks to get off.

My right ankle is sprained from kicking doors in.

This is crazy, but the last few nights, I've dreamed of chasing the enemy through scattered tents. I never catch him.

Do you remember Bomb Boy from the start of my deployment? I told you about how we lost him, but we got word today we're back on it.

We went to a neighborhood to question the locals today and it was weird. They kept smiling at me. I really can't wait to get home.

I'm starting to worry that I don't really know your daily routine at all—I've always been gone. Do you like where you work? How is your mom? Do you ever get to see her? When you write back, tell me what you do all day. I want to hear it all, so don't hold back. Every little thing.

Time might be short for me to write, but I'll try. We're going out on react missions every shift it seems.

I wish all I had to worry about was protecting my own people.

I can't wait to be with you. It's all I think about lately and I shouldn't say things like this in a letter, but when I get home, can we start a family? I know you want to and that you were just waiting for me, but I'm ready. Think about it and let me know.

Remember how I told you about that Humvee with those Marines on fire? I keep seeing that accident in my sleep.

The smell of fuel is soaked into my skin.

Civilians should see how we fight wars. They would demand their tax dollars back! We shoot last and ask questions first, but they never give us answers. Talking in circles is all they know, and when they lie to me I want to break their faces with my rifle.

Sorry. I shouldn't have written that. If I didn't already have so many days written on this paper, I'd cross that out. I don't even know why this always comes out on the end when I could start over and leave it out. I hate that I do that. We're going on a long mission, so I have to send this. I'm sorry I didn't get time to write more. I just want to see you again, so badly. Just a few more months to go and I'll be home. I love you. Don't you ever forget that.

Thumbing his last words with the edge of her nail, teardrops rained on the letters. The tone of his last few letters had been so unlike him: so sad, so lost, and angry. She wanted to forget his unhappiness, the emptiness she could feel in his words.

Her glassy eyes traced the letters of his last line again. It was the unorthodox use of you that had made her heart ache for his return years ago, and even now. Those last lines seemed an instinctive choice to her, a way to say good-bye without using the actual words. Evidence that he thought he might die before sending it.

The dire need to hold him, to comfort him and let him know he was loved, forced her to lie down. With a frantic series of long-buried cries, she held the letter closer, bowing to her pain and loss. Unlocking her love was torture, but she let some free anyway, her body trembling with the force of it. Memories of the way he had said her name made her cry a little harder, spurring recollections of lying in his arms during those mornings spent together.

"I love you," she whispered to him, hoping somehow he knew that was still true after all these years.

Staring at her engagement ring once more, the small, carefully chosen diamond glittered guilt under her review. She had said "yes" to a future out of fear that she never would love again. And now, in a few days' time she would be leaving their lost future and empty house for a new home, leaving behind every memory she and her husband had shared in every room. Leaving him.

Let your past go or tell your future you cannot embrace it, her mind whispered that advice from a counselor given years ago. It was a cruel ultimatum, a choice no one should ever have to make, and the hardest thing she would ever do. But after indefinable moments of time, the violence of her sadness gave way to heavy duty in her heart, and she lay quiet and empty.

For an even longer time she did not move, taking deep, intentional breaths with her gaze fixed on his name, realizing she had prolonged this pain unnecessarily. Avoiding the grief for all this time did not diminish its effect. Eyes clenched, she shed her last tears reluctantly, and promised him that one day they would be together again, that he was somewhere waiting for her.

Sitting upright in a gesture of strength, she placed his last letter in the box. For at that moment, she accepted the truth. There was no more fighting, no more hoping, no more grieving to be done.

Slowly closing the lid, she prayed one final chant, hoping that he could forgive her.

"Good-bye," she whispered. "I'll never forget."

And for her, life would continue.

Tiffany Madison was born and raised in Texas, USA. She has written nine fiction stories and maintains a column at Washington Times *digital news. Her work is featured at her website, TiffanyMadison.com, SpeakLibertyNow.com, and PolicyMic. She is chief operations officer of Ryan's Project, a nonprofit for wounded Marines, and has a forthcoming novel,* Black and White.

On Friendship

by Brian Henry

personal essay/creative nonfiction editor's pick

I HATE MY FRIENDS. THIS MIGHT SOUND HARSH, AND PROBABLY DOES little to endear you, the reader, to me. "They're not your friends if you hate them," you might be thinking. Perhaps you're also thinking how lucky you are not to count me among your friends (and you would be right in doing so). But you know nothing about my friends. You don't know what they've done and do to me on a regular basis. So I won't rescind. Not for your sake, anyway.

I have many friends, though I don't dare to count them for you. To do so could either open up my claim to subjection ("he doesn't have *that* many friends), or alternately make me seem boastful (as though proclaiming that "I have many friends" does not already succeed in doing so). I have many friends *now*, but I can tell you that most of my childhood, particularly the high school portion, was spent alone. I was an awkward, overweight boy with terrible acne and a sweet baritone singing voice. The latter landed me center stage in all of the school's musical productions, as well as in the crosshairs of my classmates' derision. For some reason, the wrestlers and football players at Central Mountain High School had no ear for a well-delivered Charles Strouse ballad.

Once in college, I seemed to reach my era of optimal likability. I grew trimmer, my acne cleared, and the baritone voice was suddenly a virtue in the eyes of my peers at the Penn State University School of Music. Like a pied piper, I found myself picking up single friends in every class, rehearsal—even at every frat (Phi Mu Alpha, exclusively) party I attended. Most of those people are still in my life today, one way or another.

I've never been the sort of person who thrives in group situations, and I have my high school loner days to thank for this. The adolescent thirst to belong was never quenched for me, and so I had to learn to relate to people at eye level. That is, when I wasn't relating to them from the stage in my brilliant portrayals of Albert in *Bye Bye Birdie*, Gaston in *The Beauty and the Beast*, or Jack in *Into the Woods*. As a result, most of my friendships are one-on-one, and it is the rare occasion that I can kill two (or more) birds with one stone when it comes to catching up. I must have dinner with so-and-so here, drinks with thus-and-such there, and catch a movie with what's-her-face on Friday.

As someone who values his alone time, almost above all other things, having more than one or two friends is troublesome. Alternatively, as someone whose happiness and sense of security rest solely on the reassurance and commiseration of others, firing any of these friends is hardly an option. What's more, each of my friends possesses unique virtues that cannot be replicated by anyone else in the bunch, making it doubly hard to weed anyone out in hopes of optimizing alone time.

I hate my friends.

That being said, the hatred I'm talking about isn't internal. It does not radiate *from* me. It's not a feeling that I've acknowledged and resolved to carry with me. I am no Iago. There is no black disdain festering in my heart, driving me to incite acts of malice on an innocent, unwitting Othello. No, the hatred I'm talking about is of an exterior quality. It is an attitude that has been superimposed on me by my friends, themselves. It is a conclusion that has been drawn in response to countless unanswered texts and emails, refused invitations, and canceled plans.

"You hate me," my friends will say. As a failed opera singer and failing writer, my friends are, by and large, artistic types, and given to hyperbole. But, who am I to argue with them? Whether one hates or feels hated, there still exists hatred.

What is really at the heart of this perceived hatred? I'm inclined to say that it's laziness. I am certainly lazy, and I mean that in the purest sense of the word, with none of the abstraction that I've applied to the word "hate." For instance, the other night I was invited via text message to get dinner, a drink, or see a movie with my closest friend, X. The activity wasn't important to her. It was only important that she spend some time with me: her friend. I should note that X is a Wagnerian Soprano. As such, she is the friend most given to hyperbole, and therefore the friend I hate most passionately.

Upon receiving the text message, I became irritated; almost vehemently so. While the invitation was open-ended with regards to *what* we did, it left no uncertainty as to *when* she expected to do it: "hey, u wanna do dinner/drinks/movie 2 nite?" At the time, "tonight" was less than three hours away. The text was sent at 4:06 p.m. on a Wednesday afternoon. Night, as far as I'm concerned, begins around 7:00 p.m. On a weeknight, which is what a Wednesday night is, 7:00 p.m. is an *awfully* charitable definition for the onset of night, as I can begin to feel decidedly nocturnal as early as 6:00 p.m.

By sending this text message at the time X sent it, she was assuming one of two things:

1. That by 4:06 p.m. on a Wednesday, I have not yet given a moment's thought to how I plan to spend the next four or five hours, and that I'm open to suggestions on the matter.
2. That I *had* made plans for the night, but that X's own place in my life would likely supersede them; that I would happily drop the plans for the glory of her company.

On that particular Wednesday, a sort of hybrid of these two options was true. I hadn't made specific plans for that night, other than that the night be free of specific plans. This is very different than option number one, for a good deal of thought had gone into that vacancy. I hadn't planned to sit on my bed and stare, slobbering at the wall and blissfully free of another person's company, especially that of my oldest, dearest friend. Yes, I had hoped to have that particular night to myself, but with the intention of doing any combination of the five or six things (sadly, there are that few) that make me feel like a real human being.

One of those five or six things (it's actually more like three or four things, as I've just realized that one of the things I had initially included in the bunch was masturbation, and while I enjoy and advocate it, it certainly isn't one of the things I would list among those that make me feel like a "real human being," as it is, essentially, a simulation of a real human activity) was to work on these very pages, or pages like them, in an effort to maintain my status as a writer, even if it is that of a failing one. However, if experience has taught me anything, it is that despite my most earnest intentions, I will not, in these situations, do any of the things—the real human being things—that I planned to. Experience, I should note, has taught me nothing.

The distinction between idleness and my intentions of quiet productivity is of paramount importance to the reader's comprehension of this scenario. Listen: I knew that if I answered, "Sorry, can't tonight," the way I had planned to, I would be met with a response like this: "No worries! What's going on?" Or, more pointedly: "What are your other plans?" "What is more important than *me*?" "What trumps our *years* of friendship??!!"

This leaves me with three* options:
1. Tell the truth.
2. Lie.
3. Abstain from responding to the question altogether.

(*"Concede to spend time with X at the drop of a hat" is not an option, for reasons I will clarify later.)

Each of these options comes with its own set of problems. I should note here that, though I am referring to a specific incident, this scenario has happened many times. Each iteration is a slight variation on the same resounding theme, and each of the three options has been tried to varying results.

1. Tell the Truth
If I decided to tell X the truth—that I had planned to have that Wednesday night to myself to write, do laundry, read, or take care of other business, she would have undoubtedly done her best to convince me to abandon my plans. If I successfully resisted, she would have expressed shock (hurt, even) that I would pick such mundane activities over spending time with her. The apparent flexibility of these activities would have been even more confusing. "Can't you just do that tomorrow night?" she would have asked. It's a perfectly reasonable question. But if I *did* choose to veer from my original plans, I would not have been as far along in my

reading, writing, practicing, etc., as if I had chosen to stick to my guns. Anxiety would set in. Thursday would have to be spent doing Wednesday's tasks, Friday Thursday's, and so on. Telling the truth is not ideal.

2. Lie

If I had chosen to lie to X, and made up some sort of plausible, prior engagement with parties (real or fictional), which she would have no means or reason for contacting to verify my alibi, then everything would have probably turned out just fine. I would have most likely gotten off scot-free (I have not, as of yet, been caught), though a liar. Depending on my mood, this designation bears little burden. One must never underestimate the usefulness of a well-placed lie.

3. Refrain from Responding Altogether

Option number three has proven to be the most troublesome avenue. But, because of the laziness to which I've admitted earlier, it is the road most frequently traveled. If I had chosen to abstain from responding altogether, my next interaction with X would undoubtedly be strained by the snub. The next time we saw each other, or on the rare occasion that I would extend an invitation, I would be met with icy ambivalence. The sudden frigidity would be so palpable that to do anything but address it would be excruciatingly awkward.

"What's wrong?" I would have to ask with feigned sincerity. She would tell me how much it hurt her that I had ignored the rest of her texts that Wednesday night. She would say, "it's like you *hate* me or something." I would need to apologize to her. I would need to explain that I've been depressed lately; that I hate my day job, which takes up too much of my time; that I never get enough time to write, or scout for writing competitions, or figure out what I want to do with my life, let alone to take steps in the directions necessary to accomplishing my to-be-determined goals; and then there's my music career, and so on.

She would accept my apology, probably with tears in her eyes. She would tell me that she understands. She would explain that she, too, has been depressed; that she's sorry for being so needy, but that she's lonely and just wants to spend time with me. I will say that I understand and we will most likely embrace. To ensure my absolution, I will probably commit to some sort of a weekly date with her. I will keep this date for three weeks, four at most. But I will reach a point at which I need to break the date. In doing so, I will be faced with one of the three choices again (truth, lie, abstain) and thus with the same corresponding drawbacks.

Goddammit: I can never escape friendship.

(Note: I did not include "Concede to spend time with X at the drop of a hat" among the three responses because I know that this option would probably lead to my having an absolutely wonderful time, and that would be beside the point.)

Just as the preceding situation is an amalgam of many like scenarios concerning X, there are other archetypes. Take Y, whose rays of friendship reach me from the Midwest. Like X, Y is also an artistic type. But he is an actor, and unlike X's broad accusations, hyperbolic assignations of hatred, and quick reconciliations, Y's reactions to my avoidance are more nuanced, more deep-cutting, and less easy to assuage. And, since our relationship is conducted largely over the phone, there is a constant volleying of responsibility. On whose shoulders does this precious friendship rest *today*? Mine, it would seem.

A Scene Concerning Y

I wake up to an angry, red notification on my cell phone: one missed call from Y. I get out of bed, take a shower, and get dressed. All the while, I'm thinking about the call. There was no voicemail, but it doesn't matter: a call back is expected.

I leave my apartment and ride the subway to work. I'll call Y on my lunch break, I tell myself (out loud). I consider texting and telling him to expect a call, but I quickly discard the idea. I don't want to set any immediate expectations.

The day is slow-going, which can be said of most days at my insufferable, soul-sucking office job. Still, I push my lunch break until 2:00 because it's much easier to stare down three hours than four or five (I work 9–6, which is fascist).

I head to the diner down the street and get a chicken salad sandwich and a cup of decaf coffee. I consider calling Y then, even allowing my finger to hover over his number. But there are other diners—both in their early seventies—on either side of me at the counter. I know that a conversation with Y will be long, meandering, and highly personal. His cell phone has bad reception and he lives in the Windy City, so I will probably have to ask him to repeat himself multiple times, and, as my countermates have already demonstrated their acute impatience on the poor Russian waitress, I don't want to open myself up to a confrontation. Besides, I only get forty-five minutes for lunch (also fascist) and I have to eat at *some* point, don't I?

The work day ends and I head for the subway again. I toy with the idea of calling Y on the walk (three blocks and two avenues), but I realize that I haven't called my mother in nearly a week, so I decide to devote the 15-minute window to a conversation with her. She asks me how work is going (shitty) and if I'm eating enough (plenty) and finishes by imploring me to call her more often and I promise that I will (I won't).

Once home, I throw down my work bag, take off my clothes, and dress for a run. Before leaving, I pick the phone and call Y. The decision to do so and its execution happen almost simultaneously, the same way I might rip back my shower curtain before peeing in the middle of the night, ensuring that there is no intruder with a machete waiting to pounce. I know that if I give a moment's thought to the gesture, it will be subjected to further delay.

"Hi, you've reached Y," he says. I suddenly remember (or had I remembered all along?) that it is a Tuesday and Y usually works the dinner shift at the Italian restaurant where he waits tables. "Please leave me a message and I'll get back to you as soon as possible. Thanks!"

"Hey there," I say, trying to conceal my deep sense of relief at having reached his voice-mailbox. "It's Brian. I saw that you called me last night. Just thought I'd catch you. Call me if you get a chance later. Bye."

That's all I can do, I think: I called him back. One can only be expected to return the gesture in a timely manner— under 24 hours, I believe, is the accepted deadline, after which the initial call-ee is officially an asshole.

I go for a run feeling accomplished, that I had held up my end of the bargain with minimal effort. See? Good things *can* happen to lazy people! But I return to find that Y has returned my return, only moments after I left. Oh, but I must shower before returning his return to my return. After my shower I will be hungry, probably. So I'll call him after dinner. Though, after dinner, I'll probably want to write, or read, or catch up on the new episodes of *Arrested Development* on Netflix and marvel at Portia De Rossi's unnerving metamorphosis with the rest of America. I'll spare you the rest of this: before we know it, it is Sunday night, and the ball is still in my court.

All of this isn't to say that I don't want to talk to Y. After our conversations, I invariably come away from the phone feeling rejuvenated. As I mentioned, Y is an actor. But his artistic pursuits are stunted, like mine. Though he is immensely talented, his roles in Chicago have been too few and too far between. He also works a mortally dispiriting day job, and his struggles with money are far grimmer than my own.

Even if his life mirrors mine in these respects, he seems to navigate it armed with a sage-like assurance that it is all a phase. He speaks of our shared setbacks—artistic, financial, and otherwise—confident that they will all one day be archived away in the file of our youth. We bounce our miseries off of one another until, for me, for a time, they have been whittled down from insurmountable obstacles to tiny, irritating snags that will soon be left in our dust, and I come away from the phone with the same (albeit temporary) sage-like assurance. Why, then, when my cell phone lights up with the promise of such a conversation, do I retreat?

I cannot offer a solid explanation. While the reader might not find this sort of behavior exemplary of hatred, per se, surely they will agree that it is at the very least unfriendly. What is most puzzling to me is that in my mind, I like my friends very much. I care deeply about each and every one of them individually and I place a great deal of importance in the notion of friendship (philosophically, if not practically).

Like many things in my life (not excluding my talents and virtues), I tend to hold my friendships (though not my friends) in higher esteem than I ought to. Of course, we all remember things differently, and often more fondly than they occur. But even armed with this knowledge, I hold each interaction with a friend to such high standards that, as you can see, it often precludes me from interacting altogether. For instance, what if after a telephone conversation with Y, I am *not* feeling sage-like and rejuvenated and blah blah blah? I might become afraid my situation has gotten so bleak, that there is not even solace to be found in commiseration. I would leave the phone even dourer than I had come to it. This is a prospect that I am unwilling to face.

Earlier, I supposed that I was simply lazy in putting off calls and rendezvous with my friends. But I think now that what I really meant by "laziness" was "procrastination." I *procrastinate* doing so. When one puts off doing the dishes or laundry, it's out of laziness. The banal day-to-day activities that require no skill or thought, but effort and precious time, are delayed when one is lazy. But if one puts off working on one's novel, or practicing for one's Juilliard audition, that is procrastination. Perhaps we procrastinate doing the things which we hope to do well, thinking that if we only had a bit more time, we could do those things perfectly. Or, that if we don't put pen to paper just yet, or spend a few more hours away from the piano, we'll have that much more time before we have to accept that it's all just hopeless. I want these interactions to go well, you see; I want them to be wonderful. Perhaps I stall in hopes of increasing the chance that they will all be as ideal as I expect them to be.

There is another possible motive for avoiding one's friends, which is the suspicion that there is a finite number of interactions that one can have with a friend before becoming annoyed. If this is the case (and I suspect it may be), one must sacrifice frequency for longevity.

In his essay, "On the Pleasures of Hating," William Hazlitt says, "We hate old friends . . ." going on to say that he has "observed that few of those whom I have formerly known most intimate, continue on the same friendly footing or combine the steadiness with the warmth of attachment. I have been acquainted with two or three knots of inseparable companions, who saw each other 'six days in the week,' that have broken up and dispersed." Although the title of the piece is "On the Pleasures of Hating," Hazlitt seems more to describe the inevitable boredom one feels with the people/places/things (nouns, really) to which one has been overexposed. He emphasizes the not-always-obvious truth that there is in most cases a finite supply of pleasure that can be derived from any one thing, person, activity, etc. Perhaps my subconscious has intuited this. Maybe my underlying motive for avoiding my friends is the fear that I will grow to resent them, simply from overexposure. But then again, perhaps this is an overly charitable validation for being a total prick.

At the risk of offering filial parallels in place of hard-won self-analysis (but I have already copped to my laziness), I would point out that I behave a lot like my father in my friendships. That said, his skills in the dark arts of avoidance are much keener than mine, and although I am not privy to the details of his social history, I can testify to the result: he has no friends.

Now, this isn't to say that my father isn't an affable, gregarious person. He is. Everywhere he goes (a local car dealership for free coffee or the Lock Haven Fire Hall to get ice) my dad lays the groundwork for friendship. He makes strangers laugh and catches up with old acquaintances on the spot. He asks how this or that aspect of someone's life is going, remembers the details of that person's family and inquires about so-and-so's son who's off at college, or how what's-her-name's grandmother is doing now that she's out of the hospital. Any third-party witness of these chance meetings would swear that they'd just seen two friends bumping into one another. But one mustn't be fooled: my father has no friends, and proudly so.

"Aw, shit. What do I need friends for?" he says on the rare occasion that someone (usually my mother) will be bold enough to ask. "I've got five brothers, a wife, and two kids. I'm too old for friends."

While he's got the affability, humor, and gregariousness down pat, he makes no effort to keep in touch with his old friends, let alone to foster likable acquaintances into new friends. He loathes talking on the phone, regards greeting cards as an abominable waste of resources, and would just as soon spend seven uninterrupted hours on the Susquehanna River, kayaking alone, than attend a party or go out to drinks with another couple. If it weren't for my mother's inclination towards sociability, I doubt that my father would even own a telephone.

But he wasn't always this way. At least, there is evidence that he wasn't. Seated at my grandmother's dining room table in Upper Darby, PA, I have sifted through hundreds of photographs of my dad and his five brothers through the years. There are scores of pictures that cover every age from infancy to young adulthood. My grandmother raised her children before the era of housewife scrapbooking mania, and, apparently, outside the cognizance of photo albums. As a result, the hundreds of photographs are jumbled together in unmarked shoeboxes, throwing to the wind any sense of chronology and leaving behind a narrative of my father's childhood that is decidedly Tarentino-esque.

Despite the disorganization, I can gather from these pictures that my father had, at one time, friends. Perhaps these friendships existed only because of proximity. For instance, it is possible that my dad met his best friend, Timmy, only because they lived on the same block, climbed the same trees, and ran through the same fire hydrant's sprays. Perhaps it does not bode well for the longevity of a friendship when its genesis lies in convenience.

But I know from the pictures, as well as Timmy's presence in our family's early life, that Dad and Timmy stayed friends long past the days of fire hydrants and tree climbing. The evidence is right there in the photographs: Dad and Timmy with their matching Villanova sweatshirts on the first day of freshman year; Dad and Timmy climbing on the lion sculpture that welcomes guests at the Philadelphia Zoo, my grandmother smoking to the side of the frame; Dad and Timmy in various stages of tux-shedding at one or the other's wedding, where each was the other's best man; Dad and Timmy sitting on someone's back porch, each with a beer in one hand and a sleepy newborn in the other.

Apart from the photographs, I have my own memories of Timmy. I remember my dad, before his abhorrence of the telephone reached its zenith, sitting in his chair in our living room and chatting into the night, holding a beer and laughing as if Timmy were right there with him. I remember Timmy's tiny row-house in South Philly, and how his wife, Terry, would let my younger brother and me eat Cheetos and greasy salt and vinegar chips—junk food that would have been otherwise outlawed in my father's presence. I remember Timmy and Terry bringing their girls to our house in "the mountains," as they called it, to get away from the grungy urbanity of their South Philly row home and so my dad and his buddy could catch up.

As I've gotten older, and the glaring red-eye, poor focus, and Polaroid frames have given way to the more finessed detail of digital photography, I've noticed Timmy's presence grow dimmer. In place of those late-night phone conversations, I've seen my dad mouth "I'm not here," when my mother comes to him with the phone, cupping the receiver and whispering "it's Timmy." I've seen him leave my grandmother's dinner table in a huff upon hearing the question, "Are you going to stop by Timmy's while you're down here?"

Last Easter, I overheard my grandmother quietly urging my dad to stop by Timmy's once more. "He and Terry broke up," she said as though she was describing two horny teenagers, and not a couple that had been married for 25 years and raised two children. "Please give him a call. He's been in really rough shape over it." My dad turned the page on his billowing *Philadelphia Inquirer* and I thought I saw him stifle a wince.

"Yeah," he said to my grandmother's visible surprise. "Maybe I will, then."

To my knowledge, my dad never did call Timmy after the divorce. As a result, I think that the calls and invitations from the Timmy Camp have stopped as well. But I've been able to gather scraps of the narrative that exists beyond the photographs. Words like "divorce," "alcoholic," and "debt" are often tossed off where Timmy is concerned. Usually these conversations happen in short, hushed fragments when my father has left the room, and they subside quickly upon his return.

The reason for my father's apparent distaste for his onetime best friend is unclear. I've never been able to figure out if there was some sort of a falling out, or if my dad, as Hazlitt would have predicted, simply got tired of Timmy. Had Timmy continued calling and extending invitations all these years to apologize for something? Or was he just slow to take a hint? Since my father is as reluctant to talk about Timmy as he is to talk to him, these questions might never be answered.

Although my father doesn't talk about his relationship with Timmy, and offers little explanation for his apparent friendlessness beyond disparaging the very *notion* of friendship, I believe that, somewhere, he misses his friend. At least, I want to believe that he does.

I know that despite my most fervent efforts to be left alone—to brood and bitch silently about my failures and shortcomings—I will, for a time, have to continue to ward off the pesky advances of people, like X and Y, who claim to love me. That is all right, for the time being. It's a good thing. Even though I hate my friends, I would hate even more to find myself with no one to ignore, avoid, or to force me out of my hole every now and then to be reminded of what it means to be a real human being.

Brian Henry is a New York City–based singer, performer, and writer. He received his BM from Penn State University and his MM from Manhattan School of Music in voice performance and opera. He is currently working on his first novel.

ROOF DWELLER

by Dwayne Magee

personal essay/creative nonfiction editor's pick

"The trouble is not that the world is made of fools. It's just that lightning isn't distributed right."

—*Mark Twain*

IN MANY ANCIENT CIVILIZATIONS, IT WAS BELIEVED THAT THOSE WHO were struck by lightning were being punished by God. In Greek, Norse, and Roman traditions, the gods used lightning to express power and anger. Other superstitions characterize thunder and lightning as warnings from the divine being. They exist as signs to foretell of famine, pestilence, or otherwise dark times. In some cultures, those who survive a lightning strike are ostracized from the general population. It is understood that they have been somehow singled out by God as unclean and they are deemed unfit to live in community. God has sent the lightning to mark them and their subsequent wretched lives will never be the same again. The year God sent lightning to strike the Mount Pleasant Christian Theater, He was apparently aiming at me. Of course, my assumptions regarding the purpose of the strike and my reputation with the almighty are purely speculative. However, I do regard the occasion as remarkable due largely to the fact that it coincided with the unexpected materialization of my first marriage and my eventual exile from the church.

The 1993 Mount Pleasant Easter play was a passion play. And, like all passion plays, the story revolved around the life, death, and resurrection of Jesus Christ. Due to my grace-filled, incorruptible character and my strong but gentle disposition, I was naturally cast as the lead. Or at least that is how I remember it. It also may have had something to do with my long hair, my beard, and my blue eyes as well as the fact that no one else was willing to take the part. Allegedly, the two previous Jesuses were injured during live performances. Pastor Ray, who enthusiastically always served as the play's director, had a Mel Gibson–like reputation for crucifying Jesus in the most gruesome, sensationalized productions he could contrive. Had I been aware of this, I might have instead tried out for the summer production of *The Sound of Music*. But then, I never would have met Miss Katherine Knight, my future bride-to-be and ultimate ruination of my otherwise amicable existence.

Actually, her name wasn't really Katherine Knight. The real Katherine Knight is currently detained in Australia's *Silverwater Women's Correctional Centre* for an astonishing act of violence she unleashed upon one Charles Thomas Price. After stabbing him 37 times, she removed his skin and hung it from the door frame of their living room. She also removed his head and prepared it in a pot of soup alongside his baked buttocks, and a side of gravy and vegetables. Shortly before setting this fleshy feast out for their children, she was taken away by police and has pretty much never been heard from again until this tribute. Suffice it to say that while my Katherine did not stab, fillet, or decapitate me, she did eventually and quite adeptly butcher my soul.

I met Katherine during the final week of rehearsals. She was working as Pastor Ray's assistant and doing her best to temper his lofty, theatrical ambitions. Pastor Ray wanted to make sure that this was the year we killed Jesus bigger and better than ever. He hired a makeup artist from Hollywood to do the blood and gore and also a special effects guy to engineer a cross that would levitate the dead Jesus 17-1/2 feet above the audience. He also acquired an explosives expert to incorporate some pyrotechnics that he claimed would rival any indoor fireworks display ever attempted. (Up until then, I wasn't even aware that people attempted indoor fireworks displays.) Pastor Ray rounded out his crucifixion effects team with a fourth guy named Ricky Mears, who was renowned for some lighting effects he once created for a local heavy metal rock band called Crush Hazard. Together, they were planning to make passion play history.

"More smoke!" Pastor Ray would scream during our run-throughs.

"I need more lights flashing!"

"What happened to the streaking fire ball?"

"Is that all the higher we can float Jesus?"

At our third dress rehearsal, my fellow thespians and I had finally had enough. We were refusing to participate in the crucifixion. The cast had no place to stand on stage where they weren't falling over wires, dodging sparks, or getting spattered by stage blood. The floating cross was completely unsafe. If the suspension cables elevating Jesus gave way, there was no telling how many Romans and Israelites I would take out as I plunged to my death. The Jewish historian Josephus described a crucifixion as "the most wretched of deaths." From my harrowed perch above some of Mount Pleasant's finest actors and actresses, I was questioning the extent of Josephus' knowledge of pathology. Had he even considered the distress of a forward-plunging crucifixion from almost two stories up with one and a half twists in the straight, "I wonder what will be left of my face" position? I eagerly joined the chorus of those threatening to close down the show if something was not done immediately.

That is when Katherine stepped in to help us. She convinced Pastor Ray that a slightly lower cruising altitude for the dead Jesus would be less dangerous and could possibly have a more dramatic effect by being closer to the audience. She then exaggerated when she reported that our music director Agnes Fitzwater was displaying outward symptoms of motion sickness due to some of the lighting effects. This prompted Pastor Ray to direct Mears to reposition half of the flashing lights to the rigging above me and the other half to the stage apron, where they could point back and up towards the ceiling. Then, after threatening to introduce Pastor Ray to the fire marshal, she convinced him to replace two propane flame bars with a smoke machine. It would not be the explosive moment Pastor Ray dreamed of for a scene where Satan was to ascend from hell with victorious, depraved laughter but it would have to do.

Thanks to Katherine's last-minute heroics, the show could go on, Josephus' claims would remain uncontested, and I was exceedingly grateful. Not long afterwards, Pastor Ray formally introduced me to Katherine and about a year later he married us. Eventually, it would then also be Pastor Ray who provided us with counseling services during our painful and prolonged marital implosion. He was a man who believed he could wear many hats, but his head was usually too large for any of them.

During one counseling session, he told us that an ideal marriage would be that in which both partners held similar Christian beliefs. He held out his hands with both index fingers extended and traced the image of an equilateral triangle in the air so that, if it were real, it would have been hovering just near the end of my nose. "You see," he explained, "the bottom two points of this triangle represent you and your partner while the apex represents God." Then, he slowly moved his outstretched fingers up and towards each other until they met at the summit of his imaginary geometrical illustration. "As each of you grows towards God," he concluded, "you will also grow closer together." Then he proudly returned his hands to his side and waited for a glow of recognition and understanding to reveal itself on our facial expressions.

"Perhaps," I replied after a few moments of reflection, "our marriage is more like an octagon."

I reached out my index fingers and traced this image into the space between us.

"Like this," I suggested, "you know . . . more like a STOP sign."

Pastor Ray was less than amused.

The truth is I was never very good at geometry. The mere mention of it brings back abject memories of Mr. Portman, my 10th-grade math teacher who made the learning experience painful and arduous. Anyone taking his class would more likely enjoy being slowly eaten alive by a hookworm. Any good helminthologist can tell you that the insidious hookworm disposes of its victims by lodging itself into their intestinal tract where it begins eagerly sucking out blood until there is nothing left but a heap of anemic flesh covered in rashes and the remnants of sickness and diarrhea. And this, now that I think about it, actually pretty much does describe my marriage to Katherine quite accurately. Pastor Ray may have been a better counselor than I realized.

"He'll be good for her," I once overheard him tell members of our congregation on the news of our betrothal. "She is an angry, aggressive, impatient sort of person and his calm demeanor will help to balance her out." It didn't occur to me at the time to consider the reflexive implication of his hypothesis. Would she too be *good* for me? Would our relationship help me to become cranky, ill-tempered, and sarcastic? If that was his prediction, I am happy to report that, if nothing else, the relationship furthered Pastor Ray's credibility as a seer.

I suppose if I had been a more mature person at the time we were dating, I would have seen the writing on the wall. Katherine was one of the least pleasant people I have ever come to know. When there wasn't anything about which she could disagree, she was very good at creating new opportunities. I remember one trip to the shopping mall where, as we were walking from store to store, she suddenly stopped for no apparent reason. Not immediately aware that she ceased ambulating, I continued on for another few steps until I realized she was no longer beside me. When I turned back, I found myself face to face with an impassioned demon.

"Do you despise me so much that you do not wish to be seen walking by my side?"

I fumbled through what I thought might be an appeasing response.

"Um . . . well . . . we were walking . . . and then you just . . . uh . . . sort of stopped."

"Silence mortal! Do not speak to me like that again or I will summon a darkness on you so great that, should you ever emerge into the light again, your eyeballs will burn into raisins!"

I have spent countless hours wondering what possessed me to marry her and countless more wondering what hesitation there was in leaving her. In part, I blame the church for perpetuating our misery. The church teaches a hierarchical order to sin. Divorce is usually always near the top. The list usually reads something like this:

Taking the Lord's name in vein: *unforgiveable*

Murder: *do this and you deserve to die*

Divorce: *also really, really bad.*

"What is 50–60 years of marital strife compared to what Jesus went through for you when he died on the cross for your sins?" they preach. "Furthermore, what is 50–60 years in light of all eternity?" And then, if that is not enough to convince us, they remind us of our most important marital oath: "until death do us part." Do they not realize the thoughts they are planting in people's brains? These are the thoughts they were planting in mine:

Hmmmm . . . until death do us part. Yes! Of course! Death! Why did this not occur to me before? I may not be capable of murder, but Dear God, if you could see to it that she should meet with some unfortunate accident . . .

My prayer life was suddenly invigorated.

I have sometimes wondered why we Christians emphasize the part of our marriage vows which refer to commitment while simultaneously neglecting to place any emphasis whatsoever on the other promises we make when we are married. For example, *I promise to love and to cherish.* I can't remember one person in our church who ever attempted to hold Katherine and I accountable to that promise. The implication was that so long as we stayed together, even if our marriage was a train wreck, then at least we were faithful to God and to our vows.

I recall a social movement that swept through our church back in the 1990s called Promise Keepers. They would organize rallies across the country every year and encourage churches to send all of their men to attend. By attending, married men would be declaring their unbending resolve to stay married forever, no matter what. A few of the men at my church who knew I was struggling in my marriage encouraged me to join them.

"Did you ever read that verse in Proverbs?" I asked them. "The one that tells us it is better to live outside, on the corner of a roof than to share the inside of a house with a quarrelsome wife."

They stared at me unsure of what I was getting at or where I was going with my response.

"Well," I continued, "I was wondering if I should start a social movement in the church for men like me. I would call it Roof Dwellers."

Once again I found my audience looking at me without amusement. I should have known better than to expect grace or understanding from this group in particular. After all, these were the same men who only days before had asked the ABC Men's Bowling League to hold their administrative meetings somewhere other than our church building.

"We don't like your cigarette butts in our parking lot," they ruled. "It sends the wrong message to our community."

I am fairly certain the bowlers got the right message. I never saw their butts in our parking lot ever again.

When my marriage to Katherine finally did end, despite how awful the relationship truly was, it was actually one of the saddest, darkest times in my life. I felt like I had failed. I fell into a deep depression and stopped eating. A deacon at the church pulled me aside one day and told me how sorry he was to hear about my unfortunate situation. He told me that he didn't want my divorce to negatively affect our friendship.

"However," he continued, "my wife and I have two young daughters who will soon be dating. I do not want them to perceive my willingness to associate with you as me condoning your decision to end your marriage. I hope you understand." And then he never spoke to me again.

Pastor Ray also pulled me aside. Throughout our short-lived, tumultuous marriage, I often found myself listening to his counsel. I played guitar on our Sunday morning worship team and he would advise me to work through my pain and my questions by seeking to connect with God through music.

"Now that you are divorced," he decided, "I think it would be best if you didn't play on our worship team anymore."

I was speechless.

"You see," he persisted, "I am afraid that when people come to church and see you up front, they will not be able to focus on God. Instead, they will only be able to focus on the fact that a divorced person is standing in front of our church. We can't have that."

And then he finished with a phrase that was beginning to make my stomach turn.

"I hope you understand."

That was also the last time I ever spoke with him. Being divorced, I could no longer be of any use to him or the church. I was sent back to the world from which they had saved me. I was returned to the wild to live like a feral animal. I once was found, but now I'm lost. Instead of being lost in one world, I am now lost between worlds. I am like little Susie Salmon in the book *The Lovely Bones* by Alice Sebold. I feel stuck in a place called the *In Between*. In that story, Susie dies and finds herself not quite completely gone from earth and not yet completely in heaven. The difference between Susie Salmon's experience and mine is that Susie seemed to find the place she was in to be very peaceful. I find my *In Between* to be more like a place of yearning. I yearn for a place to call home.

Will I be in church this Sunday, Pastor Ray?

Well, certainly not yours. I hope you understand.

The world of Christians and faith-based institutions was my home for a while. Now that I wear the scarlet letter of divorce, I am only left with faith. Faith is something I just cannot do without. The world of faith is a world of hope and freedom. It is the world where we bury lost loved ones with the promise of seeing them again someday. It is the world where we write songs which seek to ascribe meaning and assurance in times that are sinister. It is a world of art where simple, idealistic sojourners put on passion plays in remembrance of the one who saved us all.

Perhaps the ancient superstitions about lightning are true. Maybe the lightning that struck the Mount Pleasant Christian Theater where I first met Katherine all those years before was a sign from the Almighty. He was singling me out for exile. He was making me a marked man. I was marked by lightning so that there could be no question about what was intended.

They had just finished crucifying me the night the fire bolt hit. A horrible tempest from the bowels of hell brought down its wrath upon Mount Pleasant and upon our stage production. Vernon, who owned the laundromat, was one of six Roman soldiers assigned to secure me to the cross. He claimed afterwards to have had a bad feeling about the whole thing but he didn't know how to stop it. We were, after all, in front of a live audience.

Hollywood affixed rubber nails to my wrists while someone backstage swung a sledgehammer into a wood-splitting wedge. Performers dressed in period clothing gathered around me and gasped on cue with the metal-on-metal clanking. Sound and lighting technicians responded to their cues, throwing switches and hoisting cables. I did my best to scream out the sounds I supposed someone would make while being affixed by spikes to a wooden pole. By then the lights started to flicker and hail was pounding the building outside. The thunder came in ominous waves and it rolled constantly. Patrons could no longer distinguish the difference between what was going on outside and what was going on inside.

Pulleys turned and cables strained. The cross began its vertical ascent and I realized I would need to scream out my lines in order to be heard over the raging tumult.

"Eli, Eli, lama sabachthani?" I screamed. "My God, my God, why have you forsaken me?"

The storm suddenly surged as if my words commanded it. Wind and rain assailed the outer walls of the theater and the building moaned. A cacophony of atmospheric discharges and popping stage lights amalgamated with the rumblings of moving set pieces and actors working to remember and deliver their lines. The heavens unleashed all of their powers upon us and the audio system failed.

"It is finished!" I wailed over the bedlam as a blaze of light erupted above me and blew out all power to the building. I closed my eyes to feign death but I was no longer certain we were acting. The cross rocked and shook amidst a prolonged thunderous roar. People below me gasped in horror and astonishment. I heard weeping. I sensed fear. The bright white light assaulted my eyelids and I could feel intense heat on the back of my head.

"This is it." I thought. "It really is finished."

As I hung there suspended in darkness, the storm turned unexpectedly and abated. Silence permeated the theater. It was the sort of silence one expects in the moments after the discharge of a weapon when desperate eyes search their surroundings for reassurance. I could hear the blood and sweat dripping off my body onto the plywood expanse below. I sensed an enduring, alabaster glow around me and I began to wonder if perhaps I was in heaven. I wanted to open my eyes but the light was too intense. Besides, if I was still in Mount Pleasant, I was supposed to be dead.

"Is he dead?" I heard someone whisper.

"Turn that light off!" I heard Pastor Ray shout and whisper at the same time to a confused technician backstage.

"I can't!" came the reply. "We have no power! I can't turn anything off or on!"

"If we have no power, then why is that light on?"

"I don't know. Maybe it was the lightning."

"Here, let me try."

I caught the metallic sound of switches clicking and what was perhaps the only curse word I ever heard Pastor Ray utter. The entire town was cloaked in darkness except for a single white light radiating above me. The ominous silhouette of the Son of God crucified hovered before the dumbfounded gaze of the audience and convicted them. Pastor Ray could not have orchestrated such an imposing and breathtaking achievement. I later learned that over 200 people gave their heart to Jesus that night.

At that moment, we were no longer on script. One of the disciples below me, a fast-thinking business man who made his living selling refrigerators, began singing.

Holy Holy Holy, Lord God Almighty! Early in the morning our song shall rise to thee!

Charlotte, a beautician from the valley who was playing Mary Magdalene, joined in and they completed the verse as a duet.

Holy Holy Holy, Merciful and mighty, God in three persons, blessed Trinity!

A choir of audience members and players alike broke into song and the impromptu anthem restored peace to the room. A spirit of worship settled over us until at last, the miraculous, bright white light behind me slowly dissipated into darkness. At about that moment the building's power was restored and with an experienced hand, Pastor Ray gently illuminated the stage with blues and purples. In lavender shadows, stagehands discreetly retrieved the cross and upon its re-anchorage, my body was taken down and buried in a papier-mâché tomb. Only after the similarly fabricated stone was placed in front of my grave, shielding me from the audience, did I allow myself to open my eyes.

"What the fuck just happened?"

Actually, that is not what I said. My Christian brothers and sisters would not have taken kindly to the thought of Jesus dropping the F-bomb. I cannot recall exactly what I may have said but I am certain I sought immediate clarification from a knowledgeable source as to the exact details of the events which had just transpired.

"He's okay, Pastor Ray." I heard someone say into a radio.

"Well get him cleaned up!" came back the reply. "Jesus needs to be resurrected in four minutes!"

As my personal assistants aided me with my costume and the removal of stage blood from my tired, aching body, they did their best to explain the supernatural occurrence they had just witnessed. At the precise moment of Jesus' death, lightning had struck the building above me and all power was lost. The lighting system failed but for some inexplicable reason, the residual electricity from the lightning bolt found its way into illuminating a single, white emergency light that just happened to be pointed directly at the back of the elevated cross.

"It was as if God Himself took over our play!" my elderly makeup artist proclaimed.

"Thanks," I blurted out. "I'm fine. Thanks for asking."

They say lightning is one of the world's most underrated and unpredictable natural occurrences on our planet. It carries with it the power to amaze and to destroy. It has been observed during volcanic eruptions, forest fires, nuclear detonations, snowstorms, thunderstorms, hurricanes, and now, even passion plays. When lightning comes, it travels randomly at speeds of up to 60,000 miles per second through twisted paths at temperatures greater than five times the temperature of the surface of the sun. It is fast, it is lethal, and it is unforgiving. No one knows where or when it will strike nor are they able to predict how it will behave when it does. The odds of being hit by it are about 1 in 700,000. Those who survive tend to experience cardiac arrest, severe scarring from burns caused by the intense heat, permanent brain damage, memory loss, and even personality change. On the evening that lightning hit the Mount Pleasant Christian Theater, I was crucified and resurrected. Afterwards I was rushed into marriage, overcome by madness, and driven from the church. "All the world's a stage," William Shakespeare writes, "And all the men and women merely players; They have their exits and their entrances." In some cases, like mine, they are booed from the stage.

Dwayne Magee enjoys exploring spiritual, environmental, and social concerns through creative writing and the arts. He can often be found speaking in public libraries and elementary schools on the topic of diversity where he makes use of his award-winning children's book, A Blue-Footed Booby Named Solly McBoo. *His travel writing and fictional essays have made several appearances in the annual* Goose River Anthology *published by Goose River Press in Waldoboro, Maine, and he has written numerous songs including "Diamonds in the Rough," a song he performed for the Children's Relief Trust at the United Nations Building in New York City. Dwayne was born along with his twin sister in Williamsport, Pennsylvania, to David and Rosemary Magee, who met while working for* Grit *newspaper, now published in Topeka, Kansas. Dwayne is an author and part-time English major at Messiah College in Grantham, Pennsylvania, where he serves as director of print and mail. He is the father of two children, Garrison and Grayson. He currently resides in Mechanicsburg, Pennsylvania, with his wife Sue Frazier and their fluffy, white, smallish, poodle dog Solomon.*

ANTARCTIC WORLD

by Lynn Kincanon

poetry editor's pick

The word Arctic comes from the Greek word for bear, and Antarctic comes from the Greek meaning the opposite, without bear.

Ice Bear white against the light night
against the white of the Arctic snow.
You walk with sure, powerful footsteps
tracing back into ancient history.
Now rapidly slipping into obscurity
against the forces of greed and disregard.
More powerful than any adversary
you have ever known.
Killer whales, walrus, the starving Inuit,
do not compare for
you whose life collides in slip streams
of oil production, carbon dioxide, human desire
drowning you in forces of ignorance
and utter lack of empathy
for you, Nanuk, rider of icebergs,
naked against the melting snow.

Lynn Kincanon lives in Loveland, Colorado, where she works as a cardiovascular nurse practitioner, a wonderful profession, but her true calling is the arts. Her creative life began to blossom when she started the Artists' Collective and with inspiration and collaboration with other artists, writers, and poets she has created several art installations that include her poetry, most recently one in response to her local Loveland Art Collection. For this, she was awarded by In the Meantime Gallery and Art Space a portion of an NEA award to create a book around this installation entitled Art as Metaphor, Analogy and Allegory. *Lynn also created the first of what she hopes is an annual Loveland Loves Literature Festival, which included about 50 forms of literature from Shakespeare to original local lyricists to local high school exchange students reading the poetry of their country. Lynn hopes to continue to evolve and make poetry come alive with each new way to bring poetry into the everyday lives of the people.*

WINTER WOOD

by Carrie Tuttle

poetry editor's pick

A chill wind sweeps across the low canopy
Ahead deer tracks trail away,
Through the wood where darkness creeps
Up and up with wispy fingers,
Caressing root, bark, and bough.
Husks of milkweed stand
A silent testament to a prior autumn's bounty.
Leaves rattle on their stems
In prayer to the vibrant winter sky,
Mourning doves whistle
Their way toward the setting sun.
Onward go hares to deep thickets
With undercoats dense to warm them on the longest night
Footsteps behind, warm windows beacon.
Royal icing has crept up the stream bank
And sequined snow reflects the setting sun
We move inward now,
To where the fire burns
At the hearth of the rising moon.

Carrie Tuttle is a poet and aspiring children's book author.
She has an MS in Environmental Studies and a BS in Wildlife
Biology, both of which largely inform her writing. Carrie works

as a roving naturalist/educator and lives in Montrose, Colorado, with her family and a pride of housecats.

DEATH OF A KAYAKER

by Sam Bender

poetry editor's pick

hands thrust into fast waters
numb quickly to the shoulders
currents rage cold and deep in
unseen caverns between mountains
submerged crags, without refuge
beg revenge upon the swift or the careless
the plunge drives the kayak beneath
a renaissance reflection, the mirror of
the undersurface tasting of oxygen
narrowing, the slit of blue sky overhead is lost
tendrils of light pulling at this depth
rapidly fade, the ankle bracelet activates
sending out its now frantic
pulsing frequency of faith
there is no struggle now
no determination, no desired thrill
only degrees of observation as
amber stones flash gold, their green
mossy tint now gone
sharp lines blur into a passing as
fathoms push upward
air hunger becomes a
rite of passage, physiology tumbles
into philosophy

today passes into yesterday
a painless paradise of light
exposes a black and white negative
which, unshuttered, explodes into an
absence of thought

Sam Bender's previous work has been published in
Soundings Review, Oberon, Plainsongs, Samsara, The Poet's
Art, The Master's Work, Shepherd, *and* The Red Hat. *His
greatest circulation has come from several poems, published
over four issues, in the humanities in medicine section in the*
Journal of the American Medical Association. *His poem
"Pawnee" won the 2013 Northwest Institute of Literary Arts*
Soundings Review Founders' Circle Award. *His poetry is
derived from oral histories taken from our nation's elderly.*

GROWTH SPURT

by Jordan Lewis

short fiction editor's pick

I GASPED FOR BREATH AND FOUGHT OFF THE PAIN IN MY BACK AND knees, and, every damn part of my body, it seemed, but I kept moving; I had to make it to the Safe Zone before time ran out. I pushed and struggled, attempting to move forward through the mass of people on one of the narrow dirt paths that led to it.

The crackle of stun batons hissed through the air like downed power lines as a pack of airborne enforcement drones swarmed over the embattled group in front of me. Men, women, and children toppled to the ground in awkward, painful-looking positions, and the drone enforcers instantly pulled them to the side of the path where they lay motionless. Despite the drones' presence, a fight would break out or someone would slip and go down, knocking into others, and the drones instantly reacted. I had to ensure that no matter what, I would not go down.

The only vegetation and growth were stunted weeds that poked out in spots through dirt and rock. The last trees had been chopped down over a century ago. Now, forty-foot-high Breathers synthetically took in carbon dioxide and emitted oxygen; the air was polluted but breathable. Breathers' long winding tubes gave them the appearance of giant scarecrows that were seemingly protecting an endless and towering garden of concrete and carbon fiber buildings and high rises that ran in front of the paths which had been cordoned off for this event. Off in the distance, was the hustle and bustle of the town.

A light, early morning mist weaved through the trudging masses at foot level, as if casting a spell, adding to the dreamy, surreal-like atmosphere. This is the township of Empirebank, I thought with a grimace of regret as I recalled its original name: Yosemite National Park, California.

I moved past others who had gone down. Among those that the enforcement drones had zapped were people who were too weak or exhausted to continue. Or they looked like they had lost hope. I would not give up!

I popped a moisture-nutrient cube into my mouth, which would keep me going for hours, and was grateful that it was cloudy, blocking the sun. Still, it was a warm summer day and my jeans and button-down cotton shirt were spotted with sweat. My head ached. An undertone of muttering, gasps, and grunts reverberated everywhere like an overworked engine that drove the event.

The outdoors smelled the same as usual—mostly sterile: there just wasn't much left to give off an odor. I got a whiff of trail dirt, but mostly it reeked with the pungent smell of human sweat, brought on from excitement, fear, and anxiety. I felt for the all-valuable lottery ticket in my pocket once more, and minutes later I found my fingers wrapped around it again; I couldn't stop—the motion had become almost as necessary as taking a breath.

The controversial rules stated that finalists, like me, had to start on foot four miles away from the site where the lottery was being held. At the end was the "Safe Zone" where one became eligible for the prize. The route to the Safe Zone and the terrain were unknown so that no one could gain an advantage. You would only find out where to go by following the directions on the markers; you couldn't know how hilly or flat the trail was until you were on it.

Also, there was a time limit of only one hour and 50 minutes to get to the Safe Zone. That apparently was based on a calculation of 20 minutes for an average person to walk each mile briskly. A measly half hour was tacked on for the varied and crowded terrain.

News syndications had petitioned for the lottery to be held in this manner to heighten the drama. I flipped off the hundreds of news-affiliated camera drones and sky cars that flew overhead and reporters that lined the path. *Bunch of spurge brains* I scoffed under my breath, in reference to a common weed. Thousands of nonfinalists who wanted a glimpse of the prize had overrun barricades, and we finalists, who were only supposed to number one thousand, competed for space with them, all of us stomping, strutting, jostling, and elbowing our way along the paths.

A large holographic sign ahead proclaimed, "DISTANCE TO SAFE ZONE: 1/4 MILE TIME REMAINING: 11 Minutes"

Damn, the clock was ticking down. I had to hurry.

"Watch it, pops," a woman cried out while brushing up against my shoulder and careening ahead of me, causing me to sway.

"Watch it yourself!" I yelled back.

She turned and said, "You have spunk, pops. You might just make it, though I wouldn't bet on it."

She regarded my tall, wiry build and graying hair as if she were gauging their effect on my chances. She looked young. With age enhancers and modern medicine, it was hard to tell one's age until one got way up there in years. Hell, I was 110 and could live another few decades.

"Damn right I'll make it," I bellowed.

She was short and wore jeans with a yellow t-shirt that accented her cropped black hair and slim, firm figure. She reminded me of my youngest daughter, but with a harder edge.

An elderly woman fell to the ground, and the girl stepped around her. Without breaking stride, I pulled the fallen woman up by her arm where she stood dazed.

"You could have helped her up," I cried out to the girl as I caught up to her.

She scoffed, "Each person who goes down improves my chances of winning."

"That doesn't make it right. What's your name?"

"Why the hell do you care?"

"You remind me of—"

"Save your breath, pops, you're going to need it."

I couldn't really argue with that, however, after a long pause she said, "I'm Carla."

"I'm Artemis. Pleased to—"

"Look, pops, this isn't a social outing." With that she burst ahead.

I gazed up at the massive buildings in what had once been Yosemite Park. There was no land in sight anywhere as far as the eye could see. I sighed. How had it come to this? I had followed the different trends that had devoured the land, but like most, I hadn't done anything about it.

Unchecked overdevelopment had accounted for most of it. Rampant population growth, health advances that led to longevity, and, surprisingly, plentiful food from vertical, indoor farms added up to a current population of over 2 billion Americans! We all needed a place to live and work and shop, and drive and purchase and to be entertained and dispose of our garbage and waste—making for a huge global footprint that gobbled up land. There were small lawns that had been subdivided countlessly, but there were no more forests or fields or meadows or parks or pristine mountains or valleys and wild animals had disappeared long ago.

The only option left was to buy into a room or apartment in a mega high-rise. I looked up at the towering condos that crowned El Capitan's once majestic dome and imagined that Teddy Roosevelt must be rough riding in his grave.

I saw a commotion ahead of me and enforcement drones swooping down from the sky. There was Carla breathing hard and looking disheveled and shaken. I went up to her, and she seemed relieved to see a face that she recognized.

"I fell down and was getting trampled but forced myself up. I don't even know how," she said breathlessly.

"Sheer will, I imagine," I said taking into account my brief impression about her. I grasped Carla's shoulders to steady her and brushed hair back off her face. "You okay?"

She regained some of her bravado and growled, "Of course," but I could tell that the experience had affected her. I looked at my watch—only eight minutes left.

"Come on. We have to hurry," I implored.

I had seemingly become Carla's ally in this madness as we cut through the crowd. Carla was pushy in making her way forward, and I pressed to keep up behind her. People grumbled and cursed at us.

I caught sight of Carla's hands, which looked rough, and said, "I bet you work with your hands for a living."

"You're really a talkie, aren't you?" Carla said without turning around and showing me a blah, blah sign with her fingers.

"I'm just trying to keep my mind off the time."

She hesitated and then responded, "I'm an auto mechanic."

I nodded. "Hey, I was right. I'm a plumber."

We both spoke at a rapid pace, as if that would move us forward more quickly.

She regarded me. "You look more like the outdoorsy type."

I supposed that the lines on my face and parched, once-sunburned skin gave away my past. "I used to be a landscaper years ago," I said longingly.

If ever there was a career with no future, it was that. I had stubbornly kept at it until the bitter end. With the land disappearing, there was no need for landscapers anymore—smart machines tended to the small tracks of land that were left. The large amount of money that I made from selling my last bit of land caused me regret that had grown deeper as the years passed.

"I used to love landscaping," I said to Carla. "Designing mini-worlds was how I viewed it. I turned weeded areas into vegetable and flower gardens. Now I fix toilets," I added with a sigh. I gazed around and asked, "Are you here alone?"

"You're really nosy too, aren't ya?"

"I tried to tell you that you remind me of my daughter. I guess I feel . . . that gives me a right to, well . . . be concerned."

Carla grinned at that. "I'm on my own. Just broke up with my jerky boyfriend. He's happy living in L.A. but not me."

"Couldn't find a compromise?"

"Nah. Anyway, there were other issues; when I became a finalist in this lottery, I took it as a sign that it was time to move on. I've got to win that prize. What about you, pops, where's your family?"

"Most of them are back in Chicago. I live with my wife on the hundred and fortieth floor of a two-hundred-story high-rise by The Loop."

"That's way high up," Carla remarked.

I pointed to the sky and said, "Way too far from the ground for my taste, even if it's mostly covered with asphalt and concrete."

We had to weave through a slow group and Carla cried out, "Come on, pops!"

After we broke though she asked, "Your wife isn't with you?"

"No. She thinks that I'm crazy for coming here." I didn't mention that she had thrown me out of the apartment because she was so angry about it.

"Well, the odds are against us."

"My younger daughter, I have three, was the only one to back me. You'd like her; she's a small plane commercial pilot." Under different circumstances, I would have showed Carla pictures and told her more about my kids.

A man behind bumped into me and apologized as he caught up to stand abreast of me.

"Got your ticket?" I asked, as I checked for mine yet again.

"I didn't get into the finals. I just want to see the prize. Be the last chance to see something like it," he mentioned with a grimace.

Non–ticket holders were making it harder for us, but I understood. I tried to tune out the gasping and the sound of thousands of feet pounding the paths and the overhead whirl of enforcement and news channel drones and the whoosh of air cars owned by dignitaries and the rich and famous who were allowed to witness the event. *Bunch of spurge brains*, I muttered.

Five minutes to go. With Carla, at least I didn't feel so alone. My height enabled me to point out to her where to weave in and out of the crowd. I was in decent condition for my age; I still walked the streets of Chicago daily. Yet, my breathing was labored, my back and knees ached, and my ankles swelled. A younger man went springing by. I was about to tell Carla to go ahead on her own, but she saw the look in my eyes and shook her head, no. I kept blabbing to forget about the time limit we faced. Our conversation continued at a rapid pace between gasps of air and strides forward.

"Where are you from, Carla?" I asked.

"Utah. I grew up on a farm, one of the last in the state. Now it's a condo complex. She paused and added, "My dad left when I was young. I was one of ten kids, and we all pitched in with chores. Being one of the older ones and one of two girls, I had to take charge and help mom," she said with wrinkles etching into her forehead as she probably recalled some of the responsibilities she had had.

"You look like a mix of races."

"No shit, I'm part Spanish like most everyone in America."

"Yes. My wife is of Mexican descent."

"You're kind of light-skinned, but I see there's a mix in you," Carla surmised.

"No shit."

Carla let out a full-bodied laugh. "What about you, pops, where were you raised?"

"New York City. One of my favorite places was Central Park."

I lay on a blanket, picnicking with Sarah, one of my first girlfriends. We were on Central Park's Great Lawn, surrounded by endless, frolicking people and a spreading open area of lush grass that seemed to know no boundaries and that would last forever.

"Central what?" Carla asked inquisitively.

"What . . . oh, Park. It was in midtown Manhattan and it was beautiful; it's all apartment and office buildings now."

"Too bad."

"Years later I moved to San Fran then up the coast, trying to stay ahead of the growth spurt." I clenched my fists and added wistfully, "Never could shake it though; it kept coming like a demented, haunted spirit with unfinished business."

"Yeah."

"I met my wife on a trip to Chicago where she's from and settled there. Doesn't much matter where you live anymore; just about every place looks the same these days."

"True enough. We're getting closer to the Safe Zone, pops," Carla said.

My watch showed that we only had three minutes left. I was heartened at first at how near we were. Then I looked up. Between buildings, paths headed up a steep incline that rose so high that I could barely make out the peak. Carla careened briskly up the hill. I couldn't keep up. When it came down to it, she had saved herself; I suppose that I couldn't really blame her.

I kept moving up the slope at a slow clip. My breathing labored. My head felt woozy. Then, the hill turned into a human bowling alley—people, who had stumbled, were rolling down the hill into others, knocking them down. A large man rolled straight for me. I tried to get out of the way, but, *smack*, he hit me and cut my rubbery legs out from underneath me, and I sprawled to the ground on my back.

The very thing I had dreaded all day had happened. I was down! Damn. Within seconds, an airborne, enforcement drone was hovering overhead reaching out for me, ready to throw me to the side of the path like discarded garbage. I flailed about helplessly and struggled to get up. There was too much at stake. I had come too far. The drone was getting closer. I could hear the whirr of its electronic, aerial engine and smell its rancid lubrication. I struggled and pawed at the ground and managed to roll over onto my side and raise myself to my knees as others fell around me.

Suddenly, I was pulled up by my shirt collar. I thought that the damn drone had gotten hold of me. But the fingers weren't steel. I heard a gruff female voice yell, "Keep yer stinkin' claws off him. He's up."

The drone hovered above us for a moment before flying away. "Thank you, dear. Where did you come from, Carla?" I wheezed with relief.

"I saw what happened from up higher. I couldn't let that thing take you. We're, well . . . we're like a team or something," she said with a blush. "From now on we'll stick together . . . pops."

I smiled. "But I'll slow you down."

"It's okay. I saw the Safe Zone marker from the hilltop. Come on, move your ass."

"I can move my ass, it's the rest of me that I'm worried about."

She laughed at that. "Just keep going."

I was afraid to even look at my watch. Carla practically pushed me up the hill to the crest. Then we raced down the slope on the other side at a fast clip. Now my knees felt like they were going to pop, and my organs jounced from bouncing over the rocky trail. I felt like a martini that an angry bartender was prepping in a shaker. I could almost hear the seconds ticking off in my head. Would we make it?

Carla yelled out and pointed. "There, up ahead of us."

The largest marker of them all indicated, "WELCOME TO THE SAFE ZONE TIME TO CLOSING: 25 seconds."

We surged forward and past the marker. Damn, that was close. Land drones scanned our lottery tickets and motioned us forward. Anyone without a ticket could go no further. A holographic sign said that only those in the zone would have their numbers called, the rest of the numbers would be expunged from the system. It was hard to tell, but it appeared that a little more than half of the final contestants had made it. I was exhausted, but we trudged on.

Carla called out, "There it is!"

Large, holographic displays depicted the lottery prize that gleamed under a blaze of stadium lights. Carla kept us moving forward until we got close enough to actually see it and not just a holo of it. I choked up a bit, because it was glorious. It was surrounded by the usual buildings, but I took little notice of them. Instead, I concentrated on the prize itself, which a large billboard proclaimed: "THE LAST ACRE IN AMERICA."

It was green. Natural green. Not manmade. I could tell the difference instantly even from afar. The green of real sod, of grass. It would only cost the winner the price of the lottery ticket and some downward-adjusted taxes. Just seeing it helped alleviate most of my aches and pains. The acre glowed like an enormous emerald at the base of the long, rolling, overcrowded hill.

I wanted to cry from joy that I'd made it here to see it, and, at the same time, I wanted to scream out of anger that this really was the last acre in the country. I thought of Mark Twain who had said, "Buy land. They're not making it anymore." That statement had been unintentionally, eerily prescient.

A loud announcement was made that the Safe Zone closed. I pulled the ticket from my pocket and gazed at it. It was a plastic hologram with a waving American flag that simply said, "U.S. Government Department of the Interior— Acre Lottery Finalist."

A clerk in Washington, DC, at the Department of the Interior, had discovered it while going over old records and determined that the acre had never been sold and therefore belonged to no one. The DOI decided to offer it in a lottery, and they held a play-off type of system with hundreds of elimination lotteries to get to the last 1,000 finalists.

I reached for my good luck charm around my neck; it was a white, pressed rose embedded in amber that was given to me by my parents when I had started my landscaping business. I grasped it tightly. It was only fitting that a landscaper should win, I thought. Two stipulations for the winner were that the acre could not be sold for 20 years and that only one building could be built on it that was no higher than three stories.

Carla and I moved forward toward a stage beside the acre, pressed against the crowd as far as we could go. Enforcement drones kept people from surging closer to it. The governor of California, Lucy Rodriquez, was introduced and walked up to a podium. She commenced with the usual acknowledgments and added that the numbers had been chosen randomly by computer and would be displayed on stage and overhead in holographs throughout the area. The lottery had been sanctioned by Price Waterhouse Coopers.

Under the overcast sky, a small band in the rear of the stage struck up "America the Beautiful." Sadly, the lines referring to plains, mountain majesties, waves of grain, and wilderness had been taken out years ago, as they no longer had a reference point.

Governor Rodriquez proclaimed, "We will now commence with the DOI One Acre Lottery. Cross your fingers. Good luck."

Thousands of people became as quiet as if their tongues had been glued to their teeth; it was a silence that was willed by anticipation and hope. I had memorized my numbers, all 15 of them: "75729 04812 27057." My heart was beating even faster than when I had plodded along the trails.

Governor Rodriquez announced in an official tone, "The first number is, seven."

An enormous hologram of a black number seven appeared on the podium and over the crowd in various locations.

"Number five. Number seven again. Number two." She paused between each announcement to allow people time to check their tickets and probably to build suspense. With each number announced there were either cries of joy or moans of anguish from the crowd. I heard Carla groan.

"Damn, I lose," she said in a quiet voice filled more with sadness than anger. She continued to hold her ticket and stare at it.

I patted her shoulder and offered, "I'm sorry for you Carla, but I'm still in." She perked up and took my arm.

The number nine was announced. Amazingly, I had all of the first five numbers. My confidence was building but so was my stress. The next five numbers were announced and to my surprise and delight, I had each of them. Carla cheered and grasped my arm tighter and tighter with each winning number I had.

"Only five to go. You're going to win, Artemis!"

I looked down at the remaining numbers on my lottery ticket: "27057"

"Number two. Number seven." Carla and I cheered. "And now a Zero."

"Number five."

The number reverberated in my head. "Yes. I have it," I yelled.

"Only one more number to go, ladies and gentlemen," the governor proclaimed.

My heart raced as the ticket shook in my hand. Carla clung to my arm, quivering with anticipation.

"And now for the last number." The governor paused for a long time to prolong the effect. She probably didn't care or realize how tortuous it was. My mouth was dry. My heart pounded furiously. I grasped at my good luck charm around my neck so tightly that I almost choked. Sweat dripped off my forehead in long rivulets.

The governor cleared her throat and proclaimed, "Ladies and gentlemen, the final number is . . ."

I saw the number appear. I heard the crowd roar. I shook with disbelief.

I heard Carla cry out as she grasped my arm even tighter. Which was good, because I was about to fall down from excitement and weakness.

Locating me by the transponder in my ticket, the government air transport picked me up and flew me to the podium to claim my prize. The governor extended her hand in congratulations and offered the deed to the land that I grabbed as I ignored the dignitaries and jumped from the stage to the acre below. I sat on the grass and felt embraced by its softness. It was as if I could see each plump blade that seemed to undulate and shimmer with liveliness and the purest green. The fresh, chlorophyll smell was as intoxicating as champagne.

I chose the spot where I'd build my log cabin. I pictured my garden. I got down close to the earth and let the dirt run through my fingers. I plucked blades of grass and held them up to the bright sun, gazing at their transparency. Strangers would be welcome here.

I saw myself making piles of cut, musky-smelling grass, cut down with an old-fashioned, hand push, reel mower. My family would join me. I saw us camping out, building a fire at night and telling stories around it. We'd be close-knit again, and, without question, we'd roast marshmallows.

I envisioned some of my grandchildren playing on the lawn, under a bright, warming sun. Chasing one another, running and laughing and falling and rolling over the grass. They'd come up to me with the sweet scent of grass stains on their clothes, with happy satisfied looks on their faces and—

"Artemis! Artemis! Are you okay?" I heard someone yelling at me as if from afar, as my arm was frantically being tugged.

I turned. It was Carla. She shook her head and grasped my shirt and shook me. "You didn't win, Artemis. The winner is at the podium. Look," she said while pointing to it. "You were mumbling things out loud as if you had won."

I nodded and let my head drop. "I know. I was just imagining what could have been. It was beautiful, Carla. Why didn't I win? A landscaper should have won the last acre in America."

Carla said with compassion, "I'm so sorry you didn't win. The last number was a stupid one. You had a seven." She repeated, to make sure that I had no illusions, "Look, the winner is on the podium."

"I know. I'm sorry you didn't win either." I glared down at my ticket and scorned it as I would a lover who had betrayed me. I let it fall from my hand, and, as if blown by a gentle fall breeze, it dropped slowly to the ground like leaves used to from trees.

Tears ran down my cheeks. Carla had remained impassive and tough but when she saw me she burst into tears. We held onto one another, keeping each other steady.

The large holograms depicted enforcement drones and a metallic voice boomed, "Contestants will now be picked up by air shuttles and taken back to the entrance point. Return to your dwellings from there." The ground and airborne rows of enforcement drones were grouped in formation in front of the last acre and all around us with their menacing black stun batons waving at the ready like a stingray's tail about to strike.

The silence that had preceded the announcement of the lottery numbers was replaced with sounds of sobbing. Slight at first, then guttural and deep, a sob that reached back through centuries—ancestral—a sob that seemed to reverberate through man's earliest caves and vast wilderness: a sob of loss, irreversible loss. For us. For all the future generations.

I looked around at the others and searched their reddened eyes. There seemed to be a sense of helplessness. Disappointment. A disbelief that it had come to this. That it hadn't been stopped. Then I saw anger. Or maybe, I was just feeling all of those things.

The crowd suddenly surged forward toward the last acre in America. No longer up for grabs. They wanted to touch it. Take it for themselves. The hell with the lottery. Screams filled the air. I found myself being swept up and carried along. Carla had clamped her hand tightly in mine.

Enforcement drones remained in position. The first waves of people were downed by stun batons, but eventually, as the human tide surged forward they overwhelmed the drones and broke through their lines. Enforcement drones dropped from the skies like birds of prey about to sweep up human quarry in metallic talons. At first they did, but eventually people wrestled the batons away from the drones and beat back the mechanical pack. Carla, somehow, still held my hand as she wheeled a baton like an avenging Joan of Arc, bashing and crushing drones. There was a large cry from way behind us; the thousands of people without lottery tickets must have broken through the enforcement drone lines and were descending on the last acre.

I was rushed forward by the momentum of the masses. Eventually, I arrived at the last acre. For one fleeting moment I stood on the hallowed ground! I reached down and grasped. And came up with blades of grass. Actual grass and earth. I brought them up to my face and inhaled. It was a fresh, earthy live scent. Carla and I continued to be pushed ahead by the surging crowd, but I also felt a part of them now, and I knew that I could not go back to Chicago, at least not for a while.

Government air cars swooped down to rescue the governor and other dignitaries as the stage was wrecked, drones smashed and trampled, and people left writhing on the ground.

Carla and I still clasped hands, and we gazed at one another quietly as we were swept well past the last acre in America.

"I'm holding on, Artemis," Carla said with a look of resolve.

"Me too," I called to Carla above the clamor.

With my other hand, I still tightly clutched my blades of grass.

An early writing teacher and major influence of Jordan's was JJ McDonagh, who headed the English Department at the Berklee College of Music in Boston. He also had the good fortune to study briefly with the award-winning fantasy/science fiction writer Roger Zelazny and award-winning science fiction/fantasy writer Terry Bisson. "Growth Spurt" is Jordan's first published short story. He resides in New Jersey, and he is a member of the Garden State Speculative Fiction Writers.

HAWK BLOOD
(SOLILOQUY OF IMPERFECTION)
by Barbara Cameron

personal essay/creative nonfiction editor's pick

EVERYTHING THAT IS HAPPENING IS HAPPENING *OUT*SIDE MY WINDOW. I am in hiding. I touch the glass with my fingertips . . . yes, the odd greenish winged insect with mandibles *is* on the outside. The balled up pain I was in last night in the dark, unable to sleep, is still in the room. It left my insides, but can't get out of here until I leave, and I won't leave. The truth, I cannot leave. I have come to love this room I have been staying in for almost two weeks now. I feel safe in here. Have made it my little home.

The insect gone, off the skin of the window, now, through the glass cube I literally sit in, I see feathers floating in the circular wind tunnel created by the half-moon shape of the dormitory. Two weeks at a writer's conference in upstate New York, if there is a heaven on earth, this was mine.

The trouble started yesterday. It is my doubt. Midway through our Wednesday class, Mary Gaitskill reminded everyone to pick up the two stories we would be critiquing on Friday, one of which I wrote.

It is my *real* life away from here; I am a 54-year-old waitress—*servers* they call us now—in Beverly Hills, California. The idea of leaving here with less than what I came with (delusion or high hopes?) renders me as beaten down and bruised as my body—not to mention the mental

226

shed where I keep my survival tools—feels at the end of
what, in my business, they call a *shift*—though two days a
week I work the equivalent of three shifts in one day. My feet
ache every night. Here, I wear flip-flops every day.

Stories themselves are never confusing; they are what
happened, until the telling. My submission is a story I have
been trying to tell for 30 years. In my twenties when the
events took place, begun in a burst of wounded childlike
energy, my sense of betrayal and pain drove the telling. But
the story evolved, and I am a messy person; I cannot draw a
straight line and I cannot tell a long story short. But I tried; I
converted *me* to *she* and gave my character a name. I
thought, finally, after years of attempts, I had managed to
pull this story into a cohesive, *well-told* piece. I was wrong.
Rereading for the first time in three months, the clarity I had
hoped for wasn't there.

It is the mess, the inability to untangle and tell this story
that bothers me.

It is my knee socks losing their elasticity before my sisters
when we were in grade school, and falling at my ankles.

It is the red marks for grammatical mistakes all over my
college papers even as I received A's for content. And more.

It is my father having called me a pig, *a pig*, because my
room was always messy. My father (now dead) was a
compulsively neat man; my story is about my father. Last
night, two of my friends who had immediately read it told me
that they had been "confused" by it. "I don't know what to
say. I mean . . . I don't know how to *help*."

"Yeah, I know." Agreement was the cover: the fierce pain
had already begun to coagulate.

Jutting out of every room in the building we are housed
in is a square window with a soft, ugly turquoise cushion. All
of my worldly responsibilities elsewhere, this room is my

asylum, especially this glass capsule. I love looking out: like *Hollywood Squares*, at any given time, day or night, other writers sit in their box, knees scrunched or feet up on the wall, reading or writing. Safe little prisons with self-admitted inmates.

More feathers out there now than before, all light gray, beautifully they float, and I realize they are the aftermath of a kill. One animal fed, another has ceased to exist. It couldn't have been small either because there are so many feathers. Again, I think about leaving the room; I have to eat breakfast, don't I? No. I came for this, didn't I?

Ray said, "Your server will be right with you," but having overheard this family at the host stand, I was right there at the table where no one yet sat. The boy, maybe five, was in a stroller; how damned big he was astounded me. Inner monologue is a saving grace in my line of work. *Get that goddamned kid out of the stroller before he is 18, and make him walk.* We learn not to speak what we think, but thoughts are free, and they cross my mind like a coyote across the desert leaving indelible tracks, scars of too many things unspoken.

"You promised last time next time *I* could pick," the boy said, out of the stroller, arms folded.

The girl, about six or seven years old, said, "Not true. It's my turn," then flopped herself into the oversized stroller as the boy cried, "Outside!" The parents exchanged a look of panic. "No, honey, not today."

"It is your sister's turn to pick," the mother said.

"You promised *me* in the car," he protested.

She registered doubt. "No, I did not," she said. "The next two times, I promise, promise."

"Can I get you something to drink?" I was invisible.

The boy started up again. "Well, it is a beautiful day," the mother said. "Maybe we should go out."

The father shook his head—a *here we go* shake—and the mother snapped, "You're not the one who is going to have to deal with it, who's going to have to get up and walk him around. Can I just please eat one meal in peace."

The girl hopped up, walked to the host stand, and stuck her fist in the candy basket, came back and dumped the candy on the table.

"No, not before breakfast," the father said.

Two seconds and I walk.

"Just one."

"No."

"I'll be right back," I said.

"No, wait, we're almost ready," he directed me, then the daughter, "Take one, sweetheart, save the rest for later."

"Can I eat two now, please?"

"Okay, but only two."

"Can I have three now, and I promise, the rest for later?"

Can I go, please, daddy?

"I'll check on my new guests," I said, pointing to a newly sat couple, "and be right back."

Suddenly, realizing they were not in their home having this argument, he smiled. "Okay, but don't abandon us," he joked. Then to his daughter, "Okay, sweetie, but three is the limit, okay?" he enforced with a question.

Abandon. Inflated language is common in the restaurant business, in Beverly Hills anyway. Once a woman told me her tea press *exploded* when she pushed down (it sprinkled a little), and she had been *terrified*. It happened to be the same day one of those mine explosions had taken place, the families all truly terrified, waiting to see if their loved ones were safe. I say nothing. Ever. We are not allowed. Maybe that's why I am addicted to writing. *It exploded, and you were terrified? Really?*

I returned.

"You know, we will go outside after all. He did miss a turn to choose; it's only fair," the mother tried to convince, of all people, me. "I think I did say that in the car." She smiled at the boy.

"What about me?" the girl cried.

"Sweetheart, you're the big girl, right?" the dad said.

"Okay, then I'm gonna have four candies."

"I said *three*."

"But I am *so* hungry, and it's going to take *so* long."

"Okay, only because they're small; if they were bigger than that I would have stuck with three."

Sure you would have. Another person motioned for me. She took her fourth candy, snuck a fifth, unwrapped them and shoved them both in her mouth at once. For a few precious minutes, I fled, leaving them to Ray, catching up as they walked outside.

Drag me down means monopolize my time so that, wildly busy and the only waiter—excuse me, *server*—on the floor, I will get so far behind that no one will get decent service. The other servers weren't due for another 45 minutes, so they had closed the top half of the long outdoor patio.

"Don't you have half-shade, half-sun?" the mother asked.

The kid pointed to the end of the patio. "There, I want there!"

"I'm sorry, that's closed. We only have one server on the floor; we can't spread her out too thin," Ray explained.

"That isn't open yet, honey."

Wealthy hip parents often call their children *sweetheart* and *honey* now, no matter how irritated they are with them. When the men do it, it warms me somewhere, probably because my own father was strict—a screamer, and never in a million years would have called his children by these names. Nor would he have put up with this nonsense. I heard that creep into this father's tone when he said, "Pick a table. You wanted to be outside, we're outside."

So busy, afraid to leave, afraid to stay—*Do you want to know what the schools are like in the neighborhood before you move in?*—I followed behind them in my ugly shoes (my feet, killing me already). The woman had perfect feet—*girl feet* I call them, when you can take care of yourself that way. Her toenails, pretty with polish, in sweet pinkish-gold sandals.

"Maybe this one?"

"No, I'm cold, I want the sun."

"I want to see the Hollywood sign."

"Are you *sure* we can't sit down there at the end?" the mother persisted.

In the end, they got what they wanted; they always do in this business.

"Can I start you with something to drink?"

"Oh, we're ready to order. We're starving."

A, you are not ready to order, and B, you're not starving.

"Um, I have other tables inside, so I'll just quickly get the drinks, then be right back," I said.

"We have to order now," the mother said. "These kids have to eat."

No choice, I said, "Okay. Sure."

"I can't read the menu; the sun is too hot in my eyes," the daughter said.

In this little war, I was winning now. The illusion that hers was a perfect little family waning, she snapped—at me. "Isn't there an umbrella out here?"

"Only sun," I said, "at this time of the day at this end of the patio."

"It'll be alright, honey." The girl stuck her tongue out at her. "Don't stick your tongue out at Mommy, that's rude, sweetheart." I don't blame the children in these cases. They don't have a shot in hell.

The story I am trying to tell, the one I have converted into fiction, is about my father cheating on my mother. But more than that: about how he advertised for a new wife in the newspapers while he was still married to my mother. I was the one who found the folder marked "Real Estate," with all the pictures and letters; I was the one who stole it from his locked filing cabinet and handed the whole mess over to my mother's lawyers to secure her financial stability. The problem, after all these years, I came to realize that, not only did I love my father, but that he loved us, deeply; and that my perfect mother wasn't as perfect as I had always believed; and that I loved her dearly, as well. It's even more complicated than that. Some things are.

Some things are not. Like where to sit in a damn restaurant, and what to eat when you do.

"I can't see," the girl said.

"Sweetie, be *quiet* and order," the father said.

Her face scrunched up in deep-rooted anger: she was most likely the Queen ruling the roost until this next little creature had come onto the scene. In this family, the younger, the more power.

"Let's just get through this meal, okay."

She growled (literally). I still didn't have a drink order. Spotting my bus boy and friend Gabe, I called, "Can you ask Ray to bring the drinks to table four? They're at the bar."

Whatever else these kids would complain about, from here on out it would be my fault. If not, it would be the parents' fault; they would be bad parents. That would never happen.

It is difficult, as parents, to take responsibility for the bad behavior of your children. In much the same way, writers have to take responsibility for what they've put on the page; when it comes out fucked up it is embarrassing. For a writer, the only way to shift our sense of shame about our work is pretend it was *only a rough draft*, or something we were just *playing around with*. I believe this is never true. I believe every ounce of our being is on the line here.

Before I came here, my sister warned me, whatever you do, *don't* say you're a waitress. "People treat you differently, look at you differently." She too had been a waitress, then gone back to school and gotten her master's, is working on her PhD. The difference in the way people treat her now, she told me, she feels in her bones.

The way I feel the physical suffering from having earned my living this way for so long, mostly in my wrists, feet, and back. The mental anguish is incomprehensible. Being a server in Beverly Hills is like Vegas: the odds are against you; the house always wins. The reaction to my story, so far, not so good; what are my odds tomorrow?

Waiting at their table, I felt remiss; my other customers needed me. The parents let the kids read the menu. "They can both read," the father bragged. It is a cute game, how smart, how cute their kids are. (I have endured parents having their four-year-old recite every president of—and every state in—our nation.)

They, like many Beverly Hills parents, like many rich and quasi-rich parents these days, honestly think they are the first people ever to have given birth. It is their claimed novelty, a physical extension of their celebratory self-centeredness. I don't know what they think when they drive through less affluent neighborhoods and see children swarming around in droves, but I can guess: *others*. The pride in what they made is a direct reflection of their own pride. They revel in it: the strollers that cost more than a used car, the paraphernalia in the stroller, the mashed up organic vegetables the nanny spoon-feeds them from right little bowls atop their own plastic throw-away placemats.

There wasn't a nanny that day or the whole thing would have been a lot quicker. There is an unspoken, tacit agreement between worker-bees. As the girl shyly leaned into her mother, and the mother said, "It's okay sweetie, tell the lady what you want," the nanny would have said they would both have lemonade, for me.

Looking out my window admiring the beauty, despite myself, I think about which animal ate, and which might have been eaten.

Waiting for the damn drink order, I thought about my other 11 tables: Who had been fed, who was still waiting for their food? Minutes are hours to a waiter. So much can go wrong in one minute.

Sitting in the window at the dorm, I look at my left foot; a new blister has formed from wearing flip-flops the past two weeks, instead of the ugly black work shoes I wear daily. The sore on my right little toe that I get from those shoes has hardened and subsided.

My feet killing me as usual, I switched my weight to my other foot and said, to speed things up, "Maybe a freshly squeezed strawberry-orange juice."

"I'm sorry," she apologized for their inability to order. *How sorry?* "Is your orange juice *freshly* squeezed?"

"Yes."

"I mean *to order*. The vitamins are gone in a matter of minutes."

Gone? Table 6, inside, had gotten their food by now. I promised jam with the woman's toast. Was table 4 ready to order? I spotted Gabe, again, waved him over and said, "Can you bring jam to six and ask Ray to drop the check on eight, and take the order on four, please, if he hasn't already."

I wanted to pitch them all over the balcony. Anger, I had learned from my father's outrage, is loneliness and sadness. Anger is also stress, because of so many things you are responsible for at one time, no matter how petty the responsibility. Servers are not doctors; lives are not on the line, but tell that to the people who come to eat. They never experience *real* hunger, but being fed is a whole different story.

If we become obsessed in love, in life, without judgment about if it is healthy or not—if it feeds us, we seek it. Writing and reading feed me. So last night, in my wretched state, I sat in my glass box reading Mary Gaitskill's entire collection of stories in *Don't Cry*. "The Little Boy," I studied like a textbook: how to write about things that have happened in the past in an organized fashion, so as not to confuse the reader. Finally, sleep and the light of the day had released the pain that can only be private, never shared. But it is still in the room and won't be gone until I open that door and start to let it go. I have a love-hate relationship with this kind of deranged, disproportionate self-hatred; I want it in here now; it has made me highly productive. *I am writing.* I am rummaging, pulling out scraps of debris from the mental wastebasket where I have thrown the things that have happened to me at that job that I hadn't been able to bear to hold onto.

There is astonishing urgency now—unlike the disused urgency I suffer in the restaurant when I am slammed. *Slip-resistant* by law of the state, my highly hideous black work shoes will have a hold of my feet before I know it. Sometimes, my feet are so raw sore, at night, when my shift is over, I sit on the couch (ice pack singeing cold on my lower back) and rub them. I will have to have an attendant from a mental ward put me into a straitjacket to make me put that uniform on again; or to make me leave this room and face the other writers who, by now, have *all* read my story.

What animal killed the bird? I want to see what a satisfied *non*human looks like again.

No one waits for anything anymore when I am the server; I am that efficient. I have earned my living this way for so long—rarely do I get a complaint. Rarely do I have to be reprimanded, and never do I have to be physically dragged away from a table the way I had been in the past, in the middle of a knock-down, dragged-out verbal altercation with some asshole. The need to overpower a servant boggles me as much as my need to win with these people I serve sometimes does. But it is, I guess, a form of self-preservation. Everyone needs a win every once in a while, especially if it isn't at anyone else's expense.

This was the win I hoped for here at the conference. Affirmation is merely (or more) support. My fear: the pain that had intensified into that black ball (rotten illusion) inside of me last night had spent my soul.

Finally, having gotten the family's drink order, entered it into the computer, *promised* to return for the food order, escaped and gotten caught up inside, I was back with the drinks. I smiled, placed the strawberry lemonade in front of the daughter; the Coke—"A treat because you were so good for Mommy today and came with us" in front of the boy; coffee in front of the father; and, in front of the mother, "An iced tea with just a *splash* of lemonade," she had said, pointedly. I had clarified, "An *Arnold Palmer?*" She shook her head no. "No, no, I just want a *splash* of lemonade." Lemonade in tea makes it an Arnold Palmer; we charge more. It is not my rule, however, if, in a clothing store, you buy a blouse and just want a *tiny* scarf, you do pay for the scarf, correct? Also, define *splash*.

"I would be happy to get that for you, but it will be charged as an Arnold Palmer."

I had imagined watching her face splat on the pavement, not to mention her children motherless. She stared at me, like it was the fight that it had become for her, and for me as well, but for my *time*. The father had shaken his head at me in disgust. At a standoff, the mother figured out a way to win. She looked me up and down, my (at the time) 52-year-old self in the straitjacket I had trapped myself in, hair askew, non-lipsticked, apron smudged, heart cracked open, hoping for an act of kindness, and said, "Fine. We'll *pay* for it. We can afford it."

I drew my soul back in shock—no *hatred*—and walked away silently.

I am stronger, tougher than this, I decide in my window. I will go to Mary Gaitskill today and say (in our private conference) this: I know I write all over the place, but that is all I do. I write in the margins of books I am reading, I write in notebooks, I write on the computer, and I write on the back of menus at work. I write. Without it, I'm lost, so take what I have here, and help me. She will, I think, because she is capable. The kind of person you are a little afraid to be around, and more afraid when she isn't. I heard kindness in the memoir she read the night before called *Lost Cat*. Kind enough to be honest is my guess, which I crave after all the bullshit and silence in the job I do that earns me my keep in this world.

"Okay," I said, because the truth, when you are caught up you can ignore a lot, and you can give your best service, "so, how are you today?"

"Hungry," the mother said, pointedly. "The *kids* are hungry," she qualified in an attempt to soften her self-image, but only to herself.

I have already missed breakfast in the cafeteria. I am starving. I need lunch. Whatever happens out there— avoidance, placation, or honesty—will puncture.

The father, pissed off beyond faking it by then, said, "We're staying put. Order for Christ's sakes," and the sham was over.

"Show the lady what a big boy you are!" the mom said, insistent that he order for himself. She was going to make that family of hers normal if it killed her.

The way we all try to protect what we write, because, in a remarkably real sense, it is all we have. Like it or not, the story I submitted, is mine. I am going to own it, dress and leave the room.

The father called the host stand on his cell; he wanted a coffee refill. He had already asked "a busboy or someone," and no one had come. Ray said he was polite about it. *We're gonna have to field cell phone calls now?*

I went immediately; it would not go well for me if these people complained. The boy, up and wandering around, "starving," the mother put it, and the daughter, feeding the pigeons, "It's coming," I said, pouring the coffee. "I put the order in right away, but when things are special ordered (I had to use a *See Server* modifier for the little boy's order; it was so convoluted and complicated the poor computer wouldn't even have the available language to communicate it. I know that feeling.) it does take a little longer," I said, knowing even this slight accusation was crossing a line.

It is a rule that guests are not supposed to feed the pigeons. They get out of control and overtake the patio, shit on people and their food. When they swoop some people scream, "They're flying rats! Isn't there anything you can do?" Actually, there isn't, because harming them is against the law. I can't tell these people (it would be insubordinate) that I saw a documentary about that: they are not, in fact, dirty birds (their poop is, and even that is not a significant human threat), and they saved our ass in World War I and II. But the birds even annoy me. Others feed them because they think they are cute. The boy joined his sister, feeding crackers to the birds. More crumbs, signals sent, they flocked. The law of nature: come; there is food. The father said nothing.

"They ask us to ask our guests not to feed the pigeons. It's a Health Code thing," I said. It is.

Outside the dorm, exposed, I attempt to deconstruct my fear. The people who have read it will see, what? That I am not in control of my skills, possibly have no talent. That loathsome ball I was twisted in last night is my core fear: I will never be anything but a server.

"It's occupying them," the mother said. "The food is taking so long."

Well, you stupid cow, if you hadn't sat way back here in the first place, and taken so fucking long to order you might be eating right now!

I look to see which animal seems full, might have eaten the bird. The feathers have all fallen. I see nothing.

The huge letters, UTA, on the building across the street from where I work are silver against a white wall. They stand for United Talent Agency. The sun struck them and blinded us all for a moment. In that second, a hawk swooped in, grabbed a pigeon in its jaw, and chomped it. The blood splattered everywhere, all over the family, their skin and their clothes, on their bread and in their drinks. The perfect mother of the perfect family, her white blouse bloodied, jumped up screaming, "Someone will have to pay to get this cleaned." I—truly stunned as well—could only stare at the drops of blood she could not see, on her face, near her eyes, so terribly close to her mouth.

They kids cried. *I told you not to feed the fucking pigeons!* Also, I was thankful their father was holding them, being kind to them: it was a brutal thing to have seen; they needed comfort.

And finally, finally, in their world, I ceased to exist. I stood, familiar in the strangeness of this new peace. Even they knew they couldn't blame me for this. I knew she wasn't upset because of her clothes, but it is always telling what comes out of a person's mouth in a state of panic. I knew the restaurant would probably pay, as a gesture, to have their clothes cleaned. But they couldn't even blame the restaurant. Things like that fall under "An Act of God," because they are.

I could have stayed home, but I came. In our afternoon meeting, Mary Gaitskill said she genuinely liked a lot of my writing, and the story. I was truly taken aback. The next day in class, the students all commented on how confusing it had been for them, though *some* had appreciated *some* of the writing. Then Mary said, "I am never surprised by a student's work, almost never surprised when I read at all, but this surprised me." She said it was told in a confusing, but complex and honest way; she was moved, and thought it should be told. She read several passages out loud to the class. Some of the writers conceded that maybe they had missed something, should take another look. Later, one woman, from another group (the advanced workshop with Rick Moody), who had actually snubbed me (managing to intimidate me), approached me at dinner, and said *sweetly*, "I heard Mary really liked your story," and then parked herself at my table and ate with me. It is the law of nature, I guess. Eat or be eaten; kill or be killed. Life and death matters here.

I stood staring in awe at the hawk who, after the attack, flew across the street, perched itself on the ledge of UTA, below it, Burberry, enjoying the remains of what it had almost, actually, eaten whole. The fake ceramic owls they put all over the patio had never worked. It takes a real hawk to scare pidgins away.

And they stayed away for weeks before they had the courage to return, which they did. I think about that mother, her cover, about what she had probably genuinely wanted to scream when the bird attacked the other bird: *I am not in control and I hate myself because of it.* I think about what my father was hiding with his attempt to replace his nonworking story—his family that had not come to a good end—with a new story: just change the players.

I decide to change the *she* in my story (almost everyone had guessed it was memoir) to *I*, and begin again, with my new notes, with my new hope: my own hawk, fat and full on my anguish, will stay away long enough for all the floating parts of this story to land beautifully, the fruit of my kill.

Barbara Cameron works as a restaurant manager in Beverly Hills, CA, and wrote "Hawk Blood" after attending the New York State Summer Writers Institute workshop with Amy Hempel and Mary Gaitskill. This braided essay won first place in the Creative Nonfiction Category judged by Alice Elliot Dark, and was first published in American Literary Review's *Spring 2012 issue.*

According to Women, When to Use Knives

by Cameron Steele

poetry editor's pick

Women got to know when to use knives, when to slip metal
through their common-law men, metal words will do, but
    knives
work best sometimes when he come home too late, too wet,
those beggar eyes, yes, slippery lips, he speaking without words
clutching house keys, glass bottle against thigh and groin,
she in her tee-shirt, common and cold, and clutching at—
    what?

what newspapers leave out.

What I got? Always women want to know, words clicking
    down throats,
snapped off by sore molars, 3 a.m. cigarettes, cigars if he left
    them.
If he did, when he come home, he call her baby—thief—
    bitch—
close them wolf eyes, men always do; didn't he get worlds,
life with a girl who smile when she told, when she ain't,
she stay with him when bud's got him against walls and the
    law
What I got but a man? She knows. Left without words
and his words without love and too late but that's

what newspapers leave out.

Woman in kitchen, man is dead.
Morning headlines a day or two, three later.
The official report, they say they got, and her mug
shot: Wide, dog eyes, cigarette lips.
Woman of women who know what they got, words
refuse to forget: On slippery nights they cure the common
    cold.

what newspapers leave out.

Cameron Steele, 25, is a freelance journalist in South Dakota. After spending three years as a public safety and investigative reporter for the Anniston Star *in Alabama and the* Charlotte Observer *in North Carolina, Steele hopes to start an MFA program in poetry in fall 2014. A graduate of Washington and Lee University, she won the Academy of American Poets' College Award in 2010 for a sestina she wrote about her father.*

CASUALTIES OF NATURE

by Cameron Steele

poetry editor's pick

We lost them—
the holding hands
bodies
dancing
long hours in the yard
cool evenings on the porch
quoting from favorite
Western shows
and *La Vie En Rose.*

We lost the smells
of the house
warm and woodsy
Bill hewing some
fencepost
in the shed
Linda smoking a pipe
tapping her foot
along to hidden rhythms
an Edith Piaf record.

And it was—
on the porch
in the house

all over the yards—
La Vie En Rose.
Life's pits and stems
cast against our parents
magic.

The storm came in April.
Hold me close
Linda said.
Hold me fast.

The humming of the earth
opening up.
No one told them—
When heaven sighs,
it yawns with teeth
snapped limbs
stinking debris
looped around
the air.

We found them
in woods
next to the yard.
Every bone in Bill's
body broken—
this rough-hewn man
holding hands
with the woman
who spoke French
and smoked tobacco
from pipes.

We lost the way
every word
every day
turned into songs.

How easy they became
art. How easy they
made falling in love
with routine
and dancing next to
a wooden, sagging front door.

BUTTERFLY BOY

by Rebecca Snow

poetry editor's pick

I didn't believe
     the boy crying
         "Butterfly!"
again and again
in my front porch view,
     a book conducting my head
while four Latino children
and their mom
     walked home on the aging sidewalk,
     our edge-of-Denver street,
probably from the daycare
        down the block.
I half-listened
     to the boy's
     yells, expecting a small
white butterfly or moth,
something I couldn't see.
     The mother kept her eyes
on her shoes,
looked so depressed
     one of the little
     kids might have run
         in front of a car
     without her noticing.
The high
excitement in the boy's voice,
     the repetition trying to get
     his mother to look—

There it was,
looping a loosened spiral
in my tattered front yard,
over the sun-bright grass,
an immense, spotless butterfly,
wings gold as aspen leaves in fall.
The mother's head stayed downward.
The boy gave up but
danced
in silence,
backwards,
his dark eyes following
the butterfly's hello,
his young, brown face
forgetting all else,
open to air and shine.

Rebecca Snow's first novel is forthcoming from Conundrum Press. Her poetry has been published in the Wazee Journal, and she won first place for narrative nonfiction in the 2007 Writers Studio Contest, sponsored by Arapahoe Community College. Her piece was featured in the Progenitor. With an MFA from the University of Montana in fiction and poetry, she teaches at the Community College of Aurora and lives in Denver with her son. She is an active member of Lighthouse Writers Workshop.

Sophia and the Missing Socks

by Anthony Q. Davis

short fiction editor's pick

THERE WAS ONCE A LITTLE GIRL BY THE NAME OF SOPHIA, WHO WAS like most little girls her age. She loved to play with her friends, read books, and participate in sports. Every Saturday, when she was not cheering or doing gymnastics, Sophia loved to help her mother fold laundry. "Sophia, it is time to do the laundry," her mother would say. Instantly, Sophia would drop whatever she was doing and rush to the laundry room. "Coming, Mom," Sophia would respond. Every week, Sophia and her mother would complete their laundry folding by matching up each sock with its mate. "I will match your father's socks and my socks and you can match up your socks," said her mother.

"Yes, ma'am," Sophia responded. Sophia especially liked matching socks—she would make it into a game: "One long blue sock and another long blue sock," said Sophia.

After she would finish her matching game, Sophia seemed to always end up with a pair of socks, for which she could find no match. "Oh no," Sophia belted out, "where could the mate to these socks be?" inquired Sophia.

"Not again," said Sophia's mother with a sigh. "This happens every week. Please check the dryer, Sophia, and I will check the washer," said her mother.

"Not here," said Sophia, as she pulled a handful of lint from the dryer.

"Check your room," responded her mother.

Sophia looked under her bed, in her closet, in each of her drawers, and she even checked her smelly cheerleading shoes, but still, no sign of the missing socks. Finally, Sophia asked her father, "Dad, have you seen my missing socks?" looking to him with hope of solving the missing socks mystery.

"Sorry, Sophia, I have not seen your socks," said her father.

"Ok, thank you, Dad," said Sophia. Next, Sophia went to report the news to her mother. "Mom, I have looked everywhere and I cannot find my missing socks," reported Sophia.

"Okay, Sophia, but in the future you must be more careful not to lose your socks," said her mother.

"But, Mom—" Sophia insisted.

"Now, now, Sophia, you are seven years old now and you should be able to make sure you put your dirty clothes in the hamper," said her mother.

That evening, Sophia's mom and dad read her a bedtime story like they did every night. Once they finished the story, they tucked her in and kissed her goodnight. "We love you," said her mom and dad.

"I love you too," replied Sophia, as her parents shut her door. As she began to drift off to sleep, Sophia continued to wonder about the missing socks. Where could they be? she thought to herself.

After she was soundly asleep, Sophia was awakened by the sound of wind chimes: "Ting, ting ting."

Alarmed, Sophia opened her eyes. She heard the wind chime sound again, "ting, ting, ting." Sophia became frightened and clutched her blankets tightly as she could. "Mom, Dad, is that you?" asked Sophia, but there was no answer. Finally, Sophia decided to investigate where the strange noise was coming from. Slowly, she crept from her bed, opened her bedroom door, and peaked around the corner. "Hello?" Sophia said, but again there was no answer. All of a sudden, Sophia saw a bright flash of light, which appeared to come from the laundry room. Although she was still frightened, Sophia was way too curious not to investigate further. Carefully, Sophia tiptoed down the hall, not stopping until she reached the laundry room. Being careful not to make a sound, Sophia slowly reached for the doorknob and turned it as she held her breath.

As she eased open the door, Sophia could hardly believe her eyes. There, standing in her laundry basket, were two little men who each stood about one foot tall. Frozen in amazement, Sophia could not say a word; she simply stood there and observed the two men. The men were colorfully clothed in garments that appeared to have been made from multicolor socks. One had a knapsack over his shoulder, while the other was busy stuffing a sock into his knapsack. Unable to remain quiet any longer, Sophia yelled out, "You are taking my socks!"

Alarmed by Sophia's voice, the two men turned around and looked Sophia dead in the eye. Quickly they grabbed their knapsacks and began to run towards the dryer. All of a sudden, there was a quick burst of light and the two little men disappeared.

Instantly, Sophia raced towards the front of the dryer where the little men had disappeared, but there was no sign of them. Where had they went? Sophia thought to herself. Being the curious little girl that she was, Sophia opened the dryer door. Suddenly, there was the sound of wind chimes and a quick flash of light and Sophia disappeared.

The next thing she knew, Sophia found herself being awakened by bright sunrays shining in her eyes. Instantly,

Sophia jumped to her feet and looked all around her. *Where am I?* Being lost and scared, Sophia began to cry.

"Oh my, oh my, please do not cry," Sophia herd a strange voice say.

"Who's there?" asked Sophia.

"It is I, Mowat, guardian of the Kyoto forest."

"My who, Ky what?" replied Sophia.

"Excuse me, but the name is Mowat and you are trespassing in my forest!"

"Well, I am sorry, Mr. Mowat, but I was chasing two little men who were stealing my socks and I somehow ended up here," said Sophia.

"Who are you calling little?" asked Mowat.

"Oh I am sorry, did you happen to see them?" asked Sophia.

"No, I cannot say that I did," replied Mowat. "Oh dear, this is not good," said Mowat.

"What is not good?" Sophia asked.

"You are from the other side. It is strictly forbidden for outsiders to be in Kyoto," Mowat explained.

"Who are you calling an outsider?" asked Sophia.

"Oh my, this is not good, I must take you to the king," Mowat continued to mutter.

So Sophia agreed to follow Mowat to meet the king of Kyoto. As Mowat and Sophia forged ahead on their journey, eventually they came to a bridge.

"Wait a minute!" exclaimed Sophia.

"Oh dear, what is it now?" asked Mowat.

"This bridge is made of socks," replied Sophia.

"My dear, you are truly an observant one, are you not," Mowat said impatiently.

"Why would you build a bridge from socks?" asked Sophia.

"No time to explain," said Mowat, "we really must get you to the king. He is the only one who can answer your questions."

After walking through the forest for some time, Sophia and Mowat arrived at the Kyoto Village. Sophia could not believe what she saw. There were hundreds if not thousands of people who were the same size as Mowat. They were all busy about with their daily lives. There were builders and bakers and farmers and teachers, all hard at work. There were large houses and small houses, all perfectly lined up side by side.

"Why are all the housed covered in socks?" Sophia questioned.

"Patience, patience, patience," said Mowat. "The king will be more than happy to answer all of your questions."

As Sophia and Mowat made their way through the village, the villagers stopped what they were doing and stared in amazement at the sight of Sophia.

"Why is everyone looking at me?" asked Sophia.

"We have not had a visitor in Kyoto for some time," explained Mowat. "Now, now, the king will explain all," said Mowat.

Finally, Sophia and Mowat came to a house that did not look much different from the others. It was made from colorful socks and had a large wooden door. Mowat walked up to the door and knocked, *tap, tap, tap.* Slowly, the door opened and suddenly a man appeared. He was same height as the rest of the villagers and had a long gray and black beard. He donned a colorful cloak, which like the houses, was made from socks.

"Oh my, it is my pleasure to introduce King Femi of Kyoto," announced Mowat.

"Greetings, Mowat, guardian of the forest. I see you have brought our visitor, Sophia," said the king.

"How did you know my name?" Sophia was puzzled.

"My dear, Sophia, we have been expecting you for some time. Your being here is no accident," explained the king.

"What do you mean?" asked Sophia.

"Let me explain," replied King Femi. "Sophia, for years our people cherished and enjoyed our lush forest. However, over time we realized that we were taking our forest for granted, by cutting down trees faster than they could replenish themselves. Because of this, we knew we had to come up with an alternate solution," King Femi explained.

"But why socks?" asked Sophia.

"In our search for an alternate resource, we entered your world where we met a young boy about the same age as yourself. When we told him about our problem, he kindly offered us his socks to use. He told us that everyone loses socks in his world and no one would notice a few missing pairs now and then. Since that day, we have ventured to your world to gather socks. And as you have seen, Sophia, we have developed thousands of ways to use socks in our world," explained King Femi.

"But, you're taking socks from so many people," said Sophia.

"Hee hee hee," King Femi chuckled. "You see, Sophia, we only take what we need. Once we are done using the socks for one thing, we take and use them for something else. You see my colorful cloak here?" asked King Femi.

"Yes, it is pretty," said Sophia.

"Once I have worn it for a while, I will give it to someone else to make a dress or help build a house," King Femi continued.

"So, let me see if I get it. By recycling you are able to use the socks many more times, which prevents you from cutting down too many trees," said Sophia.

"Excellent, you got it, Sophia. Recycling helps us save the forest and helps our world," said King Femi.

"Everyone should recycle!" Sophia said with excitement and understanding.

"Oh my, it's getting dark; the gateway will be closing soon. We must get you back," said Mowat to Sophia.

"Before you go, Sophia, promise me that you will tell your people about the importance of recycling," King Femi pleaded.

"Girl Scout's honor," said Sophia.

"Pardon me, King Femi, but we really must go now." spoke Mowat.

"So long, Sophia," said King Femi.

"Good-bye," replied Sophia, as she followed Mowat back to the forest. Through the woods they hurried until they came upon the bush where Sophia first arrived in Kyoto. "Where is the gateway?" Sophia asked Mowat.

"Oh dear, hurry, just step behind the bush and you will be on your way," replied Mowat.

Before she stepped behind the bush, Sophia said good-bye to Mowat and in a flash she was gone.

The next thing she knew, Sophia found herself back in the laundry room at her house. Anxious to tell her parents what had happened, Sophia dashed from the laundry room to her parents' room. To her surprise, her parents were sound asleep; it was as if she had only been gone a few minutes. Quietly, Sophia crept back to her room and crawled into her bed and was fast to sleep after the night's adventure. That next morning, as Sophia ate breakfast with her parents, she eagerly asked, "Mom, Dad?"

"Yes, Sophia," said her mother.

"Do we recycle?" Sophia asked.

"Why, yes, we certainly do, Sophia," responded her mother.

"I learned about recycling from a little friend of mine when I was about your age," said her father.

Sophia was delighted to hear that her family had been recycling all along. From that day on, Sophia told everyone she knew about the importance of recycling. And best of all, she never got upset when she could not find the mates to her socks.

Anthony Q. Davis draws the inspiration for his stories from his childhood experiences and the mysterious world itself. Presently, Anthony is working on a geography-based picture book for children, which will dazzle the imagination. Anthony currently resides in Columbus, Ohio, with his wife and two baby daughters, but has aspirations to relocate to Denver, Colorado.

The Girl That I Walk By

by JC Lynne

personal essay/creative nonfiction editor's pick

THERE IS A GIRL THAT I WALK BY EVERY DAY. I'M GUESSING SHE'S around ten. My daughter is nine. *When Lillie was born she was a foreign, little creature that had come from my body taking me aback. All of those weeks of pregnancy, I relinquished control of my physical form; I'd talk to that creature growing inside of me. Hours upon hours of endless debate, minutes and seconds of trivial nonsense and countless songs in the shower, in the car . . . wherever. Finally, a scapegoat for those undirected comments I say aloud.* It's why I have my dogs today. *Talking to the baby, yeah, talking to the baby. Somehow, from some place I recognized her presence. I even dreamed of her once. A vivid dream of a two- or three-year-old girl with small pigtails standing on the backseat of a truck, bouncing and dancing. Déjà vu before the moment happened. Inside of me was someone connected to me in a unique, unfamiliar way. Someone whose emergence into my life would fit without question.*

Thirty-eight weeks of communion, 50 pounds of weight gain, and 31 hours of bone-crushing, exhaustive labor I laid my hands on that spiritual force in the form of seven pounds and eight ounces of flesh. For all of our connectedness, I looked on the wriggling, squalling, bruised, and wrinkled creature and felt . . . nothing. She was a complete stranger. I was shocked. Don't get me wrong, she was a beautiful baby. Bruised forehead, purple and wrinkled loveliness. From the beginning I knew that the baby was a girl. No ultrasound, no test to reveal something I intrinsically knew. The space between what I expected and what I discovered was a gaping, looming chasm. I expected to know her the way I had known her while she was in my womb. Some time between amniotic fluid and air a discreet but powerful connection had dimmed.

Walking back to my car in Fort Collins after class, I pass this girl, every day at this time, the same girl. This girl, this young stranger feels more familiar to me than my own, infant daughter did when she was born. The girl's a mirror into which I feel compelled to stare. Sandy brown hair, too-long bangs shoved to the side covering one eye, and a sideways smile that could be taken as a greeting, but it wasn't. *The whole motherhood gig was a horrible disappointment. The reality didn't match up to the expectation. I recognized my features in her tiny, infant face. The genetics were inarguable, but there was nothing familiar in the coal dark, almond eyes, replicas of my own. Eyes inherited from my great-grandmother. I spent endless hours those first few weeks staring, searching for a glimmer of the familiar presence I had shared the past nine months. I read somewhere that mothers blindfolded can identify their babies by the feel of their skin. I thought that memorizing her face, her smell, and the texture of her skin would unlock something within me.*

"Are you sure there isn't anything wrong?" I asked my mother.

"I didn't like you much either!" came the sarcastic reply.

"Very funny. You aren't making me feel any better."

"It could just be post partum, you know, baby blues," she suggested, taking the bundle lovingly into her arms. "Felt like drowning anyone lately?"

I couldn't help but laugh. "Don't be gross. It's not hormonal."

"Give it time. I really don't have any idea what you're talking about. Motherhood doesn't come naturally to anyone in our family. I was afraid my mother would eat us."

The girl is slender as girls are at that age. Coltish and gangly, she walks past me. Our eyes meet and time slows. I'm reminded of Lillie's too-long legs and her genuine smile. *Somewhere along the late-night feedings and lukewarm baths I developed a love for my baby girl that became obsession. The obsession of a mother for the soft, velvety smell of baby skin after her bath, the obsession for her so bright, soul-deep smile when I picked her up in the morning, the obsessive ache for those blurbs, goos, and ahhs that came out of her mouth as she tried to tell me the secret to all happiness. I loved her, but the symbiotic connection was dim. In its place, as Lillie grew older, an unease began to scratch at the back of my brain.*

"Lillie, honey, could you scoot over a bit. Mommy doesn't like to be crowded like that. Your elbow is hurting my knee, ouch, no, it's okay, just scoot a bit."

"Lillie, baby, please don't choke me so when you hug me. It hurts. We don't hurt people when we give them love. Love is gentle."

"Lillie, my goodness, you're three years old. Do you need to be on my lap? Mommy's tummy is full of baby and I don't have much of a lap left."

"Lillie, here's a pillow for you. Yes, we'll put the baby on it so you can hold him. Yes, this is Reilly . . . remember you picked his name!"

The girl keeps her head high as she passes me. On some days I can tell it's slung low and silent tears are building in her eyes. This girl has her emotions in a straitjacket, in a padded room with a bolt, a lock, and an electric fence. In my mind's eye, I hear Lillie's crazy laugh and see her collapse to the ground as she lets everything within her loose.

I can't remember feeling that way. Some families don't offer that chance. Crazy strolls through my family grazing its fingers casually across both maternal and paternal lines. My world was built on crazy. Crazy and lies. I don't blame any one person any more. *I didn't have this problem with my son. I was prepared for the feeling of warm, soft weight under my chin curling into a roly poly ball of trust, certain that nothing would harm him. I was conditioned by Lillie to love him on sight because I knew what transformation would take place. I was anticipating the stages that Lillie pioneered for him. I knew without a doubt how that mallow, little hunk of flesh would grow and become unwilling to cling to me. I began to worry about my daughter and what I wasn't giving her.*

"Mom, I think I'm in trouble." I start the conversation with this vague statement. I know this is dangerous territory, but sometimes I forget the ice is thin.

"How, Julia?" she says, looking over the sale ads from the paper.

"I feel cut off from Lillie. I push her away. Sometimes I get claustrophobic when she's close to me. I think it has to do with me. She's four and I was four." I hold my breath.

"Look, Target's having a sale on bath towels." She looks up at me. "Do you need some new towels? We could see if they have any in purple. You like purple, right?"

CRAACK, the ice gapes open under the weight. I plummet into the frigid water. Sliding under the ice, succumbing to hypothermia, I look at my mother through the distortion of that subzero lens. "Sure, Mom, I could use a couple of new towels." She knows I only buy white towels so they can be bleached clean. In that moment, I'm certain that Lillie won't ever feel that kind of cold.

This girl is damaged. I can see it in the swing of her arms, hands ready for fists. The boy who damaged me was broken by our father, his mother, who else he only knows. I was damaged too. Our father, my mother, and many others that I know too well participated, most unwitting accomplices. This girl that I walk by, she doesn't know that there's a way out. I could be imagining her reflection of my 10-year-old self. Imposing upon her the persona I'm remembering through the fog of perspective and adulthood.

"I'm going to a therapist," I tell my husband and await the shockwave from the bomb to overwhelm me.

"What?" he replies in that time-honored way that buys a person time to think.

"I'm going to see a therapist."

"Why? Things're fine." I resist the urge to roll my eyes, knowing full well what it might earn me.

"Things are not fine with me. I need to figure out what's wrong with me. I don't want to shut Lillie out like I've been doing." It won't mean anything to him, but I say it for myself.

"That's crazy. You know a therapist will tell you that you're crazy and that you'll have to change all sorts of things. We're doing fine."

I knew the answer before I started. I don't know what inside of me pushes the urge to step out onto that ice. I was surrounded.

"Maybe I am crazy. That's why I need to go."

"Fine, whatever, but don't be surprised to find out it's something wrong with you," the terse reply came as he snapped his paper back up in front of his face.

Alone, I began the journey from that emotionless void. Like a recovering paraplegic, I began those terrible, sweating steps. Holding my own weight up with the parallel bars, muscles burning in agony as I moved millimeter by torturous millimeter.

"It's all right, Lillie. You can sit there. Scoot closer and we'll read it together. Yes?" All the while I was struggling with the claustrophobia.

Nothing hurts this girl that I walk by because nothing surprises her, not walking down the sidewalk past a middle-aged woman pulling her books behind her on wheels. She's toughing it out. I grew tough too. Tough, but wounded. Damaged people find partners that reinforce their injuries. I learned that after thousands of hours of therapy. I moved from one controlling, functional household into another. Walking old worn paths is easier than bushwhacking. I was afraid of everything, but I never flinched. I stuck my chin out to the world and dared it to punch me. It did. I stood back up.

I love Lillie. I'd walk through fire for her. Rip your head off if you hurt her. Charge elephants to protect her. She was young, but she knew. I realized later on that she and my son, Reilly, knew everything. Even when I didn't know. Casual comments spoke volumes.

"Mommy, without Daddy here I can spread my arms this wide!"

"Mommy, we can listen to the music as loud as we want without Daddy here."

"Mommy, you never smiled that way when Daddy was home."

I felt stupid later on that my children could see more than I could. That's the grace of childhood: clarity. My theory is that as infants we so are shocked by the drastic change of circumstances after our birth that we go dim. That's why the intimate connections that I felt with my unborn children were so strong and why they dimmed those first few weeks out of the womb. They were in shock. The beauty and danger of existence is that human beings change. The power of change is terrifying. Each step we take in that direction causes vertigo that can paralyze. That's without extra damage. Those changes I made with Lillie broke open a wound that I didn't realize was festering. Like lancing a boil hurts with a hot, bubbling pain that provides relief at the same time. Each move I made toward Lillie seared through my wound, opening its raw, gangrenous edges the poisonous infection seeping out a little at a time.

"Yes, sweetie, I would love to paint your fingernails."
"Get the umbrellas out, we are dancing in the rain!"
"Sure you can have candles in your bath like I do."
I forgot to pick her up at the bus stop once, but I also let Quincey toddle about with a broken arm for a couple of days before realizing something was wrong. I've heard similar stories from every parent I've met. I was tripping along like every other parent. As my wound reopened, I began to see what good, healthy pain was. I saw how life could be if I could breathe. I was an emotional asthmatic finally getting her lungs in order. Each movement I made to close the space between Lillie and myself cracked the claustrophobic boundary I had allowed my husband to squeeze me into. My hesitance with my daughter increased his power over me.

I'm surprised by my affinity for this girl that I walk past. I'm surprised to recognize myself in every aspect of her. I thought nothing could surprise me. She walks shrouded in cynicism. Her lenses are as dark and uncompromising as my own. There's nothing I can do to help her. No warning I could offer that she'd listen too. My own kids rarely take my advice. I'm dark, cynical, and uncompromising. I can live with that because I know that I can turn my head, changing my perspective, to let in a bit more light.

JC Lynne lives and writes in Colorado. She divides her time between writing; wrangling a mostly grown daughter, two teenage boys, three dogs, and two cats; and teaching yoga.

The Esau Emergence is her first novel. For more information, to read her creative nonfiction, to find excerpts of her upcoming novels, or to contact her, please visit www.jclynne.com.

AUBADE NO.8

by Josh Hasler

poetry editor's pick

If you would register in the March half-light
The way your bar of soap dissolved into its dish,
Untended and unreplaced, a testament to Soap
And entropy and the blood-gift of energy of those
Who shop for things like solid, humane soaps like
small suns lending sensible hygiene to debris in loving orbit.
And if you saw your yellowed brush in cup,
Crossed with an arrogant Oral-B, like the bedraggled
Crest of some mad but ancient dentist's coat of arms,
Then you might gather these things in your arms,
Like child bearing broken teacup back to mom
with the first premise in the logic of fracture,
And of our puzzling new world—one and divisible.

A Colorado native, Josh grew up in Conifer, where he began writing. He currently lives in lovely Boston, where he learns about philosophy, religion, and literature, and plots courses back home.

DANCING AFTER ROY'S FUNERAL

by Margaret Watts

poetry editor's pick

Funeral guests eat Lupe's mother's lunch,
draw in breath, drop jaws,
stare as I start to dance.

They had not seen the vice-chancellor emerge kente-clad
from the church in Akropong
to dance for God and his mother.

His classical education and exulted rank
did not exclude dancing
for her who gave him life.

My husband gave me love, and another life,
taught me to dance,
would have been first to dance, if . . .

Alive,
I move
to fill the void.

Margaret Watts has taught in India, the USA, Ghana, and Trinidad & Tobago. She has always written poetry and it still tends to dominate her. She has been published in The Literary Review, The Atlanta Review, The Caribbean Review, *and other literary journals.*

NEAR ECLIPSE

by Elizabeth Sacre

poetry editor's pick

We lie, crown to crown,
on the night boat bound for Crete,
stars in our eyes,
stars in the sheen of our sleeping bags,
stars diving leaping cresting
on the surface of the sea,
shivering with each swell.

Gypsies gather in a circle,
faces gleamy in lantern light,
babies slung in taffeta shawls,
rustlings, murmurs, snatches
of song, a phrase on a fiddle,
a child's cry, a mother's
answering croon.

In this riot of constellations,
Pythagoras sought order and found
music—perfect consonance.

We fret about the drachmas
stitched inside our hiking boots,
the Homer left in Heidelberg,
estranged by what binds.

We wake, significant again,
the heavens a manageable blue.
A pair of stray cats, we wash
the sleep from each other's eyes
with the last drops from our flasks,
then amble, trailing our belongings,
untousling our hair, towards the bow.

There, where water
meets sky, we see
the scrub and stone
of earth rising, and
on the hillsides,
clusters of houses
washed chalk white.

Elizabeth Sacre lives between New York, where she practices as a psychoanalyst, and the Hudson Valley, where she writes fiction and poetry. She has been published in various journals, including Paris Transcontinental *and the* Santa Clara Review.

RAMBLING

by Elizabeth Sacre

poetry editor's pick

Above Venice, where the ground is parched,
the air heady with thyme,
right there we saw the sign—
Au Fin Du Monde—

and followed a tipsy arrow,
the only thing
to do
for two

so green,
and the moon
low and luscious,
and life as big as the stars were many.

We found
not a soul, *pas un chat*,
at the end, the end of the road.
Your shadow, my shadow
tumbled,
fumbled

among stones that once marked graves,
inscriptions
Bien-aimée
Caressé
Chérie
long claimed by elements
as lost as we.

Spring Forward, Fall Behind

by Kevin Thaddeus Fisher Paulson

personal essay/creative nonfiction editor's pick

10,000 Miles
March 28, 2004

As I drove my husband, Brian, in the big blue Saturn Vue yesterday, climbing Dolores onto Highway 280, the odometer (or *is that device called a tachometer? This is why I could never be straight. Too many useless gauges to remember*) was at 9,999. Miles passed before the numbers flashed 10,000. Ten thousand miles in the past year.

You know how people name their cars? We called the Escort the "Batmobile," and before that we called that gold '78 Thunderbird the "Queen Mary." But when Brian and I got a NEW car last year, we just kept waiting for a name to inspire us, and somehow along the miles, we are still waiting. On April 1 of last year, Brian and I sat in Alta Bates Hospital and named three babies in less than two hours. But ten thousand miles have passed and we have yet to name our big blue car.

Where were we ten thousand miles ago? Ten thousand miles ago, we were a middle-aged gay couple living in a condo, driving a budget compact. We decided to do fost/adoption, and last spring, on April 1st, a social worker called and asked us if we could take in newborn triplets, one of whom had necrotizing enterocolitis and would probably die. Within three hours, we had the duplets living with us,

272

and we visited Kyle in the neonatal intensive care unit and he was in a little plastic box, and we couldn't hold him. Every limb was connected to blood or food or oxygen or a monitor, and all we could do was sit there and pat the part of his chest where an intestine was not sticking out.

Ten thousand miles ago our biggest worry was whether Kyle would ever get out of the hospital. We spent every night at the neonatal intensive care unit, singing show tunes to a baby boy missing a section of his intestine, and we wondered whether he would ever eat like a normal baby again. Then went home to the fussiest duplets in the world.

We found a doctor who was willing to perform a reanastomis of the ileum, which meant slice his belly open, pull out the remaining intestines, check every centimeter, sew the intestine, and then put everything back in the belly. Beyond all odds, Kyle survived. He came home with us, which meant we needed a bigger car, and it was funny, because we had always ridiculed people who drove sport utility vehicles, and there we were at the Saturn dealership looking for a car big enough to hold three baby seats in back.

Ten thousand miles ago we had nothing to go on but determination. All we knew was, go into debt, and get a big car, and keep driving. Put Kyle and Vivienne and Joshua in the back seats. Drive to the pediatrician and the surgeon and the neurologist and the audiologist, and just keep putting one mile on top of the other.

A week ago, one of the deputies saw me getting into the car, and said, "I always knew you for a soccer mom." It *is* a soccer mom kind of car, a lot more middle class than we middle-aged queens drive.

The car is just one of the ways that Brian and I have changed. I am gentler than I used to be. I don't cut off quite as many cars as I used to. I don't drive through deep yellow lights. I've got the kids in the back of the car, and kids give you a conscience. I let cars in at a merge.

I like being gentle. I like smiling, and waving the pedestrian on, even when I think that he is taking his sweet time about walking across the street. In the ten thousand miles, I may have become just a little more patient. I wait for the next light.

And Brian? Well, in ten thousand miles, he complains less that he is driving with me. He has become one of those old grandmothers we make fun of, who sits in the back with the children.

My own new patience sometimes even gets out of the car with me, and walks into the house. Some nights I don't get any housework done at all, and the closest thing I do to cooking is dial Geneva Pizza. But I have the patience to sit in the living room and read *The Cat in the Hat* because even though Joshua and Vivienne don't understand the words, they like the sound of my voice. Kyle just likes the way the book tastes.

Ten thousand miles ago I began to allow for the small possibility that there was a point to being on this planet, and that my purpose just might be raising the triplets. My carefully grown cynicism began to fall apart. Maybe, just maybe, there is a force that I don't understand that makes the wheels go round.

Ten thousand miles ago, I did not know that there was a born-again Christian social worker who hated the idea of gay men raising children. Ten thousand miles ago, I would not have believed that a social worker would lie and say that an abusive birth mother who had lost her oldest son due to neglect was now cured of schizophrenia.

The hearing starts tomorrow at 1:30 at Department 14 in Juvenile Court at 1225 Fallon Street in Oakland. The hearing will be in several parts. The first part will be about the mother's suitability to parent, and Brian and the social workers and the doctors and I will testify. A lot of very mean lawyers are going to say a lot of very mean things about us. The second part, which will not start before Tuesday, will only take place if and only if the judge decides that the mother is not capable.

We are all in that big blue sport utility vehicle, and we're not sure where we're going. I like to think that the future is bright, that we have all learned a little about positive thinking and about faith. I like to think this story has a happy ending. I like to think we have got a million miles to go together.

Spring Forward, Fall Behind
April 3, 2004

Benjamin Franklin came up with the idea of daylight-saving time. For more than two centuries, we Americans just picked whatever time of day that we actually want noon to come at, and, lo and behold, it is noon. Would that the rest of the universe worked so well.

But tonight is indeed daylight-saving night, which means an hour less sleep for those of you who have to go to work on Sundays. But for me, all I need to do is get up tomorrow, throw on a pair of jeans, and sing a couple of Hosannas. Tomorrow is also Palm Sunday, the beginning of Holy Week, and the end of Lent.

Every culture has a celebration of the end of the darkness and the rebirth of hope. Before the Christians got into it, the pagans celebrated Oester (my Wiccan friend Timothy will undoubtedly correct the spelling, but just go with me on it).

The Greeks came up with the spring myth of Persephone, a beautiful mortal. Hades, the God of the Dead, took such a liking to her that he invited her to come hang out at his place, a town that we know of as Hell. Persephone's mother, Demeter, got word of this and was furious.

Demeter was not just any mother. She was goddess of the Harvest, and she told Hades that he wasn't gonna keep her daughter captive. And Hades said, "Finders keepers." Demeter replied, "Fine. I'm not happy, nobody's happy." She stopped all harvests: no wheat, no corn, no grapes. Which meant no wine, and before you knew it, everybody was talking about it, especially Dionysius. He told the big boss Zeus. So Zeus said, "Demeter, what the heck, go to Hell. Literally. Go down there and get your daughter. Just make sure that she hasn't eaten anything down there. If she has broken bread with the dead, she must stay."

Demeter rushed down to Hell, and found her daughter, Persephone, only while Persephone was sitting around waiting to be rescued, she got a little on the hungry side and she took a bite of a pomegranate, only a third, but the third was enough. Hades told Demeter that she could have her daughter back on earth, but that because she had eaten a third of the pomegranate, she must spend a third of the year with him in Hell. And for that third of the year, Demeter mourned, and gave no harvest. But at the time when her daughter came back from Hell (which just happened to coincide with the first Sunday after the first full moon after the vernal equinox), Demeter celebrated with the first fruits and the first flowers.

This tradition lives on to this day with crocuses budding, Easter bunnies dancing, and people setting their clocks forward an hour.

Brian and I very slowly return from our season in Hell. Brian mowed the lawn yesterday in our tiny little backyard in San Francisco. The lilacs are in bloom, heavy purple-scented, and the calla lilies are blossoming, in wild, tall, brilliant white crescents. Last Father's Day, our first (and maybe last)

Father's Day, I planted Ceanothus trees around the house, one for each of our foster triplets. The lawn holds three concrete flagstones, one with each of the handprints and footprints of Kyle and Joshua and Vivienne.

But Kyle and Joshua and Vivienne no longer exist. They are now Shawn and Angel and Violet, and they live a life we cannot share. But we have eaten the pomegranate together, and the piece of their souls that will always be Kyle and Joshua and Vivienne will be remembered among the lilacs and the Ceanothus.

At 3:30 p.m. on Tuesday, the judge ruled that the triplets would be moving in with the no-longer- schizophrenic-cured-of-18-years-of-smoking-crack-but-mother-who-shakes-children-when-she-gets-bored, and that we had two hours to pack the children up and say good-bye. I called Jon from just outside the court, and Jon called the family and they all rushed over to say "good-bye." Brian and I took the bridge at warp speed. I picked up Vivienne, who was crying, and the neighbors walked out of the house, and all at once, we were alone and the kids were hungry, and I heated up three bottles, and we fed them Cheerios and cereal, and changed them, and we all sat down on the couch, and Brian turned on *Charmed* and for the last few minutes of our life where the family was the family, each baby crawling over each of us, and for just a last few minutes, the world was normal.

The doorbell rang. At the door were the two social workers who had just perjured themselves on the stand. (Two weeks earlier, they had certified to the court that the mother was mentally ill and incapable of raising children. That day they testified that the mother was cured completely of schizophrenia and that shaking babies was normal cultural behavior.) Brian said, "This is it." He picked up Vivienne and walked to the van. I picked up Joshua and Kyle and followed. Brian strapped Vivienne in, and she giggled, thinking this was just another trip to the doctor's or the grocery store. Joshua clapped his hands together. I strapped in Kyle. Kyle knew. Kyle looked at me, and with his thousand-year-old eyes he told me that there would never again be another session of reading *The Cat in the Hat* on the couch. There would never again be another drinking formula in the rocking chair near the fireplace. There would never be another colostomy bag changing. There would never again be the two of us sitting in the dark at 3 a.m., singing the soundtrack to *Gypsy* or *Gilligan's Island*. And he started crying, and I started crying.

I walked back to the house to get their suitcases, and the social worker said that there was no room in the car for the statue of Saint Jude or the doll that Mom crocheted before she died or the dragon pajamas. She said that we would never see these kids again, so what did it matter? Kyle still stared at me, and I think the old soul in him was telling me that he would survive, that he had lived through heart surgery and infections and a colostomy, and that he would take care of his brother and sister for me. I whispered to him that it was okay to go on to this new life, and that I wished all three of them every joy they could have, and that it was okay to forget us with their minds, but whether he knew it or not, he would always be Kyle Thaddeus.

The social worker slammed the door. The engine roared. Somewhere in the west the sun slipped out of the sky.

The telephone rang a hundred times that night, and neither of us answered. Instead we sat on a couch, and watched the room grow dark and empty. Brian, of course, could not eat. I, of course, ate everything that was in the house. The hours ticked slower and slower, and sleep would not come.

Dawn came, and we got up and packed away their clothes, and packed away their toys, and took out car seats and dismantled the year that we had spent with the triplets.

We spend our season in Hell, because we ate a third of the pomegranate. We go on. Our nextdoor neighbor, Maureen, had a baby in January, and we gave her the doll and a lot of the smart outfits meant for our daughter, because life does go on.

We needed that season in Hell to remind ourselves that there is a spring. A few weeks ago, I told the priest that I was trying to give up my anger against the birth mother for Lent. I woke up yesterday, and I realized that I was no longer angry. Maybe, just maybe, we had scared that woman enough so that she would keep herself clean and sober and taking her medication. Maybe, just maybe, she was willing to make sacrifices herself.

Doctors have told me that Kyle would not be alive without the help and the love that we gave him. So in the middle of the night, I console myself with the hope that Kyle is destined for greatness. The Higher Powers of the Universe went through extraordinary measures to keep that kid alive, even getting an old queen like myself to spend the night in an emergency room singing the sound track to *Gypsy*. Surely he must have big plans for Kyle.

Jon called to make sure that we hadn't done any damage to ourselves. "Only our livers," I replied.

We still get weepy, because the tragedy is not us: the tragedy is what has happened to the children. I went back to work, and that helped a lot because there are so many dysfunctional people at work that I can spend my time getting angry rather than sad. Just about the only time that somebody went to jail to forget his problems.

For the first time in a year, we went out on a date tonight. Dinner (at Yet Wah's of course) and then a stupid movie, *The*

Prince and Me. It was the kind of romance that Brian likes. I was okay, until the little girl in the row in front of me turned around and started saying, "DaDa. DaDa."

Brian gets better every day. Tomorrow is Palm Sunday. Life will renew for us. We learned that despite all predictions, two middle-aged, jaded queens actually made halfway decent parents. Some day, or some year, Brian will say, "Hey, I'm ready to do this again."

In the Family Way
June 2, 2004
Here is the one answer that I have discovered in my forty-something years on the planet: there is no answer. There are only better questions and better clues. If you think that you have gotten to the right answer, then you have made the wrong conclusion somewhere along the way. The trick in life is that you'll never figure out where you are going. You might as well enjoy the journey.

We will never know anything more about the triplets. They have become part of the big mystery of the universe. There are some mysteries not meant to be solved.

In the meantime, most of our friends stood around doing what you do best: caring for us, and giving us the space to heal. Our lesbian friends from the East Coast flew us to their house in the Catskills for a weekend of pinochle and reminiscence.

Lots of things got to us. I cried every time I heard somebody sing music from *Gypsy*. And it seemed that every day, I was running into someone who didn't know, who walked up to me with a smile on his face, saying, "How are those beautiful triplets?" And each day, there was someone new to tell, from the mailman to the barber to the clerk at Safeway to the veterinarian's assistant.

A couple of other crises helped distract us. Tim has been in and out of the hospital three or four times, with pneumocystitis pneumonia and macrobacterial avian complex.

I write about hope. And it took me a while to figure out what it is that I am still hopeful about. But life does indeed go on. Harvey Milk, the first gay politician to be elected to public office, lost seven elections before he won his seat on the Board of Supervisors. In the last lost election, his opponent, Art Agnos, said after the results were in, "Harvey, you know a lot about the issues, and you can tell everybody what is wrong with what. But you make one mistake. You gotta give'em hope." And that is what Harvey did. He decided to walk in hope, to tell people about what could be and not about loss.

Which brings us to Brian and Kevin. After these weeks of drama, we return to the planet. When we lost the kids, I told Brian that I wanted to do this again. Pigs make the best bacon, after all, and it seemed that Brian and I were made to be parents. Brian took a while to grieve, and this week, he said that he was ready to start exploring again.

We thought about going to another agency. I even called a few other agencies, and was surprised in the 21st century to discover how many agencies are perfectly content to place children with adoptive parents, so long as the parents have opposing genders. But we eventually decided that we liked the people at A Better Way (all except for the above-mentioned social worker, who has been fired). So this morning we went back to the placement worker, a lovely woman named Sarah, and we talked about another placement.

Don't anyone get excited yet. Unlike the first placement, this one will take months to complete. We told Sarah that we were ready to explore another placement but that we had conditions. Mine was that the child be discovered in a rocket ship, and that all the other inhabitants of the planet Krypton had been killed. Brian, always more reasonable, asked that the child be close to the 26 hearing.

Sarah asked us about age and gender and race. We replied that we had just fostered health-compromised triplets from two different genders and two different races, so we thought we could handle any combination. Sarah then handed us "The Book." The book is a list of all the kids in the surrounding counties available for placement.

It felt a little like catalog shopping. There we were, flipping through page after page of kids in need of love, and all Sarah asked was for us to mention whether or not we were interested, and place a Post-it next to their picture. I, of course, fell in love with each of the kids and within 20 minutes had gone through a pad of Post-its. Brian, always more logical and methodical than I am, looked mainly at the sibling placements. (*A large percentage of children in the system are of African American descent and a large percentage, in California, are of Hispanic descent. Generally, the system has more difficulty placing kids in the following categories: mixed race, older, health compromised and sibling sets, because many adoptive parents want single, blond, blue-eyed, healthy babies.*)

Three hours later, we had looked at every child for 10 counties in need of a home. Sarah took down the list of children we were interested in and she will send out notes of inquiry to the social workers working on those cases, and time will pass, and then we MIGHT meet some of these kids, and they get to decide on us, and we get to decide on them. When do we get an answer? No one knows. Still part of that mystery I was writing about. But the important thing is this: We are siding with hope rather than despair. We are trying again.

Nurse Vivian said that my father never ruined a good story by sticking to the facts. In my family, everyone told stories and you got used to a little fact inflation along the way.

So, with respect to Brian, I am going to try to stick to the facts here: we are in the family way. Or at least we're heading toward that direction. Brian and I have done all the grieving that we intended to do this year, and decided that we were going back to the foster/adoption process. The first step meant looking through books of potential matches, which felt a lot like catalog shopping. The second step was even stranger. Every six months or so, the neighboring counties in the Bay Area throw a matching picnic, in which they invite potential adoptive parents and potential adoptees. Brian, as it turns out, was dancing in Hawaii that week (yes, the poor thing!), and so I got to go to this thing alone. Well, actually not alone. I went with another gay couple who are also looking to adopt. Of course, they had each other there, so I spent the bulk of the day feeling like I was back in South Ozone Park, Queens.

Both of my two older brothers were fairly athletic growing up, and I was a nelly-queen-in-training. They were ten years older than me, and pretty much the two of them ran the Irish hooligans who lived on the 130th block of Sutter Avenue, directly under the flight path of Idlewild Airport. Thus, the two of them organized all of the stoopball and basketball and stickball on the block. Stickball is just like baseball, except you use a broom handle instead of a bat, and you must block all traffic from proceeding on the block. The game begins with one brother throwing the stick to the other brother who catches it. They then go hand over hand until one of them can reach the top of the stick with the thumb. This brother got to pick whom he wanted on his team first. Well, Donald always picked Tommy McCormick, and Early picked Jimmy

Cadden, and after that they chose from all the other McCormick brothers, the McCafferys, the Caddens, Michael Carbone, Martin Campisi. Pretty soon they each had eight players, and it got down to Patrick Cadden and me. Early fretted if he got the last pick, but Donald went straight to Patrick Cadden (who was four years younger than me, and, if you ask me, just as nelly, but that would be the pot calling the kettle lavender).

I spent a lot of my youth acting as first base umpire.

So there I was at the matching picnic, and all the pretty parents talked to all the pretty children, and the social worker said to just stick it out, and I did. I actually talked to a lot of kids, and fell in love with each of them and would love to adopt any of them.

Of course, nothing turned out for any of those matches. And that is when serendipity set in. During the fight for the triplets, we met a LOT of social workers. You have read about the evil social workers who worked on the case, but we actually met some nice social workers. Unfortunately, none of those social workers had legal standing on the case.

One of the nice social workers remembered us. Leora worked for Alameda County, and thought that what had happened was a crime (well, actually perjury was involved, so technically it was a crime). She watched us take three medically fragile children and help them flower, and she decided that she wanted us to have more children.

So she called our agency, A Better Way, the very next time that she heard we were "back on the market." She had found a baby boy who she thinks would make a perfect Fisher-Paulson. Our social worker called us, and we began the matching process. BEGAN. Let me emphasize that **BEGAN**. (If Brian asks any of you, please tell him that I emphasized that this is by not means final.) We met with

Leora, and her boss, and our social worker, yesterday, and we made a plan to meet the young fellow.

Here is what we know: He is nine months old, and his hearing is scheduled for June 16. (That means that he would be legally freed for adoption six months after that.) His mother had a history of crack and methamphetamine abuse, and his father is in prison. There is no history of mental illness.

Leora really wants us to have this baby boy. He is, by the way, African American.

One of the other gay couples we met at the agency had told us that it would be very, very hard for an African American boy to grow up with two white men, because he would face the prejudices of both the black and white communities as well as the straight and gay communities. And I hesitated for a moment. Funny that the Mexican/Pakistani triplets had never caused comment with anyone.

I grew up in a conservative Catholic neighborhood in Queens, not too far from where Archie Bunker lived. It was a neighborhood with strong racial divisions. During the sixties, busing began in New York, and the white flight out of the city and into the suburbs began. I grew up thinking that African Americans were very different. I went to Saint Anthony of Padua School in South Ozone Park, and I sat next to the only African American girl in the class, Elizabeth.

In my college years, I turned out to be gay, and I found myself rejecting a lot of my family's conservative politics. I sang in choir with another Kevin, this one an African American tenor, and we toured throughout the country. We got to New Orleans on one of the tours, and the tour guide on the bus was talking about labor in the South and she talked about how "lazy the blacks were." Seeing the look of shock on our faces, and seeing Kevin sitting in the bus with us, she added, "But not black like you are. This kind was real black, shiny black." It became a standard joke with the choir, like when we sang a spiritual, we asked the conductor whether this was traditional Black Gospel or Shiny Black Gospel. Kevin used to kid me that I was not like other white people. I was shiny white.

I live in San Francisco today, and, to quote a cliché, some of my best friends are black. But when the social worker told me that baby boy was African American, I hesitated. I thought, "How will I tell my father this? How will I introduce this child to my family?" Isn't it enough that I am already a member of one minority? Do I have to keep adding minorities to the family? I spoke to other parents who had adopted cross-racially, and I learned that both the white community and the black community had criticized them.

It was at the time that I was pondering this issue that I started reading a book by Nair about Ghandi. I read the passage stating, "*Gandhi's journey on the path to a higher standard began with a simple, courageous act performed when he was a young lawyer in South Africa. He was traveling in the first class compartment on a train, when the conductor came and asked him to leave because 'coloreds' were not allowed. Gandhi refused, insisting it was his right to travel first class because he had the appropriate ticket. He was forcibly thrown off the train. At that point, Gandhi felt he had to make a decision. Should he accept color prejudice as the way of life . . . or should he work to remove the injustice?*"

The truth of Gandhi's life was shouting at me, and I chose to listen. I chose to accept my responsibility to heal the wounds of the racial divide. I chose to say, "Yes."

Kevin Thaddeus Fisher-Paulson earned a degree in American Studies from the University of Notre Dame in 1980. Kevin contributed regularly to the Sentinel, *and his stories/poems* have been seen in the James White Literary Review, Amethyst, Oberon, RFD, *and* Suburban Wilderness. *His essay "Virtue Enough for Miss Grrrl" was published as part of an anthology,* When Love Lasts Forever, *by Pilgrim Press. His plays and monologues have been produced in the* ODC Summerfest, Theater Rhinoceros, *and the National AIDS Theater Festival. Fearless Books has agreed to publish his memoir,* A Song for Lost Angels, *coming out in January 2014; this is an excerpt from that work. For more information, contact Info@fearlessbooks.com. Kevin lives with his husband Brian, their two sons, and their four rescue dogs in mysterious San Francisco.*

Adapted by permission of the publisher from A Song for Lost Angels *by Kevin Thaddeus Fisher-Paulson (Fearless Books, 2014: www.fearlessbooks.com).*